MEDITATI
YOGAS, GODS, RELIGIONS

MEDITATIONS
Yogas, Gods, Religions

RAM SWARUP

VOICE OF INDIA
New Delhi

First published 2000

ISBN 81-85990-64-6

Published by Voice of India, 2/18, Ansari Road, New Delhi – 110 002.
Printed at Rajkamal Electric Press, Delhi – 110 033.

Contents

Foreword

The exploration of consciousness is an ancient and unique specialization of Hindu spirituality which sees consciousness as the very ground and being of the entire universe. This exploration continues to be honored and practiced on a wide scale in India today, not only by organized ashrams but, often more importantly, by individual thinkers working independently in the pursuit of truth. Consciousness is the key word for the Hindu mind and meditation is the main methodology to develop it.

This pursuit of consciousness is not a religious belief or a mystical fantasy. It is a rigorous discipline approached with careful thought, reason and intention, rooted in a certain character and ethics. It requires a singular dedication of heart and mind that arises through a specific culture and way of life. It begins with deep thinking rooted in the prime questions of life, not merely with religious zeal or intellectual speculation.

In the world today we are desperately in need of such deep thinking of a spiritual nature that helps us understand the fundamental truth of our existence. As it stands we are caught in political slogans, religious dogma and scientific information that do not afford real depth and meaning to our lives. Their resultant stereotypes may comfort or stimulate us but prevent us from any real understanding of who we are and where our civilization should go. We seem to lack the real thinkers to guide us forward or, if they do exist, we have not afforded them any real recognition.

There is a new interest in spirituality today, evidenced by the popularity of Yoga and meditation worldwide but it appears as yet to be immature or naïve. People are content with adulation of personalities or general instruction that do not bring about real transformation but only perpetuate the same basic compulsions and ambitions. Only through deep thinking, not through merely sitting silently or repeating some phrase, can we enter into a truly meditative mind. While one can find meditation camps, techniques and training methods, these seldom turn out people of deep insight. The reason is that true intelligence is always something that cannot be planned, orchestrated or mass-produced. It arises on an individual basis according to its own rules that cannot be put in any formula. It arises to fulfill a Divine need in the world and dawns like the lightning bolt that cannot be predetermined.

The first principle of any deep thinking is that we must first examine and know ourselves, including the compulsions that drive us from the subconscious and from the external world. Only if we question the ego and ego-based culture from an introspective mind can a really enlightened intelligence come forth. This will produce a different type of thinker that we could call an intellectual in the real sense of the word, a seer who guides and develops culture as a vehicle for a higher consciousness that is not simply human but cosmic. This type of thinker, what the Vedas call a Rishi, has always been honored in India and has been given the main place in shaping its culture. The civilization of the country owes its impetus and sustenance to such minds and their insights.

The Limitations of the Intellect

Intellectuals are seldom truly aware or enlightened beings, though they usually regard themselves as such. While they speak in broad terms of liberalism, humanism and equality they lack a deeper vision of Self and Universe and have no real knowledge of the Eternal and the Infinite. They confuse agility or broadness of thought with a real intelligence and awareness that is beyond the mind. They mistake social, scientific or technological advancement with the real progress of the soul that is not quantifiable.

This is true not only of the intellectuals of the West — which has long been enamoured of logical materialism — but also those of the East, like the Marxist intellectuals of India. They blindly follow any leftist cause, seeing the advancement of their ideology as the greatest goal of life, oblivious to any higher truth beyond the rational mind and its historical view. Almost like devotees, they enthusiastically and uncritically imitate their Western counterparts, and produce little original of their own. They are happy to denigrate their own spiritual traditions, which are worn by time and neglect and in need of revision, and rudely reject them altogether. They are blindly destroying their own greater heritage for the current intellectual fads of the West that are unlikely to last.

The reason for this condition is that the intellect in itself is not an enlightened intelligence. It is a projection of ego, instinct and emotion into the realm of thought — at best sublimation, at worst an imposition. The intellectual rationalizes his beliefs, opinions and feelings, whether political, artistic or religious, upholding individual and collective prejudices, which are many and diverse. He may try to stand above some of these prejudices but inevitably bows down before others or invents new ones of his own that can be yet more dangerous as they are not rooted in life.

The intellect, as a manifestation of the ego, is certain and proud of its opinions and judgements. It likes to look askance at spiritual teachings and realities beyond its own realm of experience and expertise. The intellectual likes to set his personal ego as the authority and does not honor tradition, particularly of a spiritual nature. After a casual reading or by highlighting a few offensive passages, he can happily dissect the Gita, Mahabharata or Vedas and find them to be wanting from the inviolable standard of his rationalistic and humanistic views. He can glibly show how the ancient sages have failed the litmus test of the current political correctness. He feels that he is removing illusions and superstitions while trampling over the legacy of previous civilizations and presenting little meaningful or lasting in return. Such intellectuals do not take us into deep contemplation of transcendent verities but encourage us to some social protest or leave us in some agnostic limbo, with nothing enduring to guide us.

The Need of the Intellect on the Spiritual Path

On the other hand, many spiritual people, particularly of a devotional nature, are notably lacking in intellectual sophistication and sometimes miss out in common sense. While they are open to an inner reality they can naively believe any superstition of prophets, avatars, miracles and magic. They can be duped by claims of sainthood or spiritual realization, which are easy to make and difficult to verify. They are prone to uncritically accept anything that calls itself religion or mysticism, particularly once they have chosen a particular path. While they honor gurus it is more as savior figures than as teachers. While they praise traditions they seldom really study or practice them. They often turn the guru into god and themselves into his emissaries and fail to really look at themselves.

Such non-thinking devotees frequently don't know how to reason and, however profound their aspirations may be, are often incapable of articulating them in a cogent manner to a neutral audience. While this may not be a problem for them personally or for other devotees, as they may have an inner connection to the Divine, it does limit their ability to influence society or to help others. Without some positive development of the intellect, spiritual growth appears limited or one-sided, or at least mute. It easily gets lost, deceived or confused. Such uncritical spirituality gets mired in prejudice and confuses emotional highs with spiritual bliss.

Compared to the articulate intellectual such non-thinking spiritual types appear gullible, emotional and biased. On the other hand, from the standpoint of the spiritual devotee the materialist intellectual appears dry, arrogant and destructive. Both are lacking in introspection. Both have need of each other. The intellect needs a spiritual sensitivity to soften its critical edge and to turn it within. A spiritual sensitivity needs a critical mind to purify it and to take us from emotion to peace and silence.

The true thinkers of India have neither been dry intellectuals or irrational devotees. They have balanced mind and heart, reason and feeling in a higher awareness that is one with life. This is the real foundation of the spiritual path, not as a credal cult but as an individual practice that can lead one to the universal as a living communion with existence.

The Need for a New Class of Thinkers

In spite of or perhaps because of the great development of information in the world today — the internet, the media and the universities — we live in an anti-intellectual or anti-thinking society. We can find quick answers automatically at the push of a button and so do very little inner searching to find the truth ourselves. There is little introspection in our world either individually or culturally. We fail to critically analyze our culture or ourselves and don't know how to look within. If we do go in for meditation it is for stress relief, blindly applying a technique or simply trying to blank the mind. Few have the energy or the motivation for real thinking that breaks through the boundaries of the ignorance in which we live.

The creative thinker taking us forward in consciousness has been replaced with the intellectual as a well paid or highly trained apologist for various vested interests in the political, commercial or religious realms. Today thought is in service of corporations, institutions, churches or political parties. The current intellectual is like a public relations firm or advertising agency, and naturally upholds the views of those who support him. He is more like a lawyer defending a client presumed innocent than an objective observer looking for the truth.

The intellectual represents the cultural elite of the society. He or she shapes its dominant views and opinions through the media, books, the internet and the universities. The power of the intellectual to influence and mold the minds of youth is also significant as the teacher and tutor. This makes the unenlightened intellectual a dangerous influence on society. Instead of guiding us to dharma he encourages the rejection of any lasting values. To counter this, a new type of intellectual or a new class of thinkers is required that understands the great spiritual traditions but in a living way and can articulate them in clearly intelligible forms that awakens people today to the higher truth.

There is a role for a real thinker, or what we could call a true intellectual, in every society. Such an enlightened thinker does not work out of thought and the ego. He is not the product of an academic institution, nor can he be recognized by a degree or by publications in prestigious journals. He introduces new ideas and insights into the world, while at the same time carrying on the venerable traditions of the great sages who have guided humanity from the beginning of time.

A true thinker is one who follows the yogic way of *Vichāra*, what we could call "spiritually discriminating thinking", which develops out of a meditative mind. This *Vichāra* or deep thought follows a yogic methodology. To achieve it one must have control of the body, control of the *prāṇa*, control of the senses, and above all, concentration with a one-pointed mind. Such a mind can take up any problem, meditate upon it, understand it deeply and present a new comprehension of it. Such a thinker asks fundamental questions and the answers gradually unfold themselves from within by the power of the meditative mind.

The ordinary intellectual has no such control of the body, *prāṇa*, senses and mind. His thoughts are scattered and diffused, reflecting external influences and training, not internal insight. The result is that the ordinary intellectual is not a true or original thinker but the product of the times and its compulsions, often little more than a journalist or a reporter.

Curiously, particularly in the West, the ordinary intellectual shapes how we view spiritual traditions. Many people who study Eastern teachings like Yoga, Vedanta or Buddhism will read academic books on the subject, particularly as to their history, and believe that they are getting information that is authoritative and objective. It is amazing how little people question the academic establishment or the media in such matters that are outside their field of expertise or sensitivity. Sometimes spiritual people or spiritual traditions choose special individuals to train in academia, to infiltrate it in order to shape its views. While this has some effect, it has yet to make a real difference. Instead we need a new order of spiritual thinkers — spiritual intellectuals if you will — who have the sophistication of thought but coming from a place of consciousness within, and who speak directly, not relying on the intellectual establishment.

Those capable of such real *Vichāra* are not fooled by intellectual theatrics. They will not bow down to the intellectual tradition of the West that has failed to even create a concept the Atman (higher Self). Nor are they satisfied with an inarticulate mysticism or blind devotion. They have a critical edge to their thought that reflects deeper perception. Yet their thoughts have both a humor and a compassion that understands our human limitations and helps us to see beyond them.

Ram Swarup

In this context the works of Ram Swarup are notably refreshing and revitalizing to the spirit. He is a good model of the type of higher thinker that we need in the world today. Ram Swarup demonstrates a remarkable combination of sharp intellectual clarity with deep spiritual insight and sensitivity. He is a truly original voice and projects a genuine *Vichāra*, rooted in the higher mind or internalized *buddhi*. He is not an academic intellectual born of institutions, bearing titles or dispensing propaganda. His views flow from a deeper intuitive vision. In him the intellect is a helpful servant of a higher consciousness, its emissary in the world of thought and in society. He gives the intellect its place but does not let it rule him or direct his awareness. A meditative stillness and vastness inhabits his thoughts and provides them with another quality that can lift the mind beyond its habitual boundaries, affording readers a sense of the sublime.

Ram Swarup possesses a profound spiritual wisdom but has not sacrificed reason and common sense along the way. He is not seeking from an emotional level to harmonize everyone or make everyone feel good about their religion or their spiritual views. He introduces a probing analysis and sets forth several important lines of inquiry to sharpen and ennoble our thoughts, not simply to sanctify us in our present limitations. While it may be painful or disconcerting to look into our human prejudices and errors, particularly about religion, it is more transformative in the long run than pretending that we are more than what we are and that all we have done is good.

Ram Swarup presents us with a living example of a yogic thinker. His capacity for *Vichāra* is wide and many-sided, embracing religion, philosophy and spirituality, often reminiscent of Sri Aurobindo, whom he admired. He looks at things from the inside to the outside, seeing how our internal tendencies shape and control our external action.

Ram Swarup's uniqueness and power as a thinker and a seer is that he takes the Hindu mind and its comprehensive approach. Naturally this is a different mindset than the European mind or the American mind, with their intellectual and commercial trends. As representing a millennial old spiritual civilization his thoughts have a support and an energy that should not be underestimated or regarded only as personal opinions. He shows the awakened Hindu mind in the global context, aware of the past and envisioning the future. It is not the India of British rule that he reflects but a new and perennial India as the teacher or guru of nations.

The present volume — *Meditations: Yogas, Gods, Religions* — is the third in a series, following from the second volume, *On Hinduism*. Like his other works it covers a vast range of ideas. Notably, as reflected in its title, it has more focus on spiritual issues and the path to liberation. In this regard Ram Swarup's *Meditations* is a more intimate work and affords us a better view of the author's inner life and the concerns of his own *sādhanā*. From this angle, one could argue that it is Ram Swarup's most important work, particularly for those who are not concerned about the social issues that he often addresses in his other books.

The Yogic Message of Ram Swarup

Ram Swarup's meditations begin characteristically with the Yoga system of Patanjali. Patanjala Yoga is gaining much new interest all over the world along with the new interest in Yoga as a whole. There are many commentaries on Patanjali's *Yoga Sutras*. Some old commentaries are being translated. These, though useful, need updating and to be put in the context of modern views of the mind. Most of the new commentaries, however, are either academic or fanciful. Ram Swarup's comments are not specifically a commentary, yet serve a similar purpose. They go through the main topics of the *Yoga Sutras* in a broad way but getting to their essence and showing their relevance in thought and behavior for all human beings. In his essays the *Yoga Sutras* come alive as if they were written today.

Ram Swarup starts his yogic examination with *samādhi*, the yogic state of meditative absorption, which is where the *Yoga Sutras* begin in its first section *Samādhi-Pāda*. He makes this difficult subject understandable in the context of our behavior and how our minds work. In this way he shows us how to enter into the heart of Yoga as a way of self-transcendence. He offers a striking contrast to the modern emphasis on *āsana* or yoga postures that often prevents Yoga students from achieving any real interiorization and does not deal with the subject of *samādhi* at all.

Yoga is mainly a method of purification of the mind, and purifies the body and the *prāṇa* along with it, as the three are related. Ram Swarup gives the keys to the yogic purification of the mind and discusses its importance as the foundation of Yoga. Then he examines *smriti* or self-remembrance as a way of concentrating the mind. His discussion of this profound topic is quite profound and unique. Self-remembrance is perhaps the easiest way to the Self that is the core of our memory and experience. He proceeds by examining yogic equality or *samatvam*, which is aligned with detachment, and shows its difference from neutrality or compromise. It is not mere moderation but remaining in a state of balance.

His discussion of renunciation is illuminating. He shows how true renunciation is a form of self-exceeding born of joy, not a pursuit of self-denial or the rejection of life. We must give up the limited in order to gain the unlimited and we do so freely, knowing that true fulfillment can only be in the unlimited. His discussion of liberation is also practical and insightful, showing how it relates to our entire human striving. His examination of Patanjali ends with *prajñā* or wisdom, in which he clarifies the role of the *buddhi* or higher mind and shows us how to develop it properly. This is perhaps the central message of the entire book.

Ram Swarup discusses Buddhist Yoga and mentions Buddhist practices relative to Patanjala Yoga. He speaks almost as if a master of Buddhism as well as Hindu Yoga approaches. He shows the complementarity and overlap of their two approaches that can often appear quite different to the outward eye. He shows how Buddhism fits in with the Vedic and Upanishadic ethos, giving emphasis to another side of its perennial dharmic quest, emphasizing the non-ego (*anātman*) to balance the Vedantic higher Self (Atman).

Yet if we overly intellectualize Yoga it becomes dry, theoretical and incapable of really changing our nature. This is the importance of *bhakti* or devotion that is another topic of his meditations. It was the great saints of the Bhakti Movement that kept the Hindu religion alive during the dark ages of Islamic rule. True *bhakti* creates the foundation for the pursuit of spiritual knowledge to be genuine. It allows the higher teaching to enter into our human emotions and personality and ennoble them. That is why *bhakti* has been a central component of the Arya Dharma since the time of the oldest Rigveda.

This yogic message of Ram Swarup reflects depth, patience and adaptability born of a real practice of the teachings over a life-long period. Perhaps this section should be a book in its own right. It goes well with the *Antaryoga* of Sri Anirvan and has a similar flavor of living Yoga. Anyone interested in Yoga or meditation will come away from reading this material with a much deeper view of the subject.

Gods and Religions: A Psychological View

Ram Swarup in writings has perhaps pioneered the new Hindu critique of other religions, particularly versus Christianity and Islam which still seek to convert Hindu India to their more own uniform creeds. He has removed the superficial attitude — all religions are good so you might as well stick to your own — and applied the Hindu mind, the awakened *buddhi* to this difficult task. After all, religion has not only ennobled people; it has also been the main cause of genocide. It has not only produced profound thoughts and insights, but also burned libraries, banned books and prevented its doctrines from being questioned. What kind of mental and psychic formation is behind religion that can harm us if we are not aware of its compulsions?

Ram Swarup's discussion of the Gods is quite revolutionary in many ways. Much of comparative religion today is an exercise in political tolerance, as if whitewashing the differences and divisions between religions might make them go away — though the basic conflicting dogmas are not challenged and missionary aggression is not questioned. Religious teachings are often like weapons that if we don't know how to use or if we use the wrong way can wreak tremendous damage on people, both inwardly and outwardly.

What are the Gods and Goddesses and the One God? Are

they formations of the Divine or of the human mind or a mixture of both? Where does their great power come from? Is it from a higher reality or simply the pressure of our individual or collective subconscious urges and the ego's need for grandiosity? Knowing the frailty of human nature, one must expect religion to have the same limitations as any human unless we have some deeper insight.

Gods and Goddesses are formations of the individual and collective psyche as it mirrors, channels, and energizes, or even resists and perverts cosmic forces. All formulations of Divinity are not all equal or all for the good, any more than all uses of electricity or atomic power are, particularly for those who don't know how they really work. While there is a natural religion or faith innate in each person, organized or credal religion perverts and abuses this for its own vested interests of power and position in the external world. This is similar to how political ideologies like Communism and Fascism distort our natural idealism for social order and turn it into an intolerant military machine.

The danger of various Gods and Goddesses is a common subject in missionary theology that portrays the One God of monotheism as the only truth. Proponents of such monotheism see many Gods and Goddesses as imperfect formations of divinity at best, and at worst forms of superstition, idolatry and evil. Yet monotheism, with its intolerance and aggression, reflects the very lower emotional interests of human beings that its votaries like to descry in other Gods and Goddesses. Monotheism itself can appear like a crazed form of tribalism with its followers blindly seeking to impose their One God on everyone, failing to see any spiritual and religious impulse that falls outside of their narrow forms. Reducing spirituality to belief, they confuse a higher consciousness with a mere label and its emotional propagation.

Ram Swarup shows the danger of monotheism, not only for its social domination and authoritarianism that restricts individual freedom but also for its warping of the human psyche and turning religion into a force of aggression, if not vengeance. While at surface value monotheism appears as an affirmation of the unity of truth, if we look at it deeply it is usually an attempt to impose one view of Divinity on all people, and by whatever means may be necessary or possible. It is not about the unity of truth but of the singularity of one belief and its vested interests. Therefore, it avoids truth, introspection and spiritual search. It is content with an identity, institution, slogan and stereotype that arouses emotions and appeals to prejudice. It is like a tribal god arrogating the position of a universal God, not the promoting of a universal God of love, peace, and respect for all.

Belief in the One God certainly has not made people better, kinder or more intelligent. The One God, just like a primitive totem, can easily become a personification of ego-forces, a need to dominate and control, if not conquer and destroy. That the One God demonstrates such questionable traits as pride, anger and jealousy should alert us to his real nature. In the modern multicultural world it is time to set this arrogance of monotheism aside and honor all the spiritual impulses of all human beings and in all forms — and recognize the pursuit of Self-realization that transcends all beliefs, dogmas and churches. Monotheism, though it has its place, is not the highest spiritual impulse of humanity, and can serve as a channel for some of the lowest ego-urges. It has more often been used as a stick to beat people of other beliefs than as a tool for bringing the hearts of all people together.

In this examination of religion, Ram Swarup functions like a master psychologist, aware not just of ordinary human limitations but also of the psychic and occult ramifications of our religious urges. Modern psychology is ignorant of the psychic power of religious beliefs and practices. It is not aware of the forces of the psyche that extend into primal and to cosmic levels of energy and compulsion both subhuman and superhuman. Much of modern spirituality, trying to harmonize all religions, is ignorant of the danger of throwing together different beliefs, which can be like throwing together various powerful chemicals. Ram Swarup shows the psychic danger of misapplied religion and also the means to purify ourselves from their distortions.

In fact, most of our Gods, including our One God, are usually born of the ego. They are ego-formations that sustain the personal self and its desires, which include the longing for immortality. Until we question and remove that ego our religions will only reinforce it, whatever else of benefit they may claim to offer. This is the importance of the Dharmic traditions of India. They begin with an examination of our own ego, not of the beliefs of other people. They start showing us that our ego compels us to prejudice unless we question it. They don't simply channel that ego-urge to promote their own religious ego.

There are two main religious traditions in the world: the Semitic or Biblical emphasizing One God and only one path to him, and the Hindu or Dharmic, emphasizing One Truth and many paths to it. In the last section of the book Ram Swarup continues the themes as in his important work *Hindu View of Christianity and Islam*.

During his life, Ram Swarup openly and sincerely dialogued with liberal Christians and with Sufis, which communications are reflected in the present volume. While originally hoping that liberal Christianity and Sufism might offer an alternative to the prejudices of the orthodox, he eventually realized that they were just whitewashing religious intolerance with a thin coating of 'mysticism'. His critique of these trends is not born of any built-in religious prejudice. It shows how his sincere efforts at dialogue were ignored or distorted. Through repeatedly contacting their narrowness and intolerance, he learned the inherent limitations of such beliefs that left their shadows even on those who sought a wider view from them. Let liberal Christians and Sufis state that they honor Hindu dharma and its teachings as valid ways to the supreme truth. For them to honor Hinduism merely as a precursor to their own greater religion is condescending and arrogant, not tolerant and affirmative. It is only a more refined prejudice, not a real abandonment of exclusivism.

Our religions can be regarded as occult formations not only of the powers of light but those of darkness. They resemble more collective neuroses than a collective seeking of truth. They perpetuate old superstitions and hide a legacy of violence. We need to be exorcised of most of them. Though we can find good people in all religions, without a foundation of Dharma and Yogic *sādhanā* genuine spiritual growth is difficult, and religious illusions can easily distort our perception.

In all these discussions Ram Swarup is not offering any final word or last judgement. He is encouraging us to really examine the topics mentioned and find the truth for ourselves. Most importantly, his book stimulates a genuine *Vichāra* or inquiry in its readers, taking them into a state of meditation that is not fanciful or abstract but clear and adaptable. It represents a revival of the Hindu mind and its gentle but firm analysis of life, through a discerning attention. Hopefully, other thinkers will continue his line of inquiry and take Ram Swarup's dynamic thoughts to the world at large. His legacy is bound to be large for the new world and new India that are about to emerge.

May new Rishis rise again to guide humanity to a real spiritual awakening!

DAVID FRAWLEY
(Vamadeva Shastri)

June 2000,
Santa Fe, New Mexico,
USA.

Section 1

Introduction

Chapter 1

Spiritual Vocation

There is no spiritual life for those who are self-satisfied or those who are pig-happy with their circumstances and with themselves. Only those who feel a certain sense of insufficiency, a certain divine discontent in life are called to a spiritual vocation.

This sense of insufficiency could take many forms but it should not be confused with usual vexations and irritations that are part of the business of living. Unpaid bills and visits of unwelcome guests may be irritating, and we may be peeved and sored at them but they do not amount to a sense of insufficiency which could be spiritually rewarding. In fact, such hurts and offences have the savour of life rather than of the spirit.

The sense of sorrow arises when one begins to reflect on life. There is no spiritual call for the unreflecting, and the insensitive. One sees sorrow and sickness around, the pall of death hanging over all creatures. One finds life as a brief episode and death as its final end. The origin as well as the end of life is shrouded in obscurity and mystery. Is this all or is there something more to it?

Or, one was happily placed. One had health, wealth, even learning, status, popularity, friends, mates, liaisons. But suddenly something happens, some accident, some disgrace, death of a beloved, loss of position and power, desertion by friends. It awakens something in the soul. One can not take things for granted; they have their own laws. One has little control in their order.

Or nothing so sudden need happen. One may one day realize that just with the passage of time, one has less prowess, less capacity. He sees less and hears less. The young avoid him. His face is less prepossessing and it has lost the power to attract. He finds that all he thought was so intimately his own does not last and he seeks to find if there is something more abiding somewhere.

Not only is our life weary and cheerless and is subject to pain, anguish, remorse, anxiety, hunger and insecurity, but if we look at our pleasures, amusements and achievements, they are even more unsatisfactory. Think of our little games and pleasantries, our wits and quips, our gambols and antics, our monkey-tricks and joviality, our cleverness and our wisdom. A time comes when they become very insufficient, very uninteresting. In fact, they begin to bore. They look so unreal and irrelevant. The pleasures and attractions, charms and delights, bewitchery and seductions, art and learning which life has to offer begin to feel hollow and empty.

Even the money and the might of the powerful which ordinarily invite so much envy lose their charm. Surrounded by flatterers, courtiers and yes-men, they live lonely lives. They feel the poverty of their acquisitions, the powerlessness of their power. They find nothing avails, neither property, nor treasury, nor police, nor army. They feel empty, a zero, a blank. They feel a void, a sense of collapse. They feel pinched, constrained, squeezed, diminished, dwarfed.

To this sense of futility is added the sense of being unwanted, unloved. We feel we have been pushed away, discarded, banished, evicted, rejected, vomited out, even evacuated.

If we look around, we find so much insensitivity, lovelessness, hardheartedness, indifference, cruelty and brutality. Is there not somewhere a principle of more warmth, tenderness, love and friendship?

Some by chance turn their gaze inwards and they find, to their surprise that they have within their own soul all the lovelessness and callousness they complained in others. If they continued their self-examination, they find very little to be proud of. They find vanity, pettiness, smallness of the heart and paltriness of the soul. There is the usual cleverness and gimmickry masquerading as wisdom. In everything he does or thinks or moralises about, there is the mask of the Ego. They are filled with self-loathing. Is there no principle of self-transcendence?

In other case, it is not the pettiness and meanness of life nor its pain and loss present or prospective that start the process of questioning, it is its smooth-sailing and easy tenor. Everything is routine, normal, ordered, organized. Everything is taken care of from the womb to the tomb by corporate organisations. All work whether physical or mental has been reduced to easy movements and formulae. It exercises neither the brawn nor the brain. Work, recreation, emotions, travel — everything is routine, deadeningly routine. One feels one is keeping out of the business of living, of danger and challenge. One feels the need of greater self-understanding, a closer look at the definition of life.

Sometimes, in the midst of a crowd, in the midst of sociability one is filled with a sense of loneliness. He realises he is a monad; there are no outer walls but he is shut up within himself. There is a good deal of shoving, pushing, jostling but no contact. There is a lot of chatter, seminars and dialogues but no communication. The world is inhabited by people who are alien to each other. It is not that others fail, we all fail. No one can come out of oneself. We are made that way. Is there no principle of communication and intimacy, no bosom companion, no soul-mate, no comradierie?

But suppose, by an act of empathy one did enter into the feelings and ideas of others, what then? He finds them as trivial and inane as his own. Was his own ego not enough?

But if there is a real thawing of the heart and the ego and one can take a more charitable view of oneself and others, the gulf is bridged but another kind of problem arises. He is surrounded by people he cares for but he cannot wipe out the tears of those in need. He has the heart but not the knowledge and the capacity. An impotent sympathy turns into an impotent rage. He realizes that he is as impotent in selfishness as in sympathy. Again this calls for better self-understanding. Is there no principle of greater effectivity? But if limitation and incapacity are our inevitable lot, can we not accept them with greater resignation? Is there a principle of some higher fulfilment in all this?

There is something irrational about life. Just when one is bursting with riches one is assailed with unsuspected stinginess which makes him look even meaner than he is; on the other hand, when one can least afford it one is invaded by a sense of generosity which makes him feel even more helpless. What are these contradictory elements? From where do they originate? There seems to be some great Jester inside. Sometimes the Psyche throws up images, emotions and thoughts of which men cannot approve. Have they not loved and written poetry secretly and done many others things which do not agree with their self-image? All this requires greater self-understanding. A good deal of us is hidden inside us, like an iceberg. It needs a closer, more inward look.

One looks around and finds a good deal of unmerited suffering and equally unmerited happiness. One finds many good men suffering and many bad men prospering. Is there no principle of justice somewhere?

The sense of insufficiency of life is not the only motive for spiritual turning. Sometimes, in some persons, something greater than their normal life is revealed. There is a glimpse of a reality beyond. News filter through of a greater life, of a greater harmony, of a Kingdom of Heaven. A new consciousness opens up which is made up of light and life and truth and reality. By contrast, the normal reality is a shadow and counterfeit and the normal consciousness dull and opaque and alien.

This glimpse into a new consciousness feeds our hunger for a new life on the one hand and redoubles our sense of insufficiency on the other. We now know that our present consciousness is hardly awake and alive. It is somnabulist, full of make-believe and pretence, with neither light, nor life, nor joy. It is perfunctory, casual, mutilated, a garbled version of the glimpsed consciousness. We know that as long as we live in this consciousness we are in a deep, metaphysical sense disfranchised and our existence is invalid and our life unauthentic.

Or, there may even be no actual glimpse of a higher consciousness, but there is hunger for it in the soul. We do not know yet, even briefly, any higher state of the soul, yet we feel a thirst for it. This thirst may express itself in two ways, either in a sense of incompleteness and estrangement or as an attraction from the above. This estrangement and this hunger belong to the soul, or that portion in man which is most God-like. A divine principle has descended into the body and feels a divine discontent and a divine attraction.

But in most cases, the divine discontent and the divine attraction are no more than vague feelings, obscure hints and tokens. They are too weak to be convincing, much less provide knowledge and guidance of the path. And they are overlaid by another principle, the bodily principle, which exercises a constant gravitational pull in the opposite direction. It is easy to be sucked in worldliness. The weight of ordinary living is overwhelming, overpowering. The world is not without its attractions and there is something akin to it in our own soul which supports its hold on us.

We are bound to it more inextricably and in more ways than we suspect. It is not without reason that the body has been called the grave of the soul by thinkers like Plato.

Therefore, even after the soul is stirred, it needs reinforcement from outside, which could take the form of a living teacher, or a scripture or a spiritual culture in general. Without this aid, the man will end, unless the stirring is very strong and very definitive, by feeling odd and by feeling maladjusted.

Section 2

Pātañjala Yoga

Chapter 2.1

Samādhi

Yoga says that there is a secret Godhead within but it is veiled by the outer life. A vast life is locked and buried in the soul but most of the time we remain unaware of it and choose to live in shadows and illusions. The soul feels confined and this is the basic cause of its unhappiness.

Ordinarily, man never knows his free intelligence or the liberated status of his mind. What he knows are mental configurations or the mind-stuff as modified by objects. So a mind as we know it is only an image of its own objects. A man either knows the mind in its objects or its objects in the mind but never knows the mind or the objects in themselves.

Mind establishes different kinds of contact with the world. The most ordinary one which is also the best known is through the senses, and desire. The mind receives the world through the senses, carries it with itself in memory and relives it in imagination. In dream and sleep it retires from the world but it is far from being inactive in those states too. There it seems to exercise a new mode of sensibilities and enters into new worlds of experience.

Besides the impressions which it receives more or less consciously and to which it responds in the same way, there are other stimuli and responses which are going on all the time subliminally. There is a good deal of unconscious activity which partakes of intelligent adaptation at the physiological and even the chemical levels. A greater part of life is lived at these levels instinctively and reflexively. So there is a vast consciousness at work within us but of this we remain unaware for most of the time.

Besides the world which the mind receives from the outside, it seems there is another which it carries within itself on its own. There is a whole world of moral and aesthetic values which seem to form no part of the world and which are lent to it by the mind. That is why the world that Science deals with is without these values for it is difficult to imagine how they can belong to it.

But even the magnitudes like time and space and causality and the laws of Mathematics and Logic with which Science deals with such assurance and without which we cannot conceive the world do not seem to belong to it. At least this is the conclusion at which many important philosophers have arrived and to which a little reflection would lead. These magnitudes and attributes too seem to belong to the mind rather than to the world.

Then we also receive impulsions of a very different kind, impulsions which make no logical sense and yet come with an over-riding authority. They seem to be more akin to our deeper nature and aspirations and seem to hold the secret of the world. There is within us a hunger for truth and righteousness and Reality. What to make of it? Is it a token of things unseen? Deep down within us, we feel that if we had the knowledge of this world, this knowledge would be most worthy and it would be fulfilling in a way in which no other knowledge can be. Not only we know only a tiny section of the world and our mind and life, but it seems we do not know them in their best and worthiest part.

Samādhi is a method of diving deep into these unexplored and unknown regions of the mind and the psyche. But Yogic *samādhi* does not seek to extend the frontiers of knowledge as ordinarily understood, the knowledge of new facts and figures, the knowledge of all kinds of odds and ends in the psyche, but it seeks knowledge of that part which is most divine. It does not seek to know more of the mortal world but it seeks the knowledge of immortality and the path to that. And it does not seek that knowledge externally as if from the outside but by becoming that. It is an inside knowledge, a participative knowledge. It is a path of Self-knowledge.

But Self-knowledge is a process, a discipline. It does not work in a vacuum. It involves a knowledge of many relevant subjects and states: knowledge of all that liberates and that binds; or knowledge of all *klishṭa* and *aklishṭa vrittis* or *kuśal* and *akuśal* dharmas. We have to know what we are and what we have become. Our outer life is rooted in the inner. Therefore, those who take to the path of Self-knowledge cannot avoid the knowledge of these inner worlds altogether even if they do not actively seek it. It lies in their way and they grow faculties for the same. They come to know what are things and what are thoughts and what are desires and how thoughts and desires leave behind *saṁskāras* or seeds of a future becoming. When they explore these seed-states, they come to know not only their past but also their future lives.

On this path we also realize that we are not what we seem to be; that our roots spread into deeper recesses; that we are linked in a common destiny and that we are part of larger life.

All this knowledge is a part of the spiritual lore. It is not necessary that every spiritual aspirant should come by all this knowledge in its fulness but to all of them comes the message of a larger and purer life. In order to reach *ātma*-knowledge, a man has to take back the road by which he has come. This involves traversing many terrains and valleys which reveal different facts to different aspirants according to their different needs.

To enter this vaster life, *samādhi* is the key. The utility of *samādhi* is based on the truth long observed that when a mind concentrates on any object or idea, the object begins to yield its deeper secrets. Things are illumined in a state of concentrated attention which is what *samādhi* is. It is also seen that in this state not only the object but the mind too is illumined. Ordinarily, the mind is lost in its diffusion; it is dull, opaque, hazy and through its half-light, we grope and move and know — there is hardly any light left for self-awareness. But in concentration even on an object other than itself, it acquires that capacity.

Though the word *samādhi* belongs to the Yogic vocabulary, it does not mean that only the Yogis are capable of it. Concentration is a quality which is inherent in human mind. If one important attribute of *samādhi* is forgetfulness of every thing except the object of immediate attention or interest and some kind of at-one-ment with it, then *samādhi* is at work at widely different levels. Sometimes people become one with their rage or grief or joys. In sexual union, there is a kind of self-forgetfulness and at-one-ment which is taken for a Yogic *samādhi*. In all these, there is an intensified state of consciousness but these are not Yogic *samādhis*. These are called *mūḍha samādhis*.

There is *samādhi* also at more laudable levels. There is the concentration of a scientist or artist or thinker but that too is not Yogic concentration. The Yogic *samādhi* is directed to the purpose of Self-knowledge in one way or another, directly or indirectly. Lower *samādhis* generate false identifications, but the purpose of a Yogic *samādhi* is to liberate the mind from lower identification, from lower *samādhis*, from at-one-ment with the body and its desires, or even with the aesthetic joys of an artist and the intellectual joys of a researcher. Pātañjala Yoga says that the mind takes on the form of any object to which it turns and on which it concentrates. The purpose of Yoga is to liberate the mind from its own modifications and meet it in its self-status. This the *samādhi* achieves if it is directed to spiritual rather than to secular ends. To dwell with loving attention on heavenly things is *samādhi*. Buddhist Yoga defines *samādhi* as concentration of a purified mind. If we bring an impure mind or even a mind which is indifferent to higher things to the practice of *samādhi*, that *samādhi* is not Yogic.

Even the Yogic *samādhi* is discussed under two heads: *samprajñāta* and *asamprajñāta*. The words are difficult to translate but they may be called the path of Knowing and the path of Unknowing, the famous paths of *vidyā* and *avidyā* of the Upanishads. The Buddhist discuss the first under '*samādhi*' and the second under the word '*prajñā*' or wisdom.

The first kind of *samādhi* brings occult knowledge, the second one Self-knowledge; in the first the *kleśas* of the mind are weakened, in the second they are destroyed; the first wins *deva-lokas*, the worlds of Gods and Brahmā, the second one brings *nirvāṇa*, liberation. The first one leads to a deepened knowledge of the subjective and the objective worlds, the second one leads to a deepened knowledge of the Self — it opens up an inner seeing and brings wisdom. In Buddhist Yoga, the first one is also called *śamatha-mārga* or the path of pacification while the second one is called *vipaśyanā-mārga*, or the path of wisdom.

The two *samādhis* have invited a good deal of discussion in Hindu and Buddhist Yogic literature. They have been discussed from various angles and from various viewpoints — though the discussion makes a sense only to practitioners. The word '*samādhi*' itself is used to convey several connected meanings — the context determining the exact meaning. Sometimes it stands for that state of mind which cognises only the object of contemplation, the state in which the subject disappears and the object alone remains. But at other times, the word signifies all the initial aids and steps that lead to the last trance-state. The word is also used in a still higher sense, as we have seen, to designate a state in which there is no trance as such but exceeding it the wisdom-eye opens up and the man is established in the peace and unity of the Self.

From this discussion, we also learn that *samādhi* is a discipline, a process of deepening stages, each stage having its own dominant flavour or relish. These deepening stages also reveal increasingly deeper secrets and subtler truths of the world and effect lasting changes in our deeper being.

While the purpose of *samādhi* is self-exploration leading to liberation, *samādhi* itself is not easy. There are many propensities which keep dragging down the mind to lower pursuits. There are fears, phobias, greedy selfishness, egoistic grasping, clawing and hankering, violence, bitterness — they have to be conquered first before one can even think of *samādhi*. There is no spiritual life for those who have a strong desire-life and who kill and harbour deep animosity towards their brothers. They are incapable of *samādhi* and they should not take to it. *Samādhi* cannot improve them; on the other hand, instead of lifting them up, they will drag it down and they will become worse. For self-correction, they should cultivate a little more consideration of others, think more of their duties and obligations; they should cultivate brotherly feeling towards others. What can be corrected by an active moral life should not be left to contemplative life. The contemplative life serves other ends.

Even when the quality of life has been raised up by an active moral life, there still remain impediments to *samādhi*. The Buddhist Yoga specifically mentions five, a selection from a larger list provided by the Pātañjal Yoga. They are desire, ill-will, agitation and regrets, physical and mental laziness, doubt in the efficacy of the Yogic discipline.* These are mentioned in this context not because of their low moral content but because they hinder concentration. They cause distractions and restlessness.

Mind desires now one thing, now another. It flits from one object to another. Therefore, unless desire is conquered to some extent, concentration is not possible. But even if it is induced somehow through some forced and mechanical methods, it is not liberating.

There is another source of distraction, namely ill-will and spite. It seems to be the opposite of desire but in the dialectics of the mind, it is merely the other side of the coin.

It is also equally sweeping in its operation. A man bears a grudge not only against his enemies but even against his friends and benefactors; many people are permanently angry and bear a deep grudge towards everything around. The impulse is difficult to conquer. In its subtle form, it accompanies a *sādhaka* even to the very end. In that form, it arises even against one's teacher or pupil and even against Brahma. Therefore there are prayers in the Upanishads, the prayer of a teacher and pupil together: "May we bear no grudge against each other"; or the prayer of a *sādhaka*, "May I not deny Brahma" (*nirākaraṇa*).

The conquest of these propensities in their various subtle manifestations is not possible — that belongs to the mature fruits

---

*Buddhist *kāmachhanda* (desire) corresponds with *avirati* of the Pātañjala Yoga; *auddhatya-kaukritya* (agitation and regret) with *anavasthitva* and *daurmanasya*; *styāna-mriddha* (physical and mental laziness) with *styāna* and *ālasya*; *vichiktsā* (doubt) with *saṁśaya*.

of *sādhanā*. At this stage, it is enough to conquer their grosser working, to tame their potential for distracting the mind. The mind is full of other infirmities also. It is regretful; it is indolent; it is heedless; it is weary; it is agitated. In its activity, there is no poise, no method, no rationale, no science. It is nothing but restlessness.

How to conquer these weaknesses, these wanderings and downward pulls of the mind? How to acquire a state of mind which is called *ekāgra*, one-pointed, and which is also characterized by purity and which is also passive as well as alert? According to Pātañjala Yoga, the true Yogic *samādhi* begins at this level, the *ekāgra-bhūmi*, which is also the gateway to the next higher level, the *nirodha* or *nirvāṇa-bhūmi*, which gives liberation and Self-knowledge. But to enter this larger realm of the Spirit, the mind has to become one-pointed first.

To raise the mind to a minimum level of purity and to steady it, many practices are in vogue; but the essence of all those practices is to conquer bad thoughts with the help of good ones and many thoughts with the help of one thought. When bad thoughts and sentiments arise in the mind, one should reflect on their real nature, how they have their source in greed, anger and delusion (*lobha-krodha-moha-pūrvakāḥ*), how they lead to the bitter harvest of misery and nescience (*duḥkha-ajñāna-anantaphalāḥ*). This involves the 'practice of the opposite truth', *pratipaksha bhāvanā*.

Similarly, a wandering mind can be tamed by the practice of one truth or principle (*ekatattva-abhyāsaḥ*). One should choose an object and concentrate on it whole-heartedly. For this purpose, one could choose anything. One could choose God or any of his attributes, or Names or Aspects or Images; one could meditate on his chosen deity or his guru or any person who has conquered his passions; one could meditate on certain deep truths of life like Death or Dharma or certain moral and spiritual qualities like purity, truth, friendship, renunciation, courage, faith; one could meditate on any deeper psychic truth revealed in a dream or just on the emptiness of the sleeping state; one could meditate on a luminous form or sense-experience, subtle vision, sound, colour, flavour and touch; in fact, one could start with anything which is agreeable to one's deeper psyche.

One could meditate on the Elements of Nature or on natural objects like the sun, the moon, the stars, the earth, the fire. Some theologians object to this choice. But this objection is purely intellectual and lacks the insight and knowledge of Yoga. These natural objects are not what they appear at first sight. They incarnate psychic and spiritual realities. As meditation deepens, it reveals the inner Spirit informing them.

Not only celestial objects and Elements of Nature but even their representations and smaller objects and different colours could be used for initial concentration. There are called *kasins* and their various forms have been discussed in Yogic literature. To these have been added many others forms, geometrical forms, sound-forms, even intellectual conundrums called *kaons*. Various mantras, tantras, diagrams, images serve the same purpose.

'*Japa*' or the repetition of God's Name or of a Mantra is also a great help to concentration. So in watching one's own breath. *Prāṇāyāma* or breath-exercises and breath-control is also a great aid.

These objects of concentration called *karma-sthānas* are not proposed arbitrarily. Their variety conforms to the variety of human nature. People in whose nature the principle of attachment is strong (*rāga-charit*) should meditate on a dead body in different conditions and stages of decay; those whose nature is spiteful should meditate on friendliness; those in whom the ego-principle is strong, those who think too much in terms of 'I' and 'mine' should meditate on the ephemerality of the world and life.

There are also special meditations for meeting special problems. If, in a man, concupiscence is strong, he should meditate on the impurities of the body. If he is identified too much with his body, he should meditate on the truth that it is subject to death and decay. If he suffers from ill-will, he should meditate on friendliness.

This brings us to certain *karma-sthānas* which hold a very high place in *sādhanā*. They are different from *kasins* in the sense that they make a direct appeal to the psyche and are easily understood. They are *maitrī* (friendliness), *karuṇā* (compassion), *muditā* (joyfulness), and *upekshā* (indifference). One should feel friendly towards the happy ones, compassionate towards those in distress, joyful in the virtuous ones and indifferent towards the evil ones. These are the well-known four Great Abidings or *brahma-vihāras*. The practice of *brahma-vihāras* serves two purposes. One is for expansion, for growing into the likeness of those qualities, for growing into friendliness, compassion, joy and equality. This aspect is very important and it partakes of the spirit of the Upanishadic *sādhanā*. In later developments of Buddhism also this aspect began to be increasingly more emphazised. But in the Yoga of Concentration, or Rāja-Yoga, they have another utility which receives greater emphasis, namely their utility for countering the influence of certain narrowing and binding passions, *kleśas*. Through their influences, bad influences of opposite passions are countered. For example, *maitrī* destroys *dvesha* or ill-will; *muditā* destroys envy and jealousy.

But every truth of the spirit is opposed not only by its own opposite but also by its own lower version, its own kind on a lower level. For example, take compassion. Its opposite is cruelty or *hiṁsā*. While compassion counters it and in its own turn countered by it, it is liable to corruption and subversion even more insidiously from within as it were, by its own kind on another level, namely *śoka* or sorrow. It could degenerate into ignorant sorrow or condescending pity. While the heart of compassion is universality and disinterestedness, that of pity is contempt and self-congratulation.

Similarly, *maitrī* destroys *dvesha* or ill-will; but unless one is wide-awake, the feeling in turn could generate *rāga*, a doting, erotic attachment or a vulgar chumminess. *Muditā* takes pleasure in the joys of others but unless one is established in great purity, it could generate in the *sādhaka* pleasures of creaturely kind.

Upekshā is equal-mindedness towards all, friends and foes, the virtuous and the wicked; but it could degenerate into mere indifference and passivity.

We see the operation of the same principle in the working of other faculties. *Buddhi* analyses and it corrects the blindness of faith and superstition; but on a lower level, it is also akin to *dvesha*. Therefore, it begins to find faults where they do not exist. Similarly, *śraddhā* or faith could counter the excesses of doubt but unless one is very watchful, faith could become narrow, fanatic and ignorant. It is better to praise than to blame but in the world there is a good deal of *rāgātmaka* or infatuated praise which is equally unedifying. While people's blame is spiteful, their praise is equally idle and interested. It is even self-praise. People of deepened inner culture refrain from talking about others whether in praise or in blame.

The *karma-sthāna* having been chosen, one should, if it is a material object, gaze at it with concentrated attention and receive its image in the mind. With continued practice, the image gets internalized, making the outer object redundant. If one perserveres, the image begins to lose its grossness and becomes increasingly more abstract, purified and psychic. The purity is born of a deepened concentration and this in turn has a concentration-deepening quality.

One could start, according to one's predilection, with an eye-object or an ear-object, with anything visible or audible or any sense-object; eventually they all meet in the unity of the *manas*. The material becomes mental and the mental becomes psychic.

The mind has a natural tendency to dwell more easily on pleasant experiences than on painful ones. Sāṁkhya philosophy tells us that objects have their joy-forms lying just beneath their surface material and sense-forms. If through moral purity and initial Yogic effort one could get to these joy-forms, concentration becomes spontaneous and natural. The sense of strain and struggle is left behind. In the beginning, one finds it difficult to keep one's eyes closed for any length of time, but after these joy-forms are experienced, it is difficult to open them. For one reason because the *sāttvika* mind is more akin to those joy-forms than to its grosser experiences.

But even if the *karma-sthāna* chosen is not a material object but is some moral or spiritual truth like purity, truth, compassion or Dharma, or the image of a Deity like Krishna or Shiva, the nature of the problem and the process does not change. The new *karma-sthāna* has its own grossness. A lot of desires, hopes, images, sentimentalizings and conceptualizations cling to it. Through meditation, it sheds them all and acquires the purity and the fitting status of a psychic truth or meditation-form.

When the mind has sufficiently separated from the sense-form and the desire-form of a *karma-sthāna* and its abstract-form has emerged, the *sādhaka* leaves the periphery and enters the meditation-region proper. Now *samādhi* is not the name of a finished state of mind with its contents finally labelled and named; on the other hand, it is the name of a deepening process, a process which covers a very large terrain, a whole world of the unseen beyond the seen of different levels of manifestations and subtlety. It is an increasingly purer mind cognising an increasingly subtler world till both dissolve in the reality of one substance. But the two aspects have given rise to two descriptions though they both use more or less the same terminology in describing the different levels or *bhūmis* and stages of *samādhi* and meditation. The Pātañjala Yoga describes these stages in terms of the order of reality cognised and the Buddhist Yoga in terms of the dominant traits and qualities of the states of mind that emerge in each successive stage.

In presenting its thought, the Pātañjala Yoga uses Sāṁkhya categories. According to Sāṁkhya, the objective and the subjective world as we know it in our ordinary consciousness, is a modification of one principle which it calls Prakriti. While the energy and the substance of this modification is provided by this underlying reality, the impulse is provided by another principle called the Purusha. The Purusha is the conscious principle, the master but passive, which sanctions all changes but itself remains aloof from them.

The modification is in a descending order and proceeds from the inner to the outer, from the subtle to the gross, from the universal to the particular, from unity to diversity. In Yoga, with the help of concentration, we learn to retrace our steps, go over from the gross to the subtle to the causal, from the material to the mental to the intellectual, from the particular to the universal to the transcendental.

The first objects of concentration are ordinary objects, our senses and sense-objects. But as we learn to look at them with a tranquil mind and without the intervention of our desires and predilections, we arrive at the first *samādhi* and the first Yogic knowledge. In the technical language of the Yoga, this is *vitarkānugata samādhi* or *vitarka samāpatti* — *samādhi* and knowledge which are still at the discursive level.

But as meditation deepens, we go beyond the discursive level and arrive at *tanmātrā*, the five subtle Elements and subtle senses. This constitutes the second *samādhi* called *vichāra samāpatti*. In still more deepened states of *samādhi*, we arrive at still more subtle substrata, called in Sāṁkhya '*ahaṁkāra*' and '*buddhi*'. They give rise to *samāpattis* called *ānanda* and *asmitā*.

The Buddhists make similar divisions but describe the mental concomitants of those states. The mind is generally beclouded, infatuated, agitated; it is depressed or distracted. But by conquering desires and living a blameless life and by good works and good thoughts, it is freed from the servitude of its desires and becomes capable of taking to a life of meditation.

With the onset of meditation, the distractive influences of propensities like desire are weakened and minimised, and other qualities and traits appear on the scene which constitute the limbs of meditation because it is on them that it stands and by them it moves and lives and on them it is founded. They are *vitarka*, *vichāra*, *prīti*, *sukha*, *smriti*, *ekāgratā* and *upekshā*. These words are difficult to translate but the following discussion will make the sense clear.

These *dhyāna*-limbs are given in the order of their increasing depth. In the first *dhyāna*, the mind is still discursive (*vitarka*); in the second *dhyāna*, it is reflective (*vichāra*). In the first, it uses thoughts for seizing the object; in the second, it holds it and possesses it but still with the uncertain power of thought. In the first, there are separate acts, reflections and resolutions but in the second, all thoughts cease and only thought remains. In the third *dhyāna*, even thought ceases and the mind is filled with a deep satisfaction (*prīti*). In the fourth *dhyāna*, satisfaction gives way to an inner joy which is self-sprung. In the fifth *dhyāna* even joy ceases and a still more tranquil state appears which is characterized by mindfulness (*smriti*), one-pointedness (*ekāgratā*) and equal-mindedness (*upekshā*).

Beyond them lie the four infinities of deepening purity. Here one enters the infinity of mind and knowledge, a *chidākāśa* which is also the source of many *siddhis* or powers like clair-voyance, etc. Here the *sādhaka* knows things hidden from ordinary view and the limitations imposed by time and space are conquered.

Beyond these infinities lie *nirvāṇa-bhūmi* or *asamprajñāta samādhi* which are generally discussed under *prajñā* and Liberation. Here one enters self-naughting and self-annihilation and acquires Wisdom and Self-knowledge.

The above calls for some clarification on some points. In several mystic traditions, discursive reason and thought are regarded with suspicion. But this is true of thought imprisoned in desire. Once the desire-life becomes less insistent, thought comes into its own and is even a help to Yoga. In fact, the first *samādhi* is at the level of discursive mind. Whether one likes it or not, one cannot avoid discursive reason altogether, at least to begin with, till a deeper mind and a more direct seeing come into being; meanwhile the next best thing is to use thought as best as we can. In Yoga, thought is used to conquer thought.

Vitarka has now acquired a lower meaning of a contentious argumentation but in Yogic literature it has a special sense. It means verbal thought or reflection. For example, when one waits on his chosen deity with love and care, with much addressing, courting, invoking, praising, hymning, adoring to the exclusion of all other thoughts and sentiments contrary to the above, his mind is filled with one rhythm, one resonance, one thought and he experiences the first *samāpatti* or *dhyāna*. It is very high stage in Yoga and it does not come to those who are still filled with the usual clutter and chatter and noise of the mind. The mind becomes unified. In the next stage, all separate thoughts become concentrated into one single thought, into one flame of thought. Here one no longer prays with prayers; he becomes prayerful.

Here we may also refer to another important point. Different *dhyāna-bhūmis* reveal different truths. Though these truths have their own integrality and imply one another, they also have their own individual flavour and they receive different emphases in different *dhyāna-bhūmis*. No great scripture can be completely lacking in any one of these truths but different scriptures give different prominence to different truths. In the New Testament, the truths of joy, faith, a chosen luminous form, conversion, inspiration, enthusiasm, zeal, particularly of an *ishṭa* are developed; they belong to the first three *dhyāna-bhūmis*. But the truths of the fourth *dhyāna-bhūmi* like mindfulness and equal-mindedness which open the gates to the still higher truths of Universality, Liberation and Self-knowledge belong to the more mystic tradition of humanity.

Samādhi is a vast subject and in the above discussion we have no more than touched upon some of its more salient points. Its higher reaches and deeper life-power, we shall discuss under purity, equality, liberation, etc. Meanwhile, let us refer to another important point which relates to a confusion between *samādhi* and a trance. Not only are the two mistaken for each other but within the trance itself there is an inability to distinguish a religious trance from a psycho-pathological one.

Samādhi and trance are different. Because of the absence of ordinary conscious control in both and some other common features, the two are confused though they are quite different in their methods and aims. Trance is a mental condition produced involuntarily; *samādhi*, on the other hand, is a well-authenticated process of going deep into the psyche. Sometimes the methods used even for *samādhi* by some lesser Yogas are violent, mechanical and forced; therefore the state of mind induced by them is also more akin to a trance state and carries within it the violence of the methods used. And like the trance state, this state too is full of images and suggestions.

Trance does very little in the way of improving the personality. It comes and goes leaving the personality more or less unchanged. *Samādhi*, on the other hand, is a process by which to purify the normal consciousness in the light of some greater truth of the consciousness.

In the normal course, the energy of a trance comes from repression but it is not always so; it could also be an infusion of the spirit though the infusion may not be from the highest source. Only such trances which have this infusion have significance for religious life.

Modern Psychology tells us that trance is a condition of dissociation, characterized by a lack of voluntary movement and frequently by automatism in act and thought. It is based on repression though what is repressed is not a single idea as happens in many dissociations but a whole system of ideas, an organised group of experience, dissociated from the normal consciousness and functioning independently as a split-off personality. Many times, this split personality has a coherence, an inner logic of its own. From time to time, this takes over the personality temporarily; conscious control is lost and we have the phenomenon of a trance.

This is a fair description of ordinary trances but it will not do for trances which we meet in religious history. Some of the elements like the loss of the conscious control and the temporary take-over of the consciousness may be common to both but they also differ in some essential respect: repression. One cannot accuse some of the prophets most known for their trances of repression, so the energy for their trances could have come only from some other source. There was an infusion of the spirit, an expression of a hidden personality which is a part of all of us but which breaks through the common consciousness only at times and sometimes even takes control of it. Throughout antiquity, we meet trance-cultures and trance-states, in which man goes beyond the limitations of the ordinary consciousness and enters into a larger consciousness, feeling an infusion of the holy spirit, breaking into prophetic utterances, revealing something of the past and the present and giving expression to certain moral and spiritual truths of life. In the Greek world, there were oracles, soothsayers; many tribes all the world over had their *shamans*; they were called prophets in religions derived from the Semitic source.

These trances were not always involuntary. To some extent, they could be cultivated. Sometimes, herbs, inhalations were used. Isolation, fasting, moral purity helped the process. In gifted individuals, the inspiration was comparatively purer and there was genuine infusion; in other cases, this element got mixed up with a good deal which arose from a lesser source and a lower depth. Prophetic utterances have expressed piety and some moral and spiritual truths, but many times they have also bristled with lurid, colourful and picturesque imageries. They threatened people with a doomsday, aroused apocalyptic hopes and promised a Messiah and exhorted people to a new life.

The period between 200 BC and 150 AD of the Jewish history was especially marked by such prophecies. Christianity was born and nurtured for quite some centuries on this ethos. Islam was also a child of the same spirit of prophecy and in some ways improved upon it through its founder though it closed its chapter on further prophets.

On the other hand, *samādhi* of the Yoga is born of a different impulse and breathes a different atmosphere. It is not eschato-logical and apocalyptical in spirit. It also does not seek a temporary infusion. On the other hand, it is a method, a discipline for raising up the tone and quality of consciousness, of shaping life in the image of a higher truth, of calling on the hidden power of the divine so that this power assumes the lead in life. Yoga seeks a permanent change in the consciousness. Its aim is the self-revelation of the Self to the Self and its manifestation in life. Hindu Yoga is more akin in spirit to the mystic way in other religions.

Here we are not attempting to compare. A first-rate prophet may be better than a second-rate Yogi, but we should be able to see the differences of the spirit and approach of the two. They may partly arise from personality-differences and partly from cultural factors. It must also be realized that when God-impulse is very strong and pure, it can dispense with usual methods and over-power their limitations. Such people take the heavens by storm as it were.

While the above has to be admitted in principle, one should do it with the greatest circumspection. It is so easy to confuse any strong feeling or idea with divine inspiration and command. Inspiration can be a dangerous thing. Some time ago, the Associated Press reported about a Bible-toting young man of 18 years, Robert Huetti by name, belonging to Stafford, Connecticut, U.S.A. The Lord told him to cut off his right hand, which he did, because he had "raised it against the Devil". Again, I think, it is Aldous Huxley if I remember correctly, who tells us in one of his books about a man who was divinely inspired to cut off his brother's head.

We may laugh at these extreme cases though these are by far not the extremest ones. In the above cases, an impure inspiration did no harm except to the individuals concerned but in many other cases, the harm done is on a very large scale.

If inspiration comes clothed in the language of piety and is accompanied by a certain amount of sincerity and austerity and in modern savants by intellectuality, it is less easy to resist it. There has been a certain type of spirituality in which God has ordered that a whole tribe of heathens and infidels be killed and their places of worship destroyed; that their lands be invaded and their people asked to choose between true faith and death; that the light of the true faith be carried to the four corners of the earth through imperialist conquests and organized missionary work. In the religious history of mankind, such 'inspiration' has been regarded as prophetic.

According to Yoga, the field of inspiration and prophethood is full of pitfalls. And yet on the spiritual path, one cannot do without inspiration. One must therefore constantly purify it. One must cultivate modesty, discrimination and a *sāttvika* nature.

What is said about inspiration could also be said about meditation. It too could be impure and misapplied. It could be used for intensifying certain moods and ideas. And because meditation lends to those moods and ideas a certain unity and reality, shine and joy, they show all the more in the light of a concentrated consciousness. This strengthens the hold of a particular idea or doctrine or article of faith. And if that faith or belief has a certain *sāttvika* core, its grip becomes even more binding. The bondage of a *sāttvika* thought is even stronger than that of a *rājasika* or *tāmasika* thought or belief or faith.

In Yoga, a single *sāttvika* thought or image is used to conquer the wanderings of the mind. The practice gives a certain centrality, unity and purity to the mind. But this is only the first step. The consciousness should now also be broadened and universalized. If we stop short at the first step, it could lead to narrowness and fanaticism. In Yoga, concentration is only a means to an end. The Yoga of *samādhi* is important but the more important values stressed are universality, purity, liberation and *prajñā*.

Chapter 2.2

Purity

Purity has several connected meanings. It means simple, true, virtuous, chaste, honest, innocent, unstained, unadorned, genuine, guileless. If a man is essentially a soul, then purification means that he should separate his soul from all that is not soul and that in his life he should express the truths that belong to the soul.

If we accept this definition, then it involves two concepts: one is that of purgation, of giving up a lower life and lower impulsions; and the other is that of embracing a higher life and higher impulsions. The first movement involves Self-separation, the separation of the higher from the lower self; the second movement calls for Self-projection, the higher self placing itself at the forefront of life and informing all its activities and thoughts — *purohitam*. Self-expression means the expression of soul-principle in its purity.

The soul in its essence is pure but in its actual working in life, it is subject to a good deal of impurity and admixture, gross as well subtle. In fact, it needs a lot of churning before it can be separated from its more subtle admixtures.

The impurities are of different kinds and they have been differently classed and they obtain on various levels. They belong to the body, the mind and the ego; or they relate to conduct, to speech, to mind. They are outer and inner, or gross and subtle. Some are patently obnoxious to the moral sense but others take on idealist disguises and are difficult to spot. A certain stage of moral and spiritual development has its own level of purity but it may be inadequate for the next stage. Some systems of thought regard impurities as sinful, others look at sins as no more than passing impurities. Some treat them morally, others psychologically.

The other principle with which the soul get identified in its state of impurity is called in many systems the bodily principle. But the use of the word is figurative, not literal. It does not mean that the soul in order to be pure should give up the body; it only means that a man should master his passions and the attraction of his pleasures. It is a great thing to be able to face pain and dangers with self-possession but it requires a more difficult virtue and a greater and higher kind of self-mastery which arms man "against the enchantment of pleasure", as Plato tells us. Man is subject to the dictates of pain but even much more to the pull of pleasure and profit. For small gains, he is prepared to stoop to a most servile and base course, cringe, crawl, fawn and abase himself. To come out of this subjection is the major effort of a moral and spiritual life. In the language of the Upanishads, a spiritual aspirant follows what is good, *śreyas*, and not that which is merely pleasant, *preyas*.

But the good the soul follows should not be confused with any code of conduct imposed from outside which is also the more moral because it is more unpleasant; it should not even be confused with God's Commandments if it means truths revealed to a chosen few and to be obediently followed by the rest.

Fortunately, God's truths are planted in our hearts and God himself is the secret Truth of our deepest being. These truths work in us as deep-seated urges. To follow them is a kind of self-unfoldment, self-expression which is at heart a joyous process. Our being and its various instruments, its intellect, mind, heart, senses are seeking as if by an inner impulsion their own increasing purification. The eye seeks to see the good, the auspicious, the beneficent; the ear seeks the same through hearing. The speech aspires to be truthful, gentle, helpful. And behind a truthful speech, there is the seeking of a sincere heart. The mind too seeks to shed all that is foreign to it and yet by which it is heavily burdened, all that which fills it in its impure state with lust, indolence, restlessness, disorderliness and uncertainty.

But the seeking of the senses and the mind for increasingly greater purity is opposed by other counter forces in the being. These are the forces of *tamas* and *rajas*. The mind is full of negativism, desire, forgetfulness, attachment, craving. It has not yet felt the touch of the Real, the Divine. So knowing nothing better, it wallows in the lower and unregenerate experiences of the senses and the mind.

These impurities are differently classified in different literatures. According to Buddhists, they belong to body, to speech, to mind. Murder and theft, belong to the body; lying, slander, abuse and unprofitable conversation belong to speech; covetousness, malice and scepticism belong to the mind. This is merely a way of classifying them; in a fundamental sense, all impurities are mental in origin though some of them may have a more preponderant bodily expression.

In the Pātañjala Yoga, five fundamental impurities are mentioned: *avidyā* (nescience), *asmitā* (ego), *rāga* (attachment), *dvesha* (aversion) and *abhiniveśa* (gross worldliness, craving). They are mentioned in the order of decreasing subtleness. *Avidyā* is the most fundamental which supports the edifice all other impurities. In simpler language, it means that evil deeds come from evil desires; and evil desires themselves are rooted in Ego, in the illusion of a separative life; this illusion itself is supported by nescience, by a deep-rooted incapacity to distinguish the true from the false.

These are no impurities in the ordinary sense of the term. They are *kleśas*, very inadequately defined as defilements. They make us what we are at any time. All that we have desired and thought have gone into making them. They are woven into the fabric of our emotions, desires, thoughts. They keep us bound down to a particular life-cycle. They are built up of *samskāras*, impressions accumulated over repeated births. They wait in seed-form till their time comes to ripen and bear fruits. Man reaps what he sows. From bitter seeds comes a bitter harvest.

This is the famous Law of Karma. It sounds harsh and stern but it is full of hope, promise and compassion, and rationality. There are no elect here and no eternally damned. There is no particular day on which men would be judged finally and also for the first time. There is no permanent hell-fire in which the wicked will roast for all time to come. According to the Law of Karma, we are being judged every moment in every single deed and desire and thought of ours; and we are being made and unmade by them, saved and condemned by them. Every self-giving deed, every benevolent thought, every devoted and disinterested work adds something to us; on the other hand, every cruel thought and action, every self-regarding deed takes away something from us, makes us less real and authentic.

Even in the midst of our worst plight, a most evil moment, something good that we might have done in the past but which we now have even forgotten, somebody hungry we had fed, some orphan or widow we had helped, somebody in low spirits to whom we spoke words of cheer and encouragement — all that comes to our aid and shines like a beaconing light in the surrounding gloom and upholds us. In this path, there is no transgression, no waste; everything is added up and all threads are joined. This is also the path of honour; on this path we seek no undeserved remission but we want to pay our debts gladly. Suffering is no deterrent. What we fear is evil.

The Law of Karma places our destiny in our own hands. It tells us that we can make and mar ourselves. The self is its own best friend as well as its own worst enemy. We can conquer the base and the evil in us and build up the lofty and the good. This realization calls for a new sense of responsibility towards ourselves and also a deeper understanding about ourselves. Our actions should be moral but that would not come through a stubborn tug of war with ourselves; that will need silent work and self-knowledge and the knowledge of good and bad in all their manifestations, knowledge of *kuśala* and *akuśal* dharmas.

Purification of Śīla

Yoga seeks purification at various levels. The very first level is that of conduct. It seeks a moral life. One should be guided by an inner moral life, by what is legitimate and what is illegitimate. One should refrain from a life of violence, untruth, passion and greed; on the other hand, one should cultivate the path of harmlessness, gentleness, truth and rectitude.

This level is a great training ground. It trains mind's raw expressions and disciplines them. The passions of the moment bring unhappiness and retard an individual's growth, moral and intellectual. But some rough and ready rules of conduct channelize energy and give a fixed moral and social frame of references. This conserves a man's energy.

Just like the Hindus, the Greeks also believed that a man should allow the better in his nature to control the worse which also contends for the mastery of his soul. This initial principle of self-control was called 'temperance' by them. A temperate man is also a just man for he restrains himself while an intemperate man is unjust for his desires have no limits. Indeed for the Greeks, temperance was the foundation of all other virtues like courage and wisdom.

The capacity to rule over one's passions made a man to some extent his own master, a quality which was highly prized by philosophers like Socrates and Plato though there were also sophists like Collicles who thought that there was no necessity for a man to rule himself; he was only required to rule others.

But the justification of a moral life is not merely its individual and social utility. It has a deeper foundation. Through such a life, a man establishes an accord with the world around and lives in harmony with the moral and spiritual order of the universe — the *rita* of the Vedic conception. On the other hand, when he kills or steals or slanders, he sets up forces of retribution. Nemesis overtakes him. The evil done by him comes back to him. All his transgressions return to him multiplied manyfold. He is against the world, therefore the world is also against him. Through a good life, he is reconciled with his own deeper nature.

In the Pātañjala Yoga, the moral life constitutes the very first member of its well-known eight limbs. It is called *yama,* self-control; it is made up of moral qualities like *ahimsā (*non-violence*), satya* (truthful speech), *asteya* (non-stealing), *brahma-*

charya (continence) and *aparigraha* (non-possessiveness or unacquisitiveness).

These truths have increasingly deeper layers of meanings. As a man advances on the spiritual path, those meanings are revealed to him and these truths acquire purer formulations. For example, *ahiṁsā* in its outer sense only means non-killing, non-injury; but increasingly it acquires a deeper connotation. It means no retaliation, taking no revenge, bearing no anger and no malice, no fault-finding; its means being a friend even to one's enemies and returning good for evil; it means a man of *ahiṁsā* has a blessing in his heart for everyone.

Similarly, *asteya* is more than non-stealing, its outer, literal sense. It increasingly means that a man of *asteya* does not covet; he does not take what is not given to him; he does not take what is not intended for him; he does not take more than he needs; he does not hoard; he shares; he accepts with gratitude; he knows he has nothing of his own and he accepts whatever comes to him as a gift from Gods; he partakes only of the remains of sacrifice, *yajñaśishṭāśinaḥ.*

The same is true of *satya* which in the first formulation only means faithful reporting or recording of what has been seen or heard. But increasingly it stands for speaking what is pleasant, what is helpful, what is necessary, what is just. It means avoiding abusing, flattering, backbiting, tale-bearing, gossiping, swearing, idle praise and blame; it means refraining from false suppression and false emphasis; it means silence; it means speaking words that heal, that bring comfort to the needy; it also means speaking for those who cannot speak for themselves.

In Yoga, the moral truths are used in all these different senses. In their very first sense, *yamas* stand for preliminary purification which leads to a higher life of Yoga and *samādhi*. It is a preparation by an active moral life for a contemplative life. But in another larger sense, they also give, if they are perfected, powers which the advanced *samādhi* gives. When one is established in non-violence, even ferocious beasts give up their ferocity in his presence. When one is established in truthful speech, his words invariably come true and he acquires the power of conferring boons. When he stores not for tomorrow and is established in the truth of *aparigraha*, the memories of his past lives come back to him.

There is yet a still higher sense of *śīla*. In this sense, it is more than a preliminary purification or a Yogic *siddhi* or Attainment; it is the fruit and meaning of all Yogic *sādhanā*, the aim of all spiritual striving; it is the end of all crookedness. "Keep me away from all deceitful ways," is the deepest prayer of the heart which finds expression in the *Īśopnishad*. When a man is honest and straight in his thoughts and works (*riju-mati* and *riju-kratu*) he is restored to his nature and he is in tune with everything; in that state, he has his dwelling in Truth, *rita-sad*, and he is filled with truth and righteousness, *rita-sata*.

Purity has these different and deeper levels of meanings because impurity arises from correspondingly different and deeper sources. Men do not lust with their eyes and steal with their hands alone; they do these things with their mind. Violence, injury, bad blood that we see so much around come from thoughts of anger, ill-will and malice in the mind. Robbing and stealing have their source in mind's greed and covetousness. "Out of the heart proceed evil thoughts, murders, adulteries, fornications, thefts, false witness, blasphemies," says the Bible.

It means that outer purity is not enough; it is also neither possible nor effective. It has to be supported by an inner purity. True purity of conduct comes from the purification of motives, of desires; which in turn depends on the purity of aspirations and intellect. Put a little differently in the language of Indian religions, it means that purity of conduct depends on the purity of the *manas* or mind and the purity of the mind depends on the purity of the heart — heart in the Upanishads is not a seat of emotions but is the seat of *buddhi*.

Chitta-śuddhi

This leads us to the next requirement, the purification of the mind and the way to effect it. If the outer is rooted in the inner, then we should try to reach these roots and effect a change from there.

Yoga proposes several methods to suit different needs of different aspirants but all these methods are based on a deeper understanding of the human mind, its variety, potentialities and reaches. The very first method it suggests is to use thought in order to conquer thought. The outer stems from the inner but the inner too draws its sustenance from the outer. There is a two-way traffic between them. Whatever we do or desire and think leave their traces behind. Subconscious mind may throw up thoughts and desires but thoughts and desires consciously exercised are not without their power. They leave influences which sink into the depths of our psyche and exercise a shaping influence from there. If we sit regularly and think of good and holy thoughts, they will in due course become a force in our lives. They will also provide a centre, a rallying-point to refractory elements in the mind and unify life. This is the method of reaching the unknown through the known, the inner and subsonscious through the outer, the conscious.

It is a good method as a starting point. But thought is a great goose-stepper. It can go on and on indefinitely in a circle. Good thoughts are better than bad ones but they also bind. They fall short of the purity, perfection and freedom that the soul seeks.

Conscious thoughts are also not very effective. A time must come when the sole motive power of our *sādhanā* does not derive from the conscious efforts of thought but when the *sādhanā* passes into the hands of some greater truth of the soul. Within the soul are some great dissolvents, great purifiers. There is the fire of detachment, the fire of discrimination, the fire of love, the fire of aspiration, the fire of resignation, the fire of austerity, the fire of *smriti*, the fire of *samādhi*. They burn up all that is false. They should come to the force.

But like thought they too need purification as like them thought too is a power of the soul. The fact is that each truth is self-exceeding; every truth seeks a higher definition and formulation; every formation seeks a progressive purification. It is in this purified form that they aid soul-life. In their unregenerate form, they are used by the egoistic life.

I think this stage of discussion calls for a little clarification about the place and role of contemplative life. It is not an adjunct of the active life, resorted to as an aid to an active moral life. Active life is important but it is only a very small cross-section of life. A larger life is locked elsewhere in regions which are accessible only to contemplation. So the purpose of contemplation is to go beyond the limitations of ordinary mind, to open up new regions of being, to open up the mind to the influences of the deeper truths of being, to open it up to the influences of luminous thought-forms, luminous joy-forms, to the influences of *smriti, ekāgratā, upekshā*. This will give all the moral purification the mind seeks; but it will also open up new infinities and give a new birth.

But contemplative life has its own problems to be sorted out, its own sources of perversion, its own springs of lop-sidedness. In contemplation, a man enters a realm which is of the 'absolute'. Every form is soaked with that suggestion. As a result, as we see a good deal of nihilism and relativism in intellectual life, we also meet in the spiritual life a surfeit of dogmas and dicta; truths are bandied about all claiming to be sovereign; cheeky assertions are made and certainties are offered which are offensive to our modesty as well as deeper reason; chimeras parade as realities.

In contemplation, a man also does not start with a clean slate. He carries the old mind with him, with its old motives and propensities which work in even a more subtle and disguised form at this stage. As a result higher powers are used for lower ends. Piety and religious motives have inspired many wars, and inquisition and heresy-hunting have found some of their best champions in saints or at least in persons of saintly disposition.

Not only can introversion make a man worse morally, it can also unhinge him psychologically. It can open up things in the psyche which better remain shut. As people go into their interior life, thoughts tend to become things and things become thoughts. So it becomes difficult to distinguish the objective world from hallucinations unless one takes to contemplative life endowed with great spiritual discrimination.

These facts are mentioned in order to caution and not to deter. All great ventures have their risks and they should be taken; they have their problems and they should be faced. If there is sincerity and purity of aspiration, the problems will be conquered sooner or later.

Because of its importance, purity has been so much emphasised in classical Yogic literature. Though there are all kinds of *samādhis* and they serve different functions, a Yogic *samādhi* has been defined as the concentration of a purified mind. *Samādhi* is born in purity, grows in purity and finds its culmination in purity.

People know that Yoga requires purity of morals but not many of them know that it requires purity of *samādhi* too. *Samādhi* is not the name of a finished product; it is a process made up of many steps, each step requiring its own characteristic purification. It is also not a name of a state of blank though it may look like that to an outward view; nor is it a name for an abstraction though it involves abstracting from many truths of the body and the mind; on the other hand, it is the name of a state of mind at which a man arrives after journeying through various stages and to which he carries the truths of those stages and exceeds them and purifies them.

When a man takes to Yoga, he finds that the quality of his mind improve. It might have been good enough and bright enough for ordinary life but not so for a life of Yoga; for that life it is too outward-going, dull, restless, disorderly, remorseful, uncertain. All these *tāmasika* and *rājasika* qualities permeate the mind and its various constituents like the *prāṇa*, senses, *manas*. Yoga has proposed several methods to purify them. Through '*āsana*' it tries to purify the body of its lethargy and restlessness, through '*prāṇāyāma*' the nervous system and the vital body, through '*pratyāhāra*', the senses; and through '*dhāraṇā*' the *manas*. Thus different limbs of Yoga are meant to purify different members of the being.

When this purification is achieved, when the mind has

conquered its agitation, sloth, slovenliness and doubt, more *sāttvika* qualities are born — qualities like faith, zeal, concentration, discrimination. They are a great acquisition on the spiritual path but if we have too much of the one at the expense of the other, then it is detrimental to an integral *samādhi*. Sometimes, the mind lacks right qualities but sometimes a right balance between them, and that too is bad for the deepening of *samādhi*. The mind could become over-credulous or overactive or over-critical through a disproportionate development of *śraddhā* (faith) or *vīrya* (zeal) or *buddhi* (discrimination). It militates against *samādhi*.

At this point the Buddhists love to narrate a story. Bhagvān Buddha had a disciple named Vakkali. He was strong in *śraddhā* but weak in discrimination. As a result, he fell in love with Buddha's body rather than his Dharma. Once when Buddha fell sick, he taught Vakkali thus: "What is the use of doting on this impure body and making too much of it? He who sees my Dharma sees me, and he who sees me sees my Dharma."

When faith is strong and the discrimination is weak, this is always the result . They make too much of the life and death of their chosen saints and the message is forgotten. Any *samādhi* if it obtains is ignorant.

But if a right balance is struck and other factors are also favourable, then one enters the Yogic *samādhi*. But a Yogic *samādhi* too has increasingly deeper levels of purity called *samāpattis*. If there are no obstructions and if the progress is maintained and if the inner urge for self-transcendence is strong, then each step leads by an inevitable, inner movement to its next level of purity. At the initial level, the *samādhi* is discursive and reflective; with further deepening and purity it becomes ecstatic and joyful; in the third stage it becomes mindful and equanimous. Here also is the end of all materiality and particularity, however subtle. Beyond lies the infinity of mind and knowledge.

All these levels the Pātañjala Yoga discusses under four *samāpattis* of *samprajñāta samādhi*. The Buddhist Yoga has amplified them into eight made up of four *rūpa-dhyānas* and four *arūpa-samāpattis*. Beyond them lies the *asamprajñāta samādhi* or *nirodha-bhūmi* or *kaivalya* of the Pātañajala Yoga and *lokottara samādhi* or *nirvāṇa-bhūmi* or *prajñā* of the Buddhists.

All these levels are outside the reach of the ordinary consciousness or the nominal religious life though the soul in man secretly responds to their truths. Even the popular religious scriptures like the Bible develop the truths of the first few *dhyāna-bhūmis* — the truths of the rest are implied. It is only in the mystic traditions of mankind and the scriptures like the Gita and the Upanishads that the truths of the advanced stages of *samādhi* are developed, the truths of mindfulness, equal-mindedness, universality, self-annihilation and self-discovery. The Vaishnavas and the Sufis have reached the same truths by cultivating and purifying love.

According to Yoga, mind-purification leads not merely to deepened *samādhi* and self-discovery and God-discovery, it also leads to "objective thinking", to the knowledge of things as they are. According to Yoga, the mind of a man who has mastered his out-going propensities becomes crystal pure. Like a pure crystal, this mind has the capacity to reflect faithfully whatever the object that is presented to it, whether the object is gross or fine, material or mental or intellectual.[1] For proficiency in this acquirement, a *sādhaka* has to develop a particular purification called *smriti*-purification and achieve a level of concentration called *nirvitarka*, without verbal thought. When this level of purification and absorption is achieved, the mind itself disappears as it were and the object of attention alone shines in its own light revealing its own truth.[2]

When not only all verbal thoughts but also all conceptualization ends, the *sādhaka* enters into a *samāpatti* called *nirvichāra*. When this too is further purified, it brings a deep spiritual joy, tranquility and clarity — *nirvichāra vaiśāradye adhyātma-prasādaḥ*.[3] In this

---
[1]Pātañjala Yoga 1.41.
[2]Pātañjala Yoga 1.43 and 3.3.
[3]Pātañjala Yoga 1.47.

state, the mind becomes capable of bearing and holding truth —
ritambharā tatra prajñā.[4]

We have assumed in the above discussion that the progress in
meditation is unimpeded. But it is a tall order. A man's *samskāras*
accumulated over innumerable lives are there. He comes up
against them. At the time of meditation, they go underground but
they come up again at a suitable opportunity. With continued
meditation, they become weak but do not become 'seedless', do
not lose their capacity to come to life again. This requires *viveka-
khyāti*, discrimination between the Self and not-self, and
paravairāgya, complete desirelessness. This needs the birth of a
wisdom-eye which can see that nothing abides, nothing belongs to
the soul and nothing can bring it a joy which is not already its own.
At this stage, the world falls away completely from the Self.

In short, this leads to *moksha*, liberation, and *prajñā*, wisdom.

---

[4]Pātañjala Yoga 1.48.

Chapter 2.3

Smriti

Smriti is very inadequately translated as 'memory' but memory is narrow both in connotation as well as in denotation. Memory now means forgotten impression and experiences of the present life but, in Hindu thought, *smriti* stores the impression of the past lives also and therefore as a corollary even carries the impulsions of future lives as well.

Memory has also a narrower meaning. It refers to a man's trait of forgetting things and also his capacity to recall them to mind. But *smriti* also refers to his ability for a continued awareness of a particular idea, of his capacity for keeping a particular thought or truth constantly before his eyes. This sense could be conveyed by the word 'mindfulness' and the word *smriti* is very often used in this sense in the Yogic literature. But memory does not convey that meaning though it derives from older forms that did. The Sanskrit root *smri* from which we derive *smriti* is also at the base of Greek *mermera,* care, and Latin *memor*, mindful, from which the English word memory ultimately derives. But now the older sense of mindfulness has dropped from the word memory except in phrases like 'to keep something in one's memory' which means to keep that thing before one's mind. But the phrase 'full of memories' means full of an eventful past or full of remembered events.* On the other hand, the phrase '*smritimāna*', full of *smriti*, in Yogic literature, means full of mindfulness.

---

*This kind of translation creates confusion. For example, William James must have followed this translation. Speaking of the Buddhist meditation of the fourth stage, he says that in this stage, memory and self-consciousness are perfected. It must have perplexed him for perspicacious as he was, he adds: "Just what 'memory' and 'self-consciousness' mean in this connection is doubtful. They cannot be the faculties familiar to us in the lower life".

There are other differences too. Memory refer to a man's capacity for recalling a certain forgotten events or idea; *smriti*, on the other hand, consists in remembering a certain deeper truth of our Being and Spirit: that I am not my body nor my mind, that there is a high-seated Self above the flux of things, that death is the inevitable lot of everything that is born, that God is the source of our Being; remembering that the worldly attainments are undependable; remembering that man grows by the power of truth; remembering that he is the image of God and that he is also in his brother; remembering that life is a *yajña*; remembering that worship is the food of the soul; remembering that a virtuous life is the ornament of the soul; remembering the indestructible in the midst of the destructible.

In this sense, we can see, that *smriti* has very little to do with memory as ordinarily understood. One may have a wonderful retentive power, a great capacity for recalling old ideas and facts but it will not be *smriti* in the spiritual sense of the term.

And yet, even the lower meaning of *smriti* as the mind's capacity for retaining what is taught was not rejected. In fact, the memory in this sense was also cultivated. It was good in the learning of the Vedas and other scriptures and also even the more secular forms of knowledge and sciences. In ancient India, the systems of education laid a great emphasis on training the instruments of knowledge and memory was one of them.

Now we shall discuss the role of *smriti* in spiritual *sādhanā*. In *sādhanā*, it takes on many forms and it operates with various degrees of purification at various stages of *sādhanā*. In its highest culmination, it becomes *ātma-smriti*; a man realises that his true essence is Self. But generally speaking, as to be expected, in the beginning, it takes on a more modest form. It could merely begin as some word of God loudly repeated. Later on, the word still continues to be spoken but with closed lips. With further progress, it is spoken with every breath. This lends it a new rhythmic power and vitality. Then it descends into the heart. There it becomes an *ajapa-japa*, an automatic, continued utterance without being uttered. When this is properly established in the heart, one finds that whether one is asleep or awake and whether one is busy or

relaxed, the heart is going on with its *japa*. It is a great gain for it
means that some kind of *sādhanā* is going on at all hours of the
day.

It need not be a spoken word; it could as well be a sentiment, a
thought, a suggestive image, an idea, or as generally happens, a
group of ideas round a more central idea which could be present
before the mind's eyes. It could be the thought of the immortality
of the soul, or the thought of the mortality of the things, or the
beauty of a virtuous life; or it could only be a thought of truthfulness or purity or compassion. All these could do. First, the idea
comes off and on and remembered quite erratically; then it is more
recurrent till it becomes a constant presence though still in the
background. As it acquires more strength, it comes more and more
to the fore. In the beginning, the thought is very obscure, shapeless
and amorphous but increasingly becomes more fully formed.
Then it becomes even luminous. In the beginning, one could make
hardly any meaning out of it but after some time it becomes
increasingly meaningful to the soul.

All this is called *smriti* as it operates in the initial stages of
spiritual *sādhanā*. This is a necessary stage in the progress on the
spiritual path. What this kind of *smriti* does is to build a new
centre round which the psychic forces can organise themselves. In
fact, the mind in its present unevolved state has no centre. It is a
shifting field of consciousness dominated now by one idea or
desire, and now by another.

But *smriti* of a spoken word or a luminous thought introduces a
new factor in the life of the mind. This *smriti* becomes a new
gravitational force. It attracts to itself the recalcitrant forces of the
psyche which are pulling in different directions, brings them into
one orbit and organises them round some kind of a centre.

The *smriti* does another thing. It does not merely attract to
itself, it also infuses with its own life all the different psychic
forces. It informs them with its own culture. It changes them in its
own image so that it integrates the psyche by a double process of
attracting and informing.

Here a word of warning may be necessary. We should

remember that it is possible to acquire some kind of unity in life round some obsessive idea or belief or sentiment, some dominating ambition, some power-hunger, some crusading spirit, some narrowing dogma of converting the world. Therefore, we should cultivate remembrance and mindfulness of some luminous idea, some universalizing and liberating truth. Otherwise, *smriti* is used by *āsurika* forces. To purify *smriti* increasingly is one of the main tasks of spiritual *sādhanā*. And though we have to begin with some *smriti* in one form or another, its true and purified form emerges only at the end.

But before we take up *smriti* of the more advanced stage, let us continue our discussion of *smriti* in the initial stages. We have said that while advanced *smriti* is of the nature of *ātma-smriti*, in the beginning it consists of a continued rememberance of some holy name or some luminous idea or truth of life. But there is another, very different form of *smriti* that has been practised from very ancient times. This form does not consist in entertaining any particular thought however holy and luminous but to receive all thoughts, high or low, with perfect equality. It merely registers them without showing preferences for any of them in particular. It merely observes them without any approval or disapproval. The idea is to strengthen the forces of awareness within us. Our mind, though it connotes consciousness, mindfulness and *smriti*, is really woven with the forces of unmindfulness and forgetfulness. It should become true to its name.

We are what we think, desire, propose. If this is true, then we are being made and unmade every minute without our knowing it. For there is a good deal of psychic life going on all the time at the subconscious level which is the greater part of our mind. At this level, the mind continues to receive impressions, react to them. In this act, the mind is not passive. There are certain states of mind called '*samskāras*' or 'predispositions' which call forth certain impressions and respond to them selectively, and thus getting reinforced in the process. In conformity with those *samskāras*, it enters into a particular kind of relationship with the world; it assimilates it and, side by side, gets assimilated by it. It acquires a predisposition to repeat this world, be born into it again and again. It knows no other world. Thus a destiny is woven round an individual.

Smriti means that we should become aware of the things that are happening to us all the time, that nothing should occur to us without our knowing it. *Smriti* says: Be aware of all that comes to you whether from outside or even from your own mind. Just register whatever comes to you. Do not approve or disapprove. Do not enter into a relationship with the world by reacting to it and thus help it to establish its hold and itself within you. Also become aware of your own ambitions, motives, *samskāras* and disguises.

This is a step not only in the direction of self-knowledge but also in the purification of *smriti* in its other meaning of a storehouse of forgotten memories, and as a deposit of latent tendencies and *samskāras*. Our life is shaped in a large measure by forces residing in the subconscious. There can be no liberation for the mind unless this hidden mind is reached and understood.

Some writers on the *smriti* method of Yoga, in order to promote it, points out how it can help a more exact observation of facts which is the basis of modern sciences. They say, we do not know how to observe and always mix our observations with our desires and preconceived notions. The practice of *smriti* is the practice of bare attention to facts as they appear before us without ourselves getting mixed up with them.

We need not deny this advantage. But if it were all to *smriti*, it would not be much. The truth is that facts by themselves tell no story. What happens is this, that when we turn inwards through various aids, including the aid of *smriti*, new layers of mind open up, a new *prāṇa-śakti* opens up, a new heart opens up, a new intuition opens up, a new *vijñāna*-mind opens up. That does the work. If this opening does not take place, then bare facts however barely we may look at them will reveal nothing. This is as much true in the realm of science as in the realm of the Spirit. Newton did not, first observe all falling objects faithfully, then classified them together, and then drew from them a law of gravitation. He only saw one apple falling and the law came to him intuitively.

Apples had been falling from the trees long before Newton but since they opened up no intuition, they revealed no new truth.

The point we want to make is that though *smriti* makes us better observers that is not its most important value for us. It helps us in other more significant ways. It helps us by cutting at the very root of worldliness. Experience tells us that we cannot deal adequately with the world piecemeal. If we conquered one desire, there is another to replace it. Therefore, we need a more strategic approach, something which deals with the roots and the first causes. In *smriti*, we have that possibility. It is seen that the world dominates through some kind of interaction with the mind. The world grows within us because our mind reacts to it, is attracted or repelled by it. But if the mind withdraws, if it merely watches without approving or disapproving, if it becomes a spectator, then the things of the world lose their hold on it and the mind becomes free.

This is easier said than done. For the world holds within it joys and terrors that no mind can resist unless a great detachment and purity are already established in the heart. The fact is that there are no short-cuts in spiritual life. *Smriti* is one term amongst many other terms. It is a part of a larger *sādhanā* in which faith, desirelessness, surrender, all play their organic role. One cannot choose the one and cultivate it to the exclusion of the other. They all work together. It is the whole direction that matters, not a particular term. When the spiritual urge becomes insistent in man, new Gods are born in him called faith, resolve, *smriti* and wisdom — in that order. In Buddhism, they have been called the five new 'organs' (*indriyas*) and 'powers' (*balas*) that are born in the aspirant, for it is through them that he advances on the path and 'attains' and 'knows' *nirvāṇa*.

We have said above that it is in a particular context that *smriti* has a spiritually rewarding meaning. But some have tried to cultivate it in a non-spiritual context. In fact, they are attracted by it because, apparently at least, *smriti* asks you to shed nothing. Therefore, they think that through it, they can retain their unregenerate life and even add to it by becoming aware of more of it, and even enjoy it on the sly and yet be on the spiritual path. But this is a delusion. There are many writers these days who dissect their hidden thoughts and motives with the disinterestedness of a surgeon. But this kind of 'awareness' serves no spiritual purpose. It is merely intellectual wallowing.

The fact is that spiritual *smriti* is not such a 'come-all' as it has been made by some of its popularizers. In some, it is mere misunderstanding; in others, the misunderstanding is motivated — motives of which they are not aware; they are averse to anything which smacks of a moral approach. They would prefer purely a psychological approach.

But true *smriti* is different. It is more than a mechanical recording or registering. It is 'watchfulness'. And it is soul-watch and not mind-watch, which means there is deeper seeing and a deeper selection than we suspect. In every thing that comes, the mind sees what is *kuśala* (good) and what is *akuśala* (bad); what is *klishṭa* (binding) and what is *aklishṭa* (liberating or extricating); what is intrinsic and what is foreign; what is real, and what is false. No wonder that *smriti* goes hand in hand with *viveka* or discrimination and in Buddhist literature it is more often than not conjoined with *samprajanya* or right knowledge. In the same literature, *smriti* is regarded as the best watch-dog and is posted at the portals of the senses for their protection (*indriya-saṁvara*). So one can easily see that in this rendering of *smriti*, there is no indiscriminate receiving of all that comes. It is a very selective process but the selection follows a deeper seeing of the mind, the soul accepting what is akin to it and rejecting that which is foreign to it.

In the discussion above, we find that we come up again and again to the question of a purified *smriti* which is central. It seems that without purification, true *smriti* is not possible. Therefore, different Yogas tell us that while one will have to make do with a mental *smriti* initially, true liberating *smriti* emerges only at a very advanced stage of *sādhanā*. The *Chhāndogya Upanishad* tells us that first there should be *sattva-śuddhi* (purification of the inner being) through *āhāra-śuddhi* (nourishment-purity). It means that first the instruments of knowledge, the *prāṇa*, the *manas*, the *buddhi* should be purified. They should feed on good impressions and good thoughts and good aspirations and good works. The eyes should see the good and the ears should hear the good; our hearts should praise Gods and we should live a life dedicated to them. This leads to a firmly established *smriti* (*dhruva smriti*). This in turn leads to the unloosening of all the knots of the heart.

The Gita also expresses the same idea. It tells us that *smriti* is one of the last links in the chain. It is one of the very last acquisitions and, strangely enough, also one of the last to snap before one is completely destroyed. In fact, it seems one needs some kind of Yoga in the reverse to loosen it altogether. "Man muses on objects of senses, conceives an attachment to them; from attachment desire arises; from desire anger; from anger delusion; from delusion *smriti* is confused; from confused *smriti*, one loses discrimination, the capacity to distinguish the Real from the unreal; and from that he is spiritually destroyed."

Delusion (*moha* or *sammoha*) is deepened *avidyā* (nescience), a state in which one is sunk in worldliness. As delusion destroys *smriti*, in the same way *smriti* is restored when delusion is destroyed through God's grace. When *smriti* is restored, one is again established in one's self-status and goes beyond all doubts and is ready to do the Lord's bidding.

In Buddhism too, we find the same emphasis. Here as in other systems of Yoga, the practice of *smriti* can be undertaken from the start, and is very much recommended. But its true from emerges only at the end. After one has lived a life of virtue, one qualifies for a life of meditation. And though *smriti* as an element is always there in the first three meditations, it is only in the forth stage of meditation that it comes out openly in its purified form, "*smriti* purified by *upekshā* or equal-mindedness". So the principle of the purification of *smriti* is equal-mindedness when one is no more attracted by joy and repelled by sorrow.

After discussing what constitutes purity of *smriti*, we go over to another important question. In the very beginning of the chapter, we had said that *smriti* means remembering some deeper truth of the Being. What does it mean? Man's Being has many facets. It is conceived differently as *sat* or being and even as *asat* or non-being. It has been approached devotionally, ecstatically, contemplatively. It has been conceived as a Self seated above and also as an indwelling Spirit. But all these view-points use some kind of Yoga and *smriti* is an indispensable part of all of them. Whether one meditates on death or immortality, whether one takes to a Yoga of devotion or Yoga of renunciation, *smriti* is necessary.

In different Yogas, *smriti* has its place-value. In more devotional *sādhanās*, *smriti* means constant remembrances of one's *ishṭa*. "He who remember me constantly, by him I am easily reached," says the Lord in the Gita. Here the remembrance is not merely constant (*satatam*) but also of Him alone (*ananyachetas*). In Sāṁkhya *sādhanā*, *smriti* has another use, that of separating an inactive Purusha (Self) from an active Prakriti. " I do nothing. In seeing, hearing, touching, smelling, eating, moving, sleeping, breathing, speaking, giving, grasping, opening and closing the eyes — it is senses which move among their objects," is the constant *smriti* of the man who has taken to the path of the Sāṁkhya.

In Buddhist Yoga of the later times, *smriti* has found another use, an analytic use for breaking objects and mind into successive experiences and mental-states. It helps to strengthen the sentiment of *anitya* and *anātma*.

The Pātañjal Yoga uses two methods for its *sādhanā* and, therefore, *smriti* has two corresponding uses. One is the method of *ātma-smriti*, or the rememberance of *ātman*, which is used in *vivek-khyāti*, or Yoga of discrimination, at the level of *asamprajñāta samādhi*. The other may be called the method of *ātma-vismriti*, forgetfulness of the self. It is a strange way of putting it but it only means that the experiencer and even the experience is forgotten and only the object of experience is seen and remembered. This method is used at the level of *samprajñāta samādhi*. To those who perfect this method come many powers, and on whatever object they meditate, that object reveals its secrets to them.

The method of *ātma-smriti* is really the method of Sāṁkhya about which we have already spoken and which consists in separating a *kūṭastha* (seated-above) Purusha from the multifarious play of the Prakriti. But the method of *ātma-vismriti* is equally great, particularly when the object of meditation is God Himself or one of His attributes. One begins to grow in the likeness of that attribute or one disappears and God alone remains.

Chapter 2.4

Equality

"Equality" is an important spiritual category. It is both an aid as well as a mark of spiritual perfection.

Equality has several connected meanings. Its very first meaning which is also the highest is equal-mindedness. It means that through all ups and downs of life, through all its joys and sorrows, success and failure, a man remains unperturbed. He responds to them with faith, joy and understanding. Here the emphasis is on an effective, creative, high-minded response. Another meaning of equality is 'indifference' or 'disregard'; in this sense, a man is indifferent to his sorrows and joys and he regards them both of equal worth or rather he disregards them both as equally unworthy. There is a certain devaluation of the world in this view and it sounds somewhat cold. But this is an important meaning of equality and is one which has been highly valued in different spiritual disciplines. In fact, to practise equality in the first sense would be impossible without first practising it in the second sense. The mind is submerged in worldliness; it is dominated by its dualities. Unless it comes out of this domination and acquires its independence, unless the world becomes somewhat less important and the mind more important than they are at the usual, ordinary level of living, the mind cannot respond freely, effectively and creatively. The mind must first rise up, must separate itself from its own fallen condition, must first become aloof and realize its free self-status; then alone it will be able to take the world in its stride.

Besides these meanings, equality also throws up a lower image with which it is many times confused. Yogic imperturbability is not apathy or impassivity or a phlegmatic temperament hard to

arouse, or a stolid absence of curiosity and interest and respons-
iveness. But it is calm receptivity of all the touches of nature,
a serene fortitude.

To grow a certain imperviousness to outer sensations is not true
imperturbability, nor to master our responses to them, though it
may be a good training. True imperturbability comes from the
growth of the soul, from its abounding fullness. The true
foundation of imperturbability and true equality are desirelessness
and *prajñā*.

Equality is not just a mental exercise or attitude. Deep down it
conforms to the nature of things; it is merely a psychological
counterpart of a great ontological truth. In the process of world
manifestation, the reality becomes divided into separate and even
opposed objects, ideas and forces but at heart they are still one.
The spirit's equal-mindedness is the recognition of this basic unity
of the world.

But this equal-mindedness and basic unity do not abrogate
differences. In fact, differences acquire a new significance, a new
legitimacy because they express the truth of the same thing in their
own different ways. One no longer turns a suspicious eye towards
them but looks at them with a new respect. So equality at heart is
forbearance, a kind of wisdom and understanding of things
around. It accepts things not only because basically they are one
but also because their differences are legitimate, necessary part of
the process of manifestation. Why should we get angry because
things follow their own nature, because they are at different stages
of growth and manifestation? Why should one be partial to one
kind of manifestation? He should accept their variety with equal
joy.

True equality is established when a cosmic consciousness
opens up, when one begins to see that everything is a part of an
underlying reality; or when a wisdom-eye opens up when one
realizes that things have their own nature and one should not
therefore quarrel with them on that account; or when one realizes
that *duḥkha* and *sukha*, failure and success are inextricably bound
up with each other and one follows the other like the spokes of a

wheel; or when desirelessness grows within a person and he is no longer attracted by the world; or when a *kūṭastha* consciousness arises which is not involved in the things of the world; or when a great renunciation arises in the soul and one expects little from the world; or when one develops a great *titīkshā* or *kshamā-bhāva* or capacity to forbear the touches of nature; or when the heart becomes tranquil and when death loses its terror and the earth's goods their attraction; or when a great sense of self-sufficiency comes and one realizes that the source of happiness is within, not without; or when a great compassion opens up and one turns a friendly eye to all; or when a great love wells up and one sees in everything the visage of the beloved; or when a God-vision opens up and one sees the issues of all things — "And God saw everything that he had made, and behold, it was very good."

The Gita is the scripture of 'equality' *par excellence*. In this, one can notice various layers of equality. The very first one is that of *titīkshā* or fortitude, of strength to bear pain and adversity with courage. The contacts of matter (*mātrāsparśāḥ*) like cold and heat which give pleasure and pain torment not the man endowed with this quality. (Gita, 2.14-15)

A man's response to an outer stimulus is, at least, partly a matter of habit. The mind can be trained to a different response. One need not respond painfully to a stimulus customarily considered painful. Also a man is capable of enduring a good deal of pain but that is generally under the influence of another stimulus arising from the Ego. What will men not do and pass through in order to attract attention, to become acceptable, to conform to prevailing fashions and standards of beauty, riches, morality, intellect? The point of all this is that our reactions to situations are not fixed and the mind can be taught not to respond painfully to painful situations.

But this equality based on training and fortitude is not satisfying. It may compel our admiration but it does not convince our deeper mind and fulfil our deeper urge. It smacks of a continued struggle, exertion, contest, strain and even of a cold war. The very words 'fortitude' and 'endurance' etymologically mean 'strength' and 'force'. One feels that any spiritual good won through the exercise of one's own strength must be a precarious possession. A true spiritual good must be the fruit of the functioning of a deeper and more relaxed faculty, the free gift guaranteed and underwritten by the unfailing power of the great giver himself. The heart does not seek a spirituality of personal strength however superhuman it may be. It seeks the spirituality of becoming empty, of becoming nothing. If it seeks any strength it is that of the symbol of which is not rock but water which prevails through permeation, through non-resistance.

The true equality begins with desirelessness and the Gita stresses this point repeatedly. When a men is able to endure the force born of desire and passion (*kāmakrodhodbhavam vegam*), then alone he is in harmony and is happy. When he gives up all desires of the heart (*prajahāti yadā kāmān sarvān ... manogatān*), when he goes beyond all passions, fear and anger (*vītarāgabhayakrodhaḥ*), then alone he is established in true equality.

A man is submerged in nescience, in desire. That keeps him bound to the world of appearances and unreality. He loves and hates, hopes and despairs, is pleased and pained, exalted and depressed but through the two movements he remains within the orbit of desire.

By desire is designated the whole twin life of *rāga-dvesha*, (attraction and aversion), *kāma-krodha* (lust and antipathy), like and dislike. One seeks one kind of experience and shuns another kind. He is all the time choosing, preferring, emphasizing, trying to recall one experience and repress another. Between these two poles of the same pendulum, he moves alternately. But the movement is illusory for it does not take him anywhere.

Desire also gives birth to the illusion of fixed material and thought-forms. So it keeps a man bound to the world of appearances, relativity, materiality and particularity. A man can break through the hold of this world by cultivating indifference and equal-mindedness towards the two movements of desires and towards the many forms the two movements throw up. But this is not possible unless *kāma* and *krodha* are burnt up in the fire of dispassion or desirelessness. When desires are clamorous and *rajas* or passion is strong, equality is not possible. Only when they subside by cultivating desirelessness and dispassion, true equality also takes birth.

Another pillar of true equality often mentioned in the Gita is *prajñā*, a wisdom-view of things. This consists in viewing our particular experience in the light of a larger idea. We make too much of our little amusements and tragedies but if we look at them in a larger context, they lose a good deal of their poignancy. In the very first stanza in which Krishna asks Arjuna to endure (*titīkshasva*) contacts of nature, giving cold and heat, pleasure and pain" (*mātrāsparśāḥ ... śitoshṇasukhaduḥkhadāḥ*), he does not ask him to exercise his self-will but his *prajñā*. He asks him to realize that those contacts have no permanent reality; they are transitory; they come and go (*āgamāpāyino'nityāḥ*). At another place, he says that one should realize that "the delights which are contact-born are verily wombs of pain and they are transitory; the wise do not rejoice in them."

The old Stoics of Greece and Rome made noble use of philosophical ideas to cultivate a mastery over pain and pleasure. Now Stoicism is known to us through Christian eyes but in its own time it was a system of noble ethics based on a noble philosophy. It taught equal-mindedness, acceptance of all that is the lot of a man. "Everything is right for me, which is right for you, O Universe. Nothing for me is too early or too late, which comes in due time for you. Everything is fruit to me which your seasons bring, O Nature," sings Marcus Aurelius. He asks us not to care for name and fame for "all things quickly pass away and become a mere tale, and oblivion buries them".

He also gives a quotation from Plato which we reproduce here for it is relevant to the discussion in hand: That he who discourses of men should look at earthly things as if he viewed them from some higher place; should look at them in their assemblies, armies, labours on the soil, their marriages, births and deaths, the noise of the courts of justice, the desert places, the various nations of barbarians, the feasts, lamentations, markets. Thus viewed, these things would appear a good deal less important than they do today.

At this point we should remember two things. Firstly, that philosophy helps those whose lives are controlled by reason and not by sensuous pleasure. Those who live sensous life will find no help in philosophy. "The excited senses of even a learned man impetuously carry away his mind"; or again "enveloped is wisdom by this constant enemy of the wise in the form of Desire, insatiable as fire". Secondly, what we have been speaking about above is not philosophy in the ordinary sense of the term or the sense it has acquired at present; it is about 'Yogic wisdom', the sense in which philosophy was understood by old Greek sages. Philosophy to them was 'love of wisdom' which they sharply distinguished from sophistry which was merely a pretence to wisdom.

True philosophy has always loved in some measure the unseen, the unknown, the "heavenly" things as they have been called. It has also involved in some form or another a certain disregard of the seen, the known or the 'earthly' life.

So long as we lay too much store by the world, we cannot conquer desire. Where our treasure is, there will also be our heart. If we cherish the world too much, we are likely to think little of the things of heaven. The world grows within us through many channels but more particularly through its power to cause us pain and pleasure. We not only find it desirable but we also begin to desire it. Thus it enters into our emotive as well as our conative life; the free flow of consciousness is imprisoned in little desires and aversions of the world.

The Gita gives us a very comprehensive view of the imprisonment of the soul in the body. It says that the three *guṇas*, *sattva*, *rajas* and *tamas*, all born of Prakriti, bind the soul, the dweller in the body, to the body; *tamas* is born of nescience and binds the soul by heedlessness, indolence and sloth; *rajas* is born of passion; and binds the soul by attachment to action; and even *sattva* which is of the nature of purity and light and health binds the soul by attachment to knowledge and joy. True equality comes when the soul is again freed from the domination of the body at the three levels, when it rediscovers its self-status beyond the three attributes of Prakriti.

When a man goes beyond the three attributes of nature (*guṇātīta*) and rediscovers his freedom, how does he act and behave? He does not abhor light, activity and delusion when they are present, nor longs after them when they are absent. He stands aloof and unmoved and unshaken in the midst of nature's multifarious movements. He is the same in pleasure and pain, same in censure and praise, same to the loved and the unloved; to him all is alike whether it is a clod of earth or a piece of rock or a lump of gold. He is the same in honour and ignominy, same to friend and foe. He renounces all plans. He is now known as one who has gone beyond the three attributes.

So we see that true equality does not come through general ideas or through discourses on philosophy; it comes through self-conquest, through a deepened and widened being and consciousness. Hence the need of Yoga, of *tapas*, of an intense spiritual effort and aspiration.

Of this deepened consciousness, equality is the fruit as well as the root. Equality is a necessary concomitant of a cosmic consciousness but it is also its door. One enters a larger consciousness by practising 'equality'.

But the cosmic consciousness has many attributes and various *darśanas* or philosophies have emphasized them differently. Some have emphasized its transcendence, others its immanence; some its aloofness, incommunicability, otherness; some its all-inclusiveness; others tell us how it is proclaimed by all, how it is the very essence and being of everything. Consequently, different systems have practised equality differently in their *sādhanā*. There is the equality of a Buddhi-Yoga in which a high-seated Self watches everything as a play of Prakriti while itself remaining uninvolved. "The senses move among the objects of senses", or the "the *guṇas* (qualities of Nature) revolve", finds an uninvolved Self in all the movements of Nature. There is also the equality of a theistic consciousness which accepts everything as the will of God and seeks the fulfillment of this will in everything. There is the equality of the Purusha of the Sāṁkhya which finds in everything, its own otherness. There is the equality of the Buddhist *sādhanā* which looks upon everything as ephemeral, painful and phenomenal. There is also the Upanishadic equality which looks upon everything as the life of the Self. There is the equality of a Karma-Yogin who performs all works and duties without expectation of a reward. There is also the equality of a great devotee who renounces all duties, all dharmas, criterions and standards in God and resorts to Him alone with all his being: "Resort to Him alone for shelter with all thy being", or "Abandoning all duties, come upto me alone for shelter".

In the Gita, we find a highest synthesis of all these view-points and the living practices of equality in all the different weltanschauung. We also find equality as practised in its different stages. Perhaps the very first stage of equality is when a man is alike in cold and heat, in pleasure and pain (*śītoshṇasukhduḥkheshu samaḥ*). This kind of equality can be cultivated through fortitude, and self-will also. But very soon this will not suffice. To be alike to the pleasant and unpleasant sensations of the body is not enough. One must also become alike in everything that flatters or hurts one's ego. He now accepts praise and reproach equally (*tulyanindāstutiḥ*); he is balanced in honour and dishonour (*samaḥ mānāpamānayoḥ*); he is alike to foes and friends (*samaḥ śatrau cha mitre cha*).

He now becomes *sama-buddhi*, impartial-minded. He regards all impartially — lovers, friends, foes, strangers, neutrals, foreigners, relatives and also the righteous and the unrighteous. He develops an equal look. He becomes *sama-darśinaḥ*. He looks equally on a Brahamin endowed with learning and humility, a cow, an elephant and even a dog and an outcaste.

This is the highest stage of equality. Now he sees everywhere the same (*sarvatra samadarśinaḥ*). He sees the Self abiding in all beings and all beings abiding in the Self. His Self has now become the Self of all (*sarvabhūtātmabūtātmā*).

He is equal in his seeing and he is equal in his doing also. First he accepts his lot. He performs the duties of his station in life whether low or high. He gives up all expectations of rewards (*sarvakarmaphalatyāga*); then he renounces all undertakings (*sarvārambhaparityāga*) and even the formative will behind those undertakings (*sarvasaṁkalpasaṁnyāsa*). Now he no longer does anything on his own; things get done through him. The feeling of a 'doer', of an 'I' leaves him.

What is called *samatva-yoga*, Yoga of Equality, or *samadarśana*, equal-look, is known as *upekshā* in the Buddhist Yoga. Like equality in the Gita, *upekshā* operates on many levels. In *Viśuddhi-mārga*, ten kinds of *upekshā* are enumerated. We need not go into them here but only point to the underlying principle, and only refer to such of them as would amplify the discussion here.

The most important for our discussion is *dhyāna-upekshā*, the *upekshā* born of meditation. It is a late acquisition in spiritual *sādhanā* and in its turn it is a pillar of a still higher spiritual attainment. In the Buddhist Yoga, it appears at the level of the third *dhyāna* where it is combined with the *dhyāna*-joy which is difficult of attainment even by Gods. At the next level of the fourth *dhyāna*, it purifies *smriti* and both conjoined with *ekāgratā* (one-pointedness) open the door to the experience of the four Infinities.

To withdraw from pain is easy — it is the natural tendency of the mind to do it. To withdraw from joy is difficult though not impossible for one easily learns from one's experience that all joys are linked with sorrows. But when the joy is of the quality, purity and depth and intensity of the third *dhyāna*, it is a different matter. And yet at that very stage, *upekshā* is born which is indifferent even to this heavenly joy. Why? Because the soul seeks a still deeper good. In the fourth *dhyāna*, there is neither pain nor joy (*a-duḥkham a-sukham*) and which is characterized by pure mindfulness, by *smriti* purified by *upekshā* (*upekshātipariśuddham*).

That *upekshā* is indifferent even to the highest joy has to be remembered for this distinguishes Yogic Equality from more modern versions of it taught by some teachers of Yoga. Spiritual equality means a progressive withdrawal from the lower truths of the spirit. It develops progressively a deeper seeing, a faculty of choice which spontaneously rejects the lower and accepts the higher, accept that which is increasingly more akin to the spirit. But Neo-Equality is different. It is moral and metaphysical neutralism. It has no criterion, no standard of judgement. It even tries to see if it can retain the lower by treating it equally with the higher. It receives all, high and low equally — it is even more equal to the low than to the high. By Neo-Equality, its savants mean a compromise, a give and take, a broad-mindedness which will give even a devil his due. They hope, through equality, to entertain the unequal. It is an attempt at the moral and metaphysical rehabilitation of the lower truths of life in the guise of equality.

But spiritual equality is different. It does not mean doubting the higher and entertaining the lower. It means a definitive abandonment and renouncement of the lower and embracing the higher. There is the equality called the six-limb *upekshā* which renounces all the creaturely reactions of the six senses when anything, agreeable or disagreeable, presents itself before them. There is the intellectual *upekshā* (*vipaśyanā-upekshā*) of the man who is reflecting on the three attributes (*tri-guṇa*) — changeability, painfulness, phenomenality — of the five-aggregates (*pañcha-skandhas*) of being. It is decisive; it knows no quibbles; it cannot be confused by any pettifogging. It is like a man who is searching with a stick in his hand a serpent which has entered his house in the evening. He finds it lying in the hay. Trying to make sure that it is the serpent and not something else he observes three marks on its neck. This decides the matter. Now he knows it for a snake. There is no room left for a soft-headed doubt.

Next is the *saṁskāra-upekshā* of the man who sees the three worlds burning with lust, wrath and delusion, with pain and phenomenality and who, in order to escape, knows no temporizing, must not accept any of the *saṁskāras* or impressions of these worlds, must abandon them altogether. It is again like the man in the above illustration who has found the snake but who now wants to leave it without hurting it and without also being hurt by it. The situation calls for decisive action and admits of no tarrying, no dilly-dallying, no shilly-shallying.

Renunciation

The philosophy of renunciation has fallen on bad days. The very word is suspect. Some even say that the doctrine of renunciation was invented by kill-joys, envious fellows who having no pleasures in their own lives tried to poison those of others with the help of this doctrine; or by greedy fellows who taught renunciation so that they could acquire what others renounced; or by those who failed in life and therefore taught the renunciation of the acquirements of life. It is a case of 'grapes are sour'. Others are not that uncharitable and their criticism of renunciation is based on more philosophical grounds. They say that the sense-joys are all the joys that we have and the present life is all the life we know; therefore, let us make the most of these joys while the life lasts. Some would also like to add to these sense-joys the intellectual and reflective joys of the scientists and the philosophers and the aesthetic joys of the artists.

There are others who do not altogether deny the spiritual principle in life but they too seek a spirituality which, in keeping with the ethos of the present-day world, requires them to renounce nothing. And the teachers are not wanting who promise them precisely this.

Here we have merely mentioned these views and we have no intention of discussing them here. The proper place for their discussion is when materialist and spiritualist views of life are discussed. But once a spiritual approach to life is accepted, renunciation in one form or another does come in. And for those in whom the pursuit of the spirit has become an active and living force, renunciation has been an important note in their lives. True, in the spiritual tradition itself there has been a good deal of discussion about renunciation, but it has concerned itself with its more outward manifestations, with its names and forms; but renunciation in one form or another has been at the centre of many systems of Yoga and most kinds of attempts at spiritual growth.

There is in the soul itself a force or quality of self-detachment, self-withdrawal. The Self tends to withdraw from all its formations, from all that it might feel, think and dwell upon. Even in its deepest attachment, the soul remains unattached with one part of the mind, something of a spectator and an onlooker, something which remains aloof from its own formations. This 'something' is the truth at the back of all true renunciation and it also provides it with its motive force. This is a mighty and a shaping truth and it imposes its impress on different forms of spiritual *sādhanās*.

On the one hand, the soul pours itself out in forms; on the other, it also withdraws from them. It creates and it withdraws; it cherishes and it renounces. Both the principles are parts of the soul and both work in unison in a spiritual life. The spiritual life cannot advance very much without the aid of renunciation. Renunciation is a spiritual faculty, a spiritual power. It is not a conspiracy, a teaching of life-denying philosophers — though one has to admit that there is a good deal of false renunciation and there are people who deny life whether they renounce its goods or embrace them. Spiritual *sādhanā* is not possible without renunciation and renunciation cannot be practised by those to whom it is painful or who practise it for that very reason.

Renunciation is not as gloomy as it sounds to the outsiders. In actual practice, it is even a joyous process. In renunciation as taught by Yoga, something lower is given up in exchange for something higher so that in every act of renunciation there is a net profit, an unearned surplus. The pains of a wicked life are given up for the joys of a life of virtue; the joys of ordinary good life give place to the extraordinary joys of a meditative life. When craving and desire (*kāmachhanda*) are renounced, it brings concentration; when ill-will is renounced, it brings joy. When mental defilements (*kleśas*) of various descriptions are given up, different powers (*indriyas*) like faith, energy, mindfulness, concentration and wisdom (*śraddhā, vīrya, smriti, samādhi* and *prajñā*) are born in the soul.

When one renounces the pain and misery of a life of self-hood, one acquires the joy of a life of benevolence, the joy of self-finding, the joy of a universal life, the joy of the Self becoming All.

The whole of Sāmkhya and Buddhist *sādhanā* is *sukh-sādhanā* though many scholars regard the two philosophies as most pessimistic and life-negating of all Indian philosophies. But in their *sādhanā*, their renunciation is joyous renunciation: renunciation of *kāma-sukha* for the sake of the *dhyāna-sukha*; renunciation of *vitarka* and *vicāra* (ratiocination and reflection) for the fulfillment of *prīti* or joy; renunciation of even this joy for a more intense, inborn bliss of the third *dhyāna*; renunciation of even this bliss for the sake of a concentrated awareness and equanimity (*smriti* and *upekshā*) of the fourth stage of meditation; then this awareness turns from all individual forms and all materiality and becomes a seeking for progressively deeper infinities; from the infinity of the sky, it turns to the infinity of knowledge and then to an infinity where even this knowledge is negated; then it turns away from everything and sheds every trace of self-hood. The process of self-naughting, of dying-to-self, of *nirvāṇa*, of *nirodha* is a joyous process.

To some, this joy could come in the form of a pain but this is a pain of a different kind. This is a curative, liberating pain. This is the pain of those who feel the anguish of a separative life, who feel the pangs of separation from the Beloved, the pain of a stubborn self-hood which refuses to melt even in the presence of holy things. The soul sorrows not because it has to renounce but because it is unable to find. So there is a great wrenching of heart and vale of tears. There is also the sorrow of those who see and approve the better course but follow the worse. The spirit is willing but the flesh is weak. They find that God's *māyā* is as strong as God himself. They weep at their own helplessness and turn to a source of power which is all accomplishing. It is the pain of those who have made the pains of others their own pain, who have accepted a burden willingly for the sake of their brother. But this pain is a different matter; it makes a man more authentic, more akin to the life of the soul, more God-like.

Though renunciation is a soul-principle and derives its sanction and power from it, yet it is not easy. For there is another principle too equally powerful which is at work — the soul's self-identification with its own forms. The soul creates forms and identifies itself with them, forgetting its own self-status. This forgetfulness is called *vismriti* in Indian spiritual thought and is supported by yet another principle, the principle of nescience or *avidyā*.

These forms which the soul throws up are not without their own attractions and joys, however mixed and raw they may be. They also develop an ego of their own which resists their replacement even by better forms and deeper joys. The pull of the free, floating consciousness above is opposed by the gravitational attraction of the desire-life from below. The desire-life also functions as a thick veil which shuts out any glimpse of the higher life above.

According to the Indian spiritual thought, this desire-life is not a product of just one life-time. The experience and habits of innumerable past lives go into the making of the present life. Influences carried from distant past weave round a man a web, a force of destiny and impulsion, making him what he is and what he will be. It is very difficult to gainsay the propensities built over many lives. The force of spiritual renunciation is overpowered by the force of desire-forms built over innumerable lives. The soul identifies itself with those forms and it finds it difficult to give them up.

Desire is supported by ego and nescience. In fact, the two principles are so subtle, strong and pervasive that they even distort a spiritual faculty like renunciation as they do all other faculties. They make renunciation into an instrument of revenge instead of an instrument of liberation as it is intended to be. We know how the body denies the spirit but the denial of the body by the spirit can even be more ruthless. In Europe [under Christianity], it denied some very great values; it denied free inquiry; it denied even bath-tubs. It was an insufficient view of the spirit, an insufficiency which can play havoc with the life of the mind and the body.

When informed by ego, renunciation develops a morbid joy in its own self-indulgence. It does not renounce for the sake of any higher good but it becomes a stubborn denial for its own sake, for revenge, for glee. When informed by *avidyā*, renunciation becomes rabid, fanatical, a passionate need. It oversteps all bounds of reason and good sense. An ignorant renunciation denies the world: in the name of the spirit, it denies the working of the spirit in the body, the mind and the world. It turns the spirit into an instrument of revenge and destruction against the body.

So in all deeper spiritualities, renunciation is not regarded as a law unto itself. It is always combined with other qualities like purity, right aspiration, joy, tranquility and above all wisdom. In every thing one does, one should not lose his sense of proportion. He should not try to do things beyond his means and his inner preparation.

Renunciation has to be supported by the forces of Yoga, meditation, modesty, truthfulness, sincerity, self-awareness. It has to be purified before it becomes a liberating force. In certain spiritualities, renunciation is regarded as self-sufficient principle, as a matter of exercising one's self-will. As a result, renunciation becomes a painful exertion, a tug of war with one's nature, a self-defeating heroics, and imposition of an alien principle. But in the Indian Yoga systems, renunciation is conceived as a process of unfoldment and growth with the naturalness and joy that are associated with such a process. It follows an inner impulsion and an inner vision in order to effect an inner change; it does not follow an external rule or idea in order to accomplish an external effect. It makes manifest what is in the soul and it works in accordance with the nature of things and with the power of the soul. It is a process of progressive self-simplification, of self-disentanglement and self-disengagement. At no stage, it suppresses and does any violence to one's natural rhythm. In short, it works with understanding, not with self-will. It is a progressive self-transcendence. It renounces a lower form as a result of its urge for a higher one. It takes no premature step; it moves step by step.

In the process, it discovers many fairy lands, many fair forms, many benign manifestations. There is a temptation to rest in them. But each of them has within it the seed of its own self-denial, a pointer to its own self-transcendence. There is the glimpse of a higher and vaster horizon just a little ahead. Therefore, the present truth has to be given up, transcended and a higher truth embraced.

Man is bound to the world by hankering, by inertia, by *samskāra*, by duality, by a false view of things, by *avidyā*. He is bound by the tyranny of the sensible and the rational. He is bound not only by *tamas* and *rajas*, by sloth and passion, but also by goodness (*sattva*). The knot has to be loosened at all these levels. It is possible only for a man who has developed *vairāgya*. *Vairāgya* is freedom from worldly desire, indifference to carnal objects. It is a powerful weapon for shedding all those accretions that submerge the soul and make it false. It is that quality of the soul which feels dissatisfied with its imprisoned status, feels choked in a life of limitation, impotence, finitude, narrowness, duality, falsehood and bondage. *Vairāgya* is one of the two conditions enumerated by the Gita and the Pātañjala Yoga for the realization of the highest state, the other being *abhyāsa*, a constant and loving abiding in the practice of the interior life, in the practice of the holy presence of God. While *vairāgya* is a first indispensable condition of God-life, it finds its real culmination when one has seen the face of God or realized his true Self, as the Pātañjala Yoga says.

Spiritual growth is a matter of great, inner balance. It involves a delicate synthesis between different attributes of the soul. Because of the profundity and difficulty of the matter, there is no wonder that from time to time, one truth is overcultivated to the neglect of other truths. It has happened in India. Sometimes the truth of renunciation was overemphasized. And by its very success, it created an imbalance in the life of the society. The ideal of the society became monkish. It also devalued the world. The world was drowned in other-worldliness.

This overemphasis does not help. It helps neither the spiritual life as a whole nor even the particular truth overemphasized. By that very fact, that truth is distorted. For example, when renunciation is overemphasized and *prajñā* or wisdom is neglected, by that very fact renunciation becomes insufficient and even false. It becomes external; it becomes renunciation of duty, work and outer life. It becomes forced, institutionalized. People renounce without any inner preparation for leading a life of renunciation. That breeds hypocrisy. They live the same old life within the cloisters, churches and *gaddīs*. That brings into ridicule even the ideal of renunciation.

Such people renounce activity, not attachment. They are attached even in their inactivity. "They sit, controlling the organs of action, but dwelling in their minds on objects of senses" (Gita 3.6). That strengthens the grip of a deluded life still more.

So the growth of the spirit is a complicated affair. It means the growth of many attributes of which renunciation is only one attribute. Some of the other attributes are modesty, compassion, equanimity, naturalness, truthfulness, universality and wisdom.

Though spiritual life is at heart one, yet it has many peaks, each peak having a characteristic atmosphere. Different ages express their spiritual ideals differently. In India itself, recent centuries expressed their ideals in terms of the four *purushārthas* — *dharma*, *artha*, *kāma*, *moksha*; but the more ancient times expressed their spiritual ideals differently. It was in terms of paying debts, debts to Gods, debts to the teachers, debts to the parents, debts to the neighbour. The Sāṁkhya and Buddhist spiritual ideals were couched in terms of joy, renunciation, ecstasy, equanimity, *prajñā*. There is a certain otherworldliness about these ideals but renunciation alone has not much to do about it. For all the terms including *prajñā* are equally imbued with the weltanschauung of other-worldliness. On the other hand, the Vedic ideals were differently expressed. Those were *satyam*, *brihat*, *ritam*, *ugram*, *dīkshā*, *tapa*, *brahma*, *yajñam*.

In a certain spirituality, the dominant note is renunciation; in another spirituality life is conceived as a *yajña*, a free receiving and giving, freely passing on what one freely receives. Here there is no blockage, no immobilization, but it is all free circulation.

There is a spirituality which renounces the world because it is full of suffering, because there is a more spiritual world above. But there is another kind of spirituality which does not agree with this approach. According to this, the world may have its crosses and travails but it has also its own inner truth, its own deep meaning and to deny that truth does not belong to the fullness of spirituality.

But behind the two formulations, there is also a good deal in common. The Yogic ideals give no solace to those who seek a hedonistic and self-regarding life and who think that this is all the life the earthly existence has to offer. The Vedic ideal of life is extremely noble, high-minded, upright. It is an ideal of a holy and consecrated life. It knows nothing mean and narrow. It covers a good deal of common ground with the Sāmkhya and Buddhist approach. Whatever the differences, they appear at the summit. But in both, the lower life has to be renounced. In both, there is no place for craving, greed, hatred, malice, ingratitude, envy, fear, cowardice, spite, indolence, egoism, selfishness, boasting, vanity, pretensions. The sordid worldliness of ordinary pursuit has no place in both the ideals and both teach its renunciation. The only difference is that while one seeks the kingdom of heaven, the other also seeks its fulfilment in the earthly life of man. Both call for purification of the inner instruments of the soul, a purification which can be effected only by renunciation. The word 'pure' comes from the same source as the word 'fire', fire which purifies by burning. Renunciation is that inner fire, that power of the soul which consumes everything that is false, foreign and narrow.

Renunciation is not opposed to joy; rather, they go together. The world cannot be enjoyed by greedy possession; it is enjoyed by generous renunciation. Therefore, the Vedic teaching is: enjoy by renunciation, by self-giving. True joy finds its fulfilment and culmination in renunciation, renunciation of all that is false, unreal, crooked and dark.

Chapter 2.6

Liberation

The aim of spiritual life has been expressed in two different ways: (1) in becoming more God-like and (2) in release from bondage, in freedom from all that limits and incapacitates. Different spiritual cultures and disciplines have used different metaphors and figures of speech in stating their spiritual aims but in the main they conform to the above classification.

In the Gita and other Hindu scriptures, the two ideas are constantly repeated and they appear almost antiphonally in a creative response, the one bringing out, reinforcing and enriching the sense of the other. The highest state of spiritual illumination is described by phrases which mean freedom from lower impulsions and also the assumption of higher qualities. People who have 'arrived' are described by such epithets as *vīta-rāga-bhaya-krodhāḥ* (gone beyond worldly attachments, fear and anger), or simply *vīta-rāgāḥ* (gone beyond desires); they have destroyed their doubts (*chhinna-saṁśayāḥ*); they have conquered the vice of attachment (*jita-saṅga-doshāḥ*); they are without pride and delusion (*nirmāna-mohāḥ*); they are freed from dualities (*dvandvairvimuktāḥ*) and their doubts are cut off (*chhinnad-vaidhāḥ*); their desires are pacified (*vinivritttakāmāḥ*); they have conquered their senses (*jitendriyāḥ*) and their afflictions and doubts are gone (*gatavyathāḥ*, and *gatasandehāḥ*); they are freed from Names and Forms (*nāmarūpāvimuktāḥ*), or freed from the knots of the heart (*guhā-granthibhyo vimuktāḥ*); they are purified from sins (*pūta-pāpāḥ*) and liberated from them (*sarvebhyo aghebhyo vimuktāḥ*). In the more positive language, they are described as constantly dwelling in the Self (*adhyātma-nityāḥ*); they are seated in the Self (*ātma-saṁsthāḥ*), Self-satisfied (*ātma-*

triptāḥ), happy within (*antaḥ-sukhāḥ*), rejoice within (*antarā-rāmāḥ*), illumined within (*antarjyotiḥ*); they have become Brahma (*brahmabhūtāḥ*); they have become immortal and eternal (*brahmamayāḥ, amritamayāḥ*).

In the ancient world of Greece, we find the two aims stated in a language startlingly Hindu. Orphism, the Mystery religion of this region, spoke of *'Lusis'*, or release or freedom or liberation; and Phaedo in Plato preached that the destiny of man is to "dwell with Gods", and to become as "God-like" as possible.

If we reflect a little on the problem, we shall find that both mean the same thing and they are referring to the same process. Spiritual life is both a growth in being from one viewpoint as well as a release from bondage from another viewpoint. We grow in the measure of our liberation from the limitations of the body and the heart.

Though there will be little disagreement on the above point but how to achieve the end could cause a good deal of difference both in emphasis as well as in approach. Also most people have rather a limited idea of the scope of the problem. Some people think that spiritual growth involves no giving up but only adding a few more desirable traits. Others are not so self-satisfied. They suffer from certain negative feelings and attitudes like boredom, fickleness, and capriciousness which they would like to give up; on the other hand, they would like to cultivate certain positive qualities like confidence and cheerfulness. Some would like to give up the more obvious infidelities and insincerity of character — these do not agree with their self-image. Some also suffer, particularly the intellectuals, from doubts, disbelief and uncertainties and they find them burdensome; therefore they are prepared to take to the certainties of faith. Not many feel the same justification about continence, a value emphasized by many spiritual disciplines; but if it has to be a package deal, some are prepared to give it a try too off and on. Some feel the sting of unsatisfied desire and therefore, in a huff, would like to give up desire itself.

For such people, there is no liberation understood in the Yogic sense. Their effort might bring about some self-improvement and resolve some surface conflicts and bring about a certain harmony and self-mastery but it is far from being a liberation of the Yogis. Liberation lies far beyond the cogitations, ambivalences and moral dilemmas, mixed sincerities and aspirations of an ordinary life; it lies even beyond the intensities of religions and interesting and extraordinary 'experiences' of a successful trance. Liberation belongs to the very last stages and stations of Yoga and mystical attainments. It involves a complete transformation of the present level of consciousness.

There are three levels at which life is lived. One is the ordinary, active life. In its lower rung, it is rather unregenerate, full of passions, envy, strife, strong attractions and revulsions, or what the Bible calls the life of rioting and drunkenness, chambering and wantonness, strife and envying, but in its higher expressions, work is informed by a sense of duty and idealism; activity is self-restrained, dedicated, brotherly, ethical. Here some persons also consecrate themselves to particular vows of a discipline and adopt a certain lofty way of life.

But to some this active life even at its most exalted is not enough. They have a feeling that the active is rooted in the contemplative. They take to a life of meditation, *dhyāna*. In fact when the clamour of passions subsides and one leads an ethical and disciplined life, one automatically enters into the calm and joy of a meditative state. In this state there are new intensities, visions, joys; there is faith, piety, self-melting; there is the news of a higher life. He also sees in these states the source of a great deal of the truths of the ethical life. Of course, he need not give up works but works have to be done in the spirit of truths revealed in meditation.

The truths up to this point are not wholly unfamiliar to man. These have elements of life which he knows and which in some measure he can intuit. But there is also a third level which is less known and yet which is the basis of the second level, the fountain-source of all that is good and great in action and devotion. Equanimity, passionlessness, desirelessness constitute this level.

People understand bad desires; they also understand desire for good things. Both are part of their experience and aspiration. But they do not know what to make of 'desirelessness'. It lies too much beyond their ken. They even distrust it. To them, it is a life-negating category, a world-denying thought.

Most people seek a warm-hearted spirituality. The psychic principle in them is fulfilled by a life of dedication, confidence, joy, fellow-feeling, brotherliness, purity. Therefore, popular religious scriptures mainly deal in the truths of faith and ethics. The word 'desirelessness' does not even occur in the Bible except by implication; on the other hand, there is plenty of exhortation to avoid bad desires and follow good ones, like 'let us not be desirous of vain glory', etc.

But there is a rare minority who seek a still higher fare. They have a more single-minded urge for a more unitive life, a consuming passion for self-naughting, a more clamorous sense of immortality. They seek no edifying truth but a truth in all its nakedness. They seek annihilation in the beloved; they seek awakening, rebirth, resurrection. Phoenix-like, they seek to rise from their own ashes. They seek a region where the sun shines not, nor the moon, nor the stars; they seek a light which is neither on the seas nor on the land. They seek more than brotherliness — they seek to become the life of all. This urge finds its fulfilment in Yoga, and in the Upanishadic and mystic traditions of mankind. These teach *samādhi*, self-reflection, self-awareness, self-knowledge, wisdom, liberation, *nirvāṇa*, *advaita*, desirelessness, *vairāgya*.

But the people who take to this single-minded search for truth discover that the search is not easy. It is not enough to be good or to cultivate some amiable traits. On the other hand, our life must become luminous. It should become universal; it should transcend its limitations; it should throw away the bondage of pain, hunger, thirst and mortality. The soul is submerged in the world and it must come out of its orbit.

But when we go about this business, we find that we are bound to the world in more ways than we suspect. In fact, it is not something outside of us; it exists inside us. We are bound to it by desire, by ego, by duality. We carry it within us in a subtle form wherever we go. It is stored away in us as *saṁskāras*, as impressions and dispositions. According to Hindu scriptures, we are bound to the lower life by a triple-knot and for true liberation all these knots have to be unravelled. The world is no part of us, yet it is within us. However hard we may try to throw it out, it clings to us, comes back to us. No physical change in outer circumstances, nor even physical death effects escape from the world for it lives within us in a seed state and it comes to life again and recreates its own concomitant circumstances and puts its own meaning into them. It is 'reborn'.

It is in this context that in Indian spirituality, one of the important aims of liberation is liberation from repeated births. Man wanders aimlessly in *saṁsāra*, in a world created by himself, by his thoughts and desires and actions, reaping what he has sown. Liberation means liberation from this wandering; it means home-coming. Through sustained spiritual discipline, one becomes *anāgāmī*, one who does not return. The Gita speaks of two paths, the path of *anāvritti*, the path from which one returns not and the path of *āvritti*, the path from which one returns. These are also called the paths of light (*śukla*) and darkness (*krishṇa*). One who takes to the path of light returns not but one who takes to the path of darkness returns.

In the same spirit, different systems of Indian philosophy have described the aim of 'liberation' as liberation from pain. But pain here is not used in an ordinary sense. It is a short formula used to describe all conditioned and partial existence whose fruit is 'pain'. It stands for unreality, for falsehood, for separative existence, and even for those exalted states which are luminous and blissful but which fall short of the absolute free status of the soul. A spiritual aspirant should rise above *sukha* and *duḥkha*, pleasure and pain not by a stoic exercise of the personal will but by realizing that these do not belong to the soul. The liberated status of the soul or the world beyond (*uttarataram*) is called formless and painless, (*arūpam, anāmayam*). To this abode of bliss (*padam anāmayam*) go those who are liberated from the bonds of rebirth (*janmabandhavinirmuktāḥ*).

What binds the soul to a lower consciousness, to repeated births, to the pain of separative existence? How does the soul which is free in essence become a slave? How is its liberation effected? These are some of the questions that have been raised and answered by various spiritual philosophies and disciplines.

That which keeps the soul in a state of bondage is evil life, evil deeds, evil desires, ego, clinging to life, nescience. The principle is one though it is called by many names in order to bring out the different nuances. It is called *kashāya,* a defilement or impurity that cleaves to the soul, or because it afflicts (*kashṭa*) it. It is also called *samyojana* because it binds the soul to the world. Buddhists also call it *upādāna* because it is a form of grasping and clinging to existence. It is caused by *trishṇā*, desire, which in turn leads to *bhava,* a new birth. It is also called *anuśaya* because consequences are closely related to their causes and therefore the results of all that one has done and desired lie waiting in his soul which makes it take to new bodies when their seeds mature. The Jains call it *āsrava* and define it as "a door through which action enter the soul". Put a little differently, it also means the action of the senses which impel the soul towards external objects. According to Jains, action is not passive; it lends its quality to the soul of the doer; action is even material. It enters the soul. If action is bad, it affects the soul in many different ways; it obscures the doer's wisdom, his intuition, his faith, his joy and brings him into the subjugation of pleasure and pain; it effects his next birth, its length, status and circumstances. It even lends a particular colour to the soul. In fact, each soul is born with a colour of its own which is lent to it by the kind of actions he has performed in the past.

The Pātañjala Yoga used the word *kleśa* for the principle of impurity in the soul which keeps it in bondage. It takes on many forms and exists in different states of subtlety. It is an actively shaping force but it can wait for aeons in the psyche before it begins to bear fruits. Sometimes it has a conative tone, sometimes affective, sometimes intellectual. *Kleśa* is a multi-significant term and no single translation can convey all the richness of its meanings. Therefore, it is best to retain the word as it is and allowing the context to define its meanings. Following Sāṃkhya the Pātañjala Yoga enumerates five *kleśas*. In the descending order of subtlety and potency, they are *avidyā*, *asmitā*, *rāga*, *dvesha* and *abhiniveśa* each preceding one supporting the working of the following while *avidyā*, the first one, is the field in which they all prosper and grow. *Avidyā* is the very first defilement which arises in the involution of nature. It is a form of forgetfulness by the Purusha of its true nature. As a result, a defilement or affliction arises which regards the impermanent to be permanent, the impure to be pure, the painful to be blissful, the unconscious to be conscious.

This nescience is the first to come and the last to go. It operates on every level. It is because of *avidyā* that a man makes so much of the goods of the world and thinks that he can own them. His body, his mind, his intelligence are vehicles of the spirit but he mistakes them for the spirit itself.

Avidyā gives rise to another *kleśa* called *asmitā*, by which the knower wrongly identifies itself with the instruments of knowledge. According to Sāṃkhya philosophy, there are two principles: Purusha and Prakriti. Purusha is conscious, integral, independent, inactive, unconditioned and knows no modification. Prakriti is unconscious, composite, dependent, active, conditioned and undergoes modifications. Purusha is *kevala*, alone; Prakriti is triune. Purusha is the master, Prakriti is the property. According to Sāṃkhya even *chitta* (mind-stuff) or *buddhi* (intelligence) is material and is Prakriti's first modification. It is also called *mahat*. It is unconscious but it is so full of the *sattva* quality that it faithfully reflects the light of the Purusha. But because of the working of *avidyā*, it confuses this light or rather shadow with the Purusha itself. *Chitta* or *buddhi* thinks it is conscious or a seer, but it is only an instrument of seeing. This is called *asmitā kleśa* and gives rise to a false sense of personality. This *kleśa* too is very subtle. Wrong identification with the body and its passions is relatively easier to conquer than wrong identification with the *mahat*, with *buddhi*.

This *asmitā* is not the Self of the Upanishads, but the *anātma* about which Lord Buddha speaks. It is the self which is enmeshed in the world, which is in bondage to nature. This *kleśa* is the author of a false individuality or personality. At the level of *asmitā*, it is full of *sattva* and luminosity but as it casts its shadow on lower planes like the desire-plane, it becomes darksome and intractable. *Asmitā* supports *rāga*, desire, hankering after pleasure, attachment to objects of pleasure. When we begin to think we are the body, the senses or the mind, we develop a hankering for things and objects which bring them pleasure. And by the same token, we avoid objects which are painful. This gives rise to a *kleśa* called *dvesha*, aversion.

Rāga and *dvesha* go together. They are two sides of the same coin. We seek pleasure and avoid pain. We are attracted by one kind of contacts of nature and we shrink from another kind; we grow a liking for the one and a dislike for the other. But like and dislike both bind. When we desire something inordinately, we are enslaved by it. In desiring it, we also want to possess it but in the process we get possessed by it. Similarly, simply because we dislike a thing, we do not win our independence from it. We may avoid it physically but we cannot avoid it psychologically. The more we dislike and resent a thing, the more it grows within us; its grip on us tightens.

We should notice one important characteristic of *rāga* and *dvesha* as they operate on desire-plane or *kāma-bhūmi*. Here pleasures and pains are mixed and what we desire we also detest. Satisfaction leads to satiety and every desire has within it the seed of its opposite. So our attitude to our surroundings is ambivalent. There is festivity in every funeral and vice versa. We desire and dislike a thing alternately and even simultaneously.

We should also remember another thing. A simple theory of pleasure and pain will not explain *rāga* and *dvesha*. *Rāga* and *dvesha* are at the service of Ego, the shadow cast by *asmitā* on the desire-plane. Men are prepared willingly to accept a good deal of pain and forgo a good deal of pleasure in response to current opinions and fashions so long as that feeds their pride and self-opinion. Similarly, it is possible by training our nervous system and by certain ascetic practices not to pursue pleasures and not to shrink from pain — and even to take pleasure in pain — but it does not necessarily diminish our sense of ego.

As *tamas* increases, *rāga* and *dvesha* degenerate into a still deeper *kleśa* called *abhiniveśa*. It is sordid worldliness, a craving for life and fear of death. And though it is afraid of death, this *kleśa* is the cause of repeated lives and deaths. At this level, *rāga* no longer seeks pleasure; it seeks repetition, perpetuation of a particular form. Similarly, *dvesha* is no longer shrinking from pain; it is resentment and hostility for their own sake. Ego too here is perverted into pure self-aggrandisement.

The naming of *kleśas* is not merely a scholarly digression; it has a practical bearing. They hold us in their grip. They embrace us on all sides. They clip the spiritual wings. They keep us bound to the gravitational pull of carnality. We cannot cross over the ocean of *saṁsāra*, becoming, when our hands and feet are tied. We must understand them in order to conquer them.

They bind us by pain but even more firmly by pleasure. Their grip is sometimes rough, sometimes smooth, sometimes hard, sometimes soft but it is always sure; sometimes their sway is open, sometimes disguised but it is ubiquitous. As a man advances on the spiritual path, he begins to see these *kleśas* more clearly and he makes progress to the extent he is able to see them. Those who feel comfortable in the lap of *kleśas* have no call for a spiritual life.

How to conquer *kleśas* is the central problem of Yoga. Therefore, it must understand them and know their various expressions; it must find out how they arise and what strengthens them and what weakens them; it must discover the process by which the soul is bound and also the process by which it is liberated.

We have already said that the soul is bound by a triple-knot. It is bound by desire, by duality, by ego. In the language of the Gita, it is bound by *tamas*, *rajas*, and even *sattva* while its true status is beyond the three qualities — *guṇātīta*. *Tamas* binds by inertia and pain, *rajas* by action and passion, *sattva* by knowledge and joy. The last sounds rather curious — knowledge, learning and joy binding the soul. But it is only a way of expressing a great mystic truth that the soul does not merely seek goodness; it seeks liberation. The truth of the matter is that *sattva* is a great purifying force and a good deal of the initial Yogic *sādhanā* consists in increasing the force of *sattva* in us. It is a great *kuśala dharma*, a great *aklishṭa dharma*. It releases the soul from its gross bondage. It stands for all that is generous and good in our actions and luminous and joyful and *ekāgra* in our *samādhi*. But it too tends to leave its *saṁskāras* behind which the soul finds binding. So the soul enters into *nirodha samādhi* and denies those *samaskāras* too for its liberation. According to Sāṁkhya, *sattva* is a purity-force of Prakriti and it takes the mind to the very portals of the Self but for the last step it too is inadequate and must retire. That requires a different faculty, a different operation, a different movement. That requires self-naughting, *nirodha, nirvāṇa, pralaya, pratiprasava*.

Kleśas exist externally in our actions; they exist more internally in our desires and they exist more centrally in our intellect. They have to be conquered on all these levels. The three-fold bondage calls for a three-fold liberation.

Lord Buddha is asked: Man is criss-cross with *kleśas*; they have woven a web round him and within him. How can one unravel their threads, defeat their grip? Buddha replies: The man who is wise and heroic, who is established in *śīla*, who engages in *samādhi* and who exercises wisdom alone can cut through their web. The science of liberation is built on the triple foundations of *śīla, samādhi* and *prajñā*. Their combined action constitutes the famous *viśuddhi-mārga* — *mārga* is the way to *nirvāṇa* and *viśuddhi* is that state of being which is free from all taints.

In all mystic traditions, Indian or non-Indian, the aim of spiritual life is stated to be 'liberation' and the way to attain it has been taught to be the exercise of certain deeper faculties of the soul in which virtue and wisdom or *prajñā* occupy a premier place. According to Plato it is virtue which purges the soul from error and which effects her conversion from darkness to light, while wisdom is the highest combination of virtue and intelligence. It is a rare possession but most people think they have it in plenty.

In India itself, even in traditions other than Brahmanical and Buddhist, virtue and knowledge got full emphasis for soul-liberation. Says an old Jain text: the passions are the fire; knowledge, virtuous life, and penance are the waters; sprinkled with the drop of knowledge, the fire of passion is extinguished. Another important text says: right knowledge (the knowledge of things as they are, *samyak darśana*), right wisdom (*samyak jñāna*) and right conduct (*samyak charitra*) constitute the way to liberation

In Pātañjal Yoga, we meet the same scheme. *Yama* and *niyama* constitute the first foundation. *Yama* is ethical life. Harmlessness, truthfulness, abstention from theft, continence, non-covetousness are its limbs. *Niyama* is a name for an adopted way of life, of great vows undertaken which include purity, external and internal, contentment, askesis, bodily and mental, scriptural study and spiritual reading, and surrender to God. They taken together are also called *kriyāyoga*. They help to weaken the hold of *kleśas* and strengthen an interior life, and promote *samādhi*. *Samādhi* reveals many luminous and joyous forms, reveals many hidden powers of the soul like *śraddhā*, *vīrya*, *smriti*, *samādhi*, *prajñā*. Equipped with these powers, it enters a still higher path, the path of liberation, of desirelessness, of Self-discovery, of *nirvāna*, *nirodha* and wisdom.

Samādhi is not mentioned in all *darśanas* but all Yogas which aim at liberation make use of it in one form or another. The reason is simple. A diffused, scattered mind is weak and feeble; it can accomplish nothing, and is a poor guide. In order to be effective, it must grow in intensity and concentration, *ekāgratā* — and for the purposes of Yoga, there should also be purity in this *ekāgratā* and its aim should be a holy life.

There are other reasons also why *samādhi* is a necessary

concomitant of Yoga. The purpose of Yoga is liberation from desire and other *kleśas* but the roots of these *kleśas* lie deep in the *chitta*, in those recesses of the mind which are accessible only in *samādhi*. Ordinarily, we know only the more external expression of desire, its conative and affective aspect, as an active hankering for a pleasant experience. But it also exists in a more mentalized form, as a *samjñā*, as a *samskāra*, as a concept, as a state of mind, as a propensity, as a *drishṭi*, as a way of looking and evaluating the world. Unless we learn to go deep into the mind and catch desire in these subtle, mentalized forms, we cannot adequately cope with it. Purification of desire calls for purification of *samskāras* and *drishṭi*, purification of all proclivities, thought habits and thought formations. *Samādhi* promotes objectivity and develops a seeing which is inner and direct. This makes evasion and concealment difficult. *Kleśas* cannot put on the cloak of rationalization and idealization, subtle and mental, with the same ease.

Samādhi helps in other ways too. It brings vision of a higher and holier life. By repeated contemplation of such a life, its impressions on the mind are strengthened and the impressions of an opposite life are weakened. It builds up *śubha samskāra*, *kuśal samskāra*, *aklishṭa samskāra* or *samskāras* that are auspicious, meritorious and liberating. People who reach this stage enjoy celestial joys in their inner being and when they die they are born in the realm of Gods.

All this is very meritorious and liberating but not yet liberation. A subtle sense of 'I' still clings to the stage and a luminous nescience still subsists in the background. A *sādhaka* experiences heavenly joys and the accumulated *samskāras* for a lower life are weakened; but in the process, he also begins to accumulate *samskāras* for a life on a higher plane. He develops a taste for that life and wants to perpetuate it. He does not see that that too must come to an end and that that too does not belong to the essential nature of the soul. The Self is not yet liberated; it is identified with not-Self, with *anātma*. Therefore, the Yoga declares a further ideal, the ideal of *moksha* or liberation.

For liberation, one enters into another territory called *nirvāṇa-bhūmi* by the Buddhists and *nirodha-bhūmi* by Pātañjala Yoga. But between this and the previous stage there is an intermediate ground, a no man's land. It is at the apex of *samprjñāta samādhi* and at the beginning of *asmaprajñāta samādhi*. This has a very high place in Pātañjala Yoga. Here by a sustained practice of the Yoga of discrimination or *viveka-khyāti*, which separates the seer from the seen and the instruments of seeing, Purusha is seen for the first time as separate from Prakriti and its formations including *chitta* or *buddhi* though it continues to exist as a bare configuration, as a *saṁskāra*. When this knowledge arises, the *asmitā kleśa* is destroyed. So long as the seer is seen as an object of cognition and identified with it, it gives rise to *asmitā kleśa*. But when the *chitta* or the *buddhi* knows that it merely reflects a light which belongs to someone other than itself, the spiritual man is born. The *asmitā kleśa*, known as the heart-knot in the Upanishads is destroyed. Now a mind steeped in the knowledge of its separateness from nature (*vivekanimna*) moves effortlessly towards self-illumination (*kaivalyaprāgbhāram*). It no longer flows towards worldly objects; it becomes its own destination. It is established in *param vairāgya* (supreme non-attachment).

What is the analogue of *viveka-khyāti* in Buddhist Yoga is difficult to say, for here the two Yogas emphasize two different aspects. While the Pātañjala Yoga speaks of the self-same identity of the nominal 'I' the Buddhist Yoga speaks of the complete otherness of the phenomenal 'I'. In neither, they meet except under *moha* and *avidyā* and they always exclude each other.

But what we have called the intermediate no man's land above has a rough and ready sort of Buddhist analogue in its eighth *samāpatti*: *naivasaṁjñā nāsmajñā*, neither knowing nor unknowing. It means the *saṁsāra* has ended but the *nirvāṇa* has not begun; the mind has ended but the Self has not begun. What is called *asaṁjñā* here is called *asamprjñāta* in Pātañjala Yoga.

Pātañjala Yoga says very little about *asmprajñāta* Yoga and even less about the knowledge it gives. It gives no method, no direction, no guidance. The reason is that here we enter a pathless path. The process is self-guided and a knowledge arises which is untaught (*anaupadeśika*), which is spontaneous. It is a knowledge by which one crosses over the ocean of the world.

The path that the soul enters here is called the path of *avidyā* or *asambhūti* or *vināśa* (annihilation) in the *Īśopnishad*. This is the path of *nirodha*, of *nirvāṇa*, of ceasing to be. Here the soul turns away, withdraws, stands back; here it leans on no particular truth; it cultivates nothing, receives nothing; it is merely intent on denuding, divesting and shedding. It subjects everything that has gone before and of which there still remains anything in the form of *saṃskāras* to the continued influence of a supra-mundane 'unknowing' and desirelessness. This burns up all impurities and even their traces. It enters into a state of rest and silence, a state like a suspended animation (*virāma-pratyaya*) from which it comes out completely renewed. The sway of *avidyā* ceases and Self-knowledge is born. *Kleśas* which were merely weakened by *samādhi* and which were seed-burnt in *viveka-khyāti* are completely eradicated in *asmaprajñāta samādhi*.

Buddhism is not as laconic about this stage as the Pātañjala Yoga. The reason is easy to understand. Buddhism is not describing an actual state of liberation, a state which goes beyond description; it is describing the state of bondage, the process by which a man has come to this bonded stage and the process by which he can extricate himself, the process of deepening entanglement and the counter process of increasing disentanglement — things which can still be expressed in the language of thought. In fact, the discussion is so copious and full of details and classification that there is a danger of losing sight of the essential truth and the underlying principle, losing sight of the wood for trees. When a man is perfected in *samādhi*, he begins to see things as they are; he begins to see that they are transient, painful, blind; he sees their arising (*udaya*) and their passing away (*vyaya*); he attains to the knowledge that all things dissolve (*bhaṅga jñāna*); he finds this knowledge frightful (*bhaya jñāna*) — the whole world is like a pit of burning ember; he arrives at the knowledge of the wretchedness of the deluded world (*ādinava jñāna*); from this arises a feeling of disgust (*nirveda jñāna*) which gives birth to a strong will for deliverance (*muñchitamayatā jñāna*); then he begins to meditate on the transience, sorrowfulness and vanity of conditioned things (*pratisaṃkhyā jñāna*); this brings about a complete indifference to the things of the world (*saṃskāra upekshā jñāna*); this brings him *nirvāṇa*.

Ordinarily a man feels quite restful in his *kleśas*. But a mind purified by *samādhi* begins to mirror their true nature, their ubiquity and evil power. This mind sees that every thing is on fire: The eye is on fire: the form is on fire; the eye-knowledge is on fire; the contact of the eye with its object is on fire; the feelings of pleasure and pain that arise from that contact are on fire; similarly the ear is on fire; the nose is on fire; the tongue is on fire; the body is on fire; the *manas* is on fire — they are burning with the fire of attachment (*rāgāgni*), with the fire of aversion (*dveshāgni*), with the fire of delusion (*mohāgni*); they are burning with the fire of birth, with the fire of old age, with the fire of death.

Similarly, this mind sees that the eye is blind, the ear is blind, the nose is blind, the tongue is blind, the body is blind, the mind is blind; their respective objects are blind; their respective knowledge is blind; their respective contacts with their objects are blind; the pleasant and unpleasant experiences born of those contacts are blind. Knowing all this, he develops a distaste (*nirveda*) for the world; from *nirveds* comes desirelessness; from desirelessness comes liberation (*vimukti*); from liberation comes the saving knowledge of the liberated and the bonded states. The *sādhaka* now knows that he has 'arrived', that *kleśas* are destroyed. The world falls (away) completely from him, not only from his desires and affections but also from his intellect too. He attains to *nirvāṇa*, to desirelessness. "That state alone is *nirvāṇa* where there is annihilation of desire, aversion and delusion (*rāga-kshaya, dvesha-kshaya, moha-kshaya*) — that is how Saṃyutta Nikāya defines *nirvāṇa* in 'nibbāna sutta'.

This is also the famous purification of insight or wisdom or *vipaśyanā*. With this the process of purification is complete. The *sādhaka* becomes a *siddha*. He sees with an inner eye the "maker of the illusion", its rafts and shafts. He discovers that the foundation of this world is 'desire' which itself is built on a deep nescience, a nescience or *avidyā* which continually creates *vismriti* or forgetfulness of his true nature. But when the yogic insight or *bodhi* eyes open he finds that the life of the body and the mind, is not 'real'. It is a concatenation, a *skandha*. It is subject to change and pain; he can not own it or store it. Chasing it is like chasing a shadow. With this realization comes utter renunciation (*para vairāgya*) and one is liberated.

On more than one occasion, Buddha spoke of the liberated state as a state which brings wisdom and wins immortality, and assuages all hunger and thirst and ends the sway of old age and death but in most cases he described it as liberation from *kleśas*, liberation from sorrow, liberation from illusion, liberation from nescience. This way of expression does not suit certain types and temperaments but let it be remembered that this is an important way, even a necessary way for expressing some of the truths of the Spirit. It cannot be dispensed with particularly by those who have taken to the mystic path. The truth of the *kleśas* in its deeper aspects and ramifications comes only to those who lead a profoundly interior and introspective life. It is easier to know the more obvious entanglements of desire but it is difficult to know the subtler and more disguised knots of *asmitā* and *avidyā*. This insight is not so well developed in those who merely seek piety and ethical life.

The insight of *kleśa* also promotes better understanding of words like 'Spirit' and 'God' which we use rather in a sloppy and loose manner. They are used as blanket terms but they include different ideas belonging to different levels of mind and they mean different things to different minds. For example, to the Yoga the highest concept of God is that of a being who is free from all *kleśas*, *kleśāprāmrishṭaḥ*, but in actual practice in most cases we have God who is joined with *kleśas*. Even to regard him as 'one' is a form of *kleśa*.

There are all kinds of Gods belonging to all kinds of levels. There are 'desire Gods' and 'Ego Gods' thrown up by *kāma-*

bhūmi. When the God of Moses has brought him and his followers to the land of the Hittites, Amorites, Canaanites and others and delivers these people into their hands, He tells them: "Thou shalt smite them, and utterly destroy them; thou shalt make no covenant with them nor shew mercy upto them", and "ye shall destroy their altars, and break their images, and cut down their groves, and burn their graven images with fire."

There are also more benign Gods thrown up by different *dhyāna-bhūmis.* There are Gods of faith, the faith itself differing in its level of purity. In some cases, it is no more than an induced belief but in other cases it represents a deep truth of the soul. In the *dhyānas* of *rūpa-bhūmi,* the God does not rise above particularity and form. The God is the God of a particular people, a particular church; He has preferences; he enters into special covenants with special people; He exalts certain people and equally arbitrarily condemns certain others. But at his best he still represents a great luminous form. He is an ethical God who demands compliance to the moral laws he reveals to his people. He also inculcates piety, faith, joy, consecration. But in his less purified form, he is joined with the *kleśa* of *dvesha.* He is a jealous God. He seeks elimination of other Gods. He does not rise up to the concept of a universal God because he does not yet come from the universality of the mind, from the universality of *dhyānas* of *arūpa-bhūmi* in which all forms are transcended and reconciled. He knows no other way of universality except that of conquest, crusades and proselytizing.

We first know God through his luminous forms, through his works and creation, through his goodness and greatness, through his signs and miracles. Then we know him in his universality and transcendence, above all forms, good and bad. Then we also know him as the secret of our own inner being. We first know the creatures, then the creator, first the manifestations then the manifestor; then we go to the great Unmanifest, the great Abyss, the Transcendental.

True worship generates *ekāgratā.* It makes us *ananyachetas;* we worship Him alone. This is great devotion. But we soon rise to the level of understanding; we realize that there is no other than

He. Similarly, when we have gone beyond *rūpa* and *arūpa samāpattis*, we arrive at the Advaitic truth that 'I am He'. But it soon deepens into a still greater truth that He alone is. Here we experience God without any admixture of *kleśas*.

So we see that the problem is more complicated than many of us believe. Some believe that the theology of 'one God' is superior to the theology of 'many Gods'. They claim that their scriptures contain a deeper concept of God but the fact is that they have a shallower knowledge of their own minds. God is not a name for a finished something given once for all. It has to do with growth in soul-life. With increasing purity, with increasing conquest of *kleśas*, Gods change — the unchanging changes. When the knots of the mind and the heart are loosened, when one has gone beyond the three *guṇās*, when one is established in *śraddhā*, *smriti* and *prajñā*, one's object of worship changes beyond all recognition. He no longer worships what the other people here worship — *naidam yadaidam upāsati*.

The knowledge of *kleśas* is a purifying knowledge; it is an enlightening knowledge; it is a liberating knowledge.

Chapter 2.7

Prajñā

In most people, life is buried in the physical and sense-body. It is lived in nescience. It is a product of stimulus and response. It is identified with the capacity for sensation, with the feelings of pain and pleasure. In a small minority, it rises to the level of rationality. Such people are capable of generalising their experience and establishing a relationship of cause and effect between its different constituents. They are capable of arriving at general truths and from those truths also deduce particular conclusions. But neither the sensate nor the logical mind represents the highest possibilities of consciousness. At a certain stage, pain and pleasure may give us a measure of the intensity of life, but they can hardly plumb its depths. The capacity for sensation is only one expression of life and that too not a very satisfactory one. The logical mind too has its sharp limitations and man's reason if it is modest knows this. Beyond this is another mind, a larger mind whose seeing is deeper and more direct.

Ordinary mind is subject to the bondage of the body, to its attachments and aversions; it is heavy, opaque, bound to desire-objects; it is caught in rigid logic-forms and narrow and lifeless concepts. But beyond this is a free, living consciousness, a disembodied life of Self-awareness and World-awareness. It is the aim of Yoga to liberate this larger, freer consciousness from its bondage, its downward pull. There are thoughts without consciousness; but there is also a consciousness without thoughts. This can be released by the practice of desirelessness, equal-mindedness, by worship and adoration. By them the mind is nourished and strengthened; it sheds weight, becomes light, bright, limpid; it becomes self-aware; it is restored to its Self-nature which is a concentrated illumination, consciousness and knowledge, *prajñāna-ghana*.

Prajñā is knowledge but not all knowledge is *prajñā*. Only spiritual knowledge is *prajñā*. It destroys the illusion of a separative existence. *Kleśas* which were merely weakened by *samādhi* are completely burnt up by *prajñā*. *Prajñā* is liberating knowledge *par excellence*; it is also the knowledge which comes with liberation. *Prajñā* is Self-knowledge.

But Self-knowledge could mean two things. It could mean knowledge of the Self qua Self, knowledge of the Self in its isolation, *kaivalya jñāna*, Spirit's knowledge of itself in its transcendence. This knowledge is difficult to describe though the mystics have tried to do it through suggestive images, metaphors and symbols and also more often by telling us what it is not than by what it is.

Self-knowledge could also mean all the knowledge contained in the Self or the knowledge of all that is contained in the Self.

But if all knowledge is contained in the Self as mystics tell us, then in that sense all knowledge is Self-knowledge. It was in this sense that Plato called all knowledge 'recollection'. But this is too wide a use of the term and by this use it loses its usefulness. Only that knowledge is spiritual which refers back directly to the Spirit and not to any of its instrumentalities like the reason and the senses. But there is a good deal of knowledge, sometimes very interesting and recondite, which has only an indirect reference to the Spirit. This includes scientific, artistic and even occult knowledge. This is phenomenal knowledge or *aparā vidyā*.

In an important sense, there are no spiritual and profane subjects but there could be a spiritual and profane approach or knowledge. There is a spiritual knowledge of things considered ordinary but there is also a phenomenal or mental knowledge of things considered spiritual. The last one is the pasture-grounds of theologians and schoolmen.

Sometimes a dichotomy is established between the two approaches, between Science and Spirit. In Medieval times, in Europe, the Church tried to dictate to Sciences in the name of the

Spirit; but it was not the Spirit but the ecclesiastics who took over. A narrow spirituality with a limited view both of reason as well as of the soul dominated the scene.

In India, there was no such opposition between the two. Both had their own validity and both were good in their own spheres, time and place. Spiritual knowledge was for those in whom the spiritual urge had come to the fore, who were now seeking a different dimension in life, who were asking questions about life and death, truth, being and immortality. It is interesting to see the change that comes in life once the soul's face turns. With this turning, two things happen. Firstly, areas of experience hitherto neglected occupy the forefront position. Faith, charity, adoration, self-discipline, worship, self-giving, brotherliness acquire a new meaning and urgency. The questions of Gods, Self, *brahma, anātma, rita*, dharma become important. Secondly, even the old, familiar things acquire a new face. The Sun, the Sky, the Earth, the Fire, the Directions, mountains, rivers and such objects of every-day experience — they now appear in a different guise and convey a different experience. They lose their alienness. They becomes figures and images of the Spirit. We see that our senses are really divinities, that the Purusha that is within the Eye is the same as the Purusha in the Sun, that at heart we are all one.

We also believe that this kind of experience holds a deeper truth of things and of ourselves than does a most objective and empirical investigation of them by a rigorous, analytic intellect. The latter has its own importance but it does not give us that Insight or Self-knowledge or *prajñā* which an awakened soul seeks.

The soul has several modes of awareness depending on its state of purity. First it knows itself through its objects; it is reflected in them. This too is a kind of Self-awareness though rather of a rudimentary kind and it is modified by the medium in which it is reflected. But when through Yoga, forms dissolve, the soul experiences itself as a mind. But this mind too is soaked with the life of the non-self or *anātma* and the experience does not rise to that Self-knowledge which the soul seeks in its selflessness, transcendence, aloneness and nakedness. The last knowledge has to be won through *sādhanā*.

Spiritual *sādhanā* is expressed in a 3-terms formula: *śīla*, *samādhi, prajñā*. The words are borrowed from Buddhist Yoga but they apply in one form or another to most Indian systems of Yoga. *Śīla* is moral life and it is the first indispensable foundation. It also includes vows of a particular way of life or discipline one has voluntarily chosen for oneself. On this foundation is built another life of a greater inner discipline, mind-concentration and mind-purity. This in its turn leads to *prajñā*, the knowledge that brings and accompanies liberation.

As the path of *samādhi* lies through *yama* and *niyama*, the path of *prajñā* lies through *samādhi*. Unless one dives deep into one's psyche, one cannot grow into *prajñā*. *Samādhi* gives knowledge of things as they are, *yathārtha jñāna*; This opens up the doors of higher knowledge, *prajñā*. *Prajñā* destroys all impurities, particularly *avidyā* which is the source of all impurities. This brings *moksha*, liberation.

So in this way of presentation, *prajñā* is the mature fruit of a spiritual life and in its fulness it comes only at the end of spiritual *sādhanā*. Its aim is not merely ethical improvement or spiritual edification; it is to go beyond the life of self-hood, a self-hood which is fed by a deep-seated *moha* and *avidyā*, delusion and nescience. It is not enough to conquer passions; it is necessary to develop a greater power of seeing, to cut at the root of nescience. Passions as we know them are only the first veil but there are other more luminous veils too which are difficult to conquer except through *prajñā* which is inborn knowledge of the soul about itself and about the world. Philo said: The rout and destruction of the passions, while good, is not the ultimate good; the discovery of Wisdom is the surpassing good. Earlier Plato had preached that Wisdom is the virtue which effects the conversion of the soul from darkness to light and enables her to behold true being.

While we must make a distinction between *śīla* and *prajñā* for the sake of analysis, we must also remember that they are intimately related. While *śīla* leads to *prajñā, prajñā* perfects *śīla*;

while *prajñā* is the natural flowering of *śīla* and *samādhi*, *śīla* reveals its self-basis in *samādhi* and *prajñā*. Without *prajñā*, *śīla* is blind; without *śīla*, *prajñā* is lame. In fact, it is not possible to achieve any considerable proficiency in the one without the help of the other.

Prajñā makes explicit only that which is already contained in *śīla*. If *śīla* consists in disinterested works and in the spirit of unity without merely following our bodily appetites and passions, it is because, as *prajñā* makes explicit, the Spirit is free and in some way we are one and in a deep sense we are more than our body. When *prajñā* arises, one is no longer good by 'habit' but by 'knowledge'.

In becoming explicit what was merely implicit, so much new happens and so much new is added that it truly bears a name. *Śīla* becomes *prajñā*. Action becomes knowledge. In *prajñā*, a new divinity is revealed, a new 'togetherness' is revealed. Life becomes deep, wondrous, blessed. Personality is healed and made whole. The seed-*kleśa* of *avidyā* or nescience which is the source of all other *kleśas* is destroyed. Moral life becomes natural and spontaneous. There is no longer any fear of relapse into old ways. The fear of death is conquered. A new infinity is added. A new knowledge or wisdom is born.

This wisdom or knowledge is an essential attribute of the soul but as the Gita says, it is "enveloped by desire which is insatiable like fire", enveloped as a "flame is enveloped by smoke or a mirror by dust". Because of lust and hate, both born of *rajas*, it suffers degeneration in its expression in ordinary life. In fact, according to Yogic thought, knowledge is one but its character is modified according to the plane on which it is reflected. When reflected on the *kāma-bhūmi*, knowledge is scattered, *vibhrānta*; it merely gives knowledge of diversity; the knowledge is also painful; it is also surface-knowledge. It may also give a knowledge of a sort of ethics, of ideals, of Gods; but since this knowledge is mixed up with passions of a lower life, it is generally their instrument, their rationalization.

But when the same knowledge is reflected in *dhyāna-bhūmi*,

the knowledge is joyful, trustful, restful; the knowledge also penetrates the surface of things and knows their luminous source in *tanmātrās*. When knowledge is reflected in *arūpa-bhūmi*, the knowledge is one-pointed and disinterested; in this knowledge all forms dissolve and it is the knowledge of an infinite mind and intelligence. But according to Sāmkhya, this mind or this intelligence is still *jaḍa*; its light is borrowed; it is merely a shadow of the Purusha beyond which alone is truly conscious. The Buddhists say the same thing using another expression. To them this mind or intelligence is still *anātma* though it is source of extraordinary knowledge and powers. Beyond lies the *nirodha-bhūmi* where the Seer is seated in its own self-status (*svarūpa-avasthā*), where there are no more reflections and shadows and where knowledge shines in its own right.

That knowledge has different levels and is of different kinds is maintained in one form or another by all Yogic thought. *Buddhi* or intellect according to the Gita is of three kinds: *sāttvika, rājasika* and *tāmasika. Sāttvika* intellect can discriminate rightly; it knows true activity and true abstinence; it knows what is to be done and what is to be avoided; it knows what binds and what liberates; *rājasika* intellect does not know *dharma* and *adharma*, the right and the wrong as they are; but *tāmasika* or deluded intellect insists that the wrong is right and thinks all things in a perverted way. At another place, but maintaining the same distinction, the Gita brings out other characteristics of the three-fold knowledge. *Sāttvika* knowledge sees one Being in all beings, the inseparate in the separated; *rājasika* knowledge sees diverse things as separate; but *tāmasika* knowledge clings to each part as if it were the whole.

The three *guṇas* exist together on all levels though in different combinations. *Tamas* predominates in ordinary knowledge of *kāma-bhūmi* where cults of passion, malice, hedonism, violence, class war, economic determinism, and the divine rights of priests, plutocrats or the proletariat are preached as gospels and pass for absolute truths of history; but it is also retained even on *dhyāna-bhūmi* which is relatively *sāttvika* in character as a whole. It accompanies here luminous forms. A particular luminous form, a particular spiritual truth is regarded as the whole truth. A doctrine, a faith, an *ishta,* a *guru,* a prophet, a particular theology — each claims to be absolute.

Knowledge also differs in its contents and mode at different *bhūmis.* On secular level, knowledge is object-directed and the knower is known only as a reflection of that knowledge. On the spiritual level, the knower itself is the object of knowledge and the world is known in the reflection of the Spirit, just as if in a mirror. The mode of knowing also becomes more direct as knowledge becomes more spiritualised. The soul first knows itself in its good and luminous works; then it knows itself in the purity and clarity of its mind *(adhyātma-prasāda)*; then in the universality of the *mahat* or *chitta* or *buddhi*; and lastly in its selflessness, aloneness, and nakedness.

All are knowledge but the last one is *prajñā.* In the technical language of Yoga, *prajñā* is that knowledge which pertains to *nirodha-* or *nirvāṇa-bhūmi.* It is transcendental knowledge.

Prajñā is transcendental knowledge but the word 'transcendent' should not suggest some mystifying knowledge, some highly intriguing, heaven-storming knowledge; it is unadorned, inornate, simplified knowledge. Nor is it knowledge of a far-away, dreamland; on the other hand, it is intimate knowledge of the Self by the Self, knowledge of man's secret being, knowledge of the meaning and significance of life, knowledge of its origin and destiny. It is knowledge of God in man.

It is non-sensuous and non-logical knowledge. It is knowledge about something which is more subtle than the subtlest, which transcends the limitations of time and space and which therefore cannot be expressed in the language which conforms to ordinary ways of thinking. The Spirit exists in many modes and it has many a status. It is single, dual, multiple. Therefore, it is described in contradictory ways: It is greater than the great and smaller than the small; it is inside as well as outside; it is far off and yet nearer than our hands and feet; it is aloof from all and yet it is source of their very existence; it is itself stationary and yet everything moves in it; it is stable amongst the unstable; it is the seer in everything; we see by its light though it itself remains unseen; one could not reach its end even though one flew with the speed of mind; yet it could be contained in a single act of love, of compassion, and disinterested action.

In a rough and ready sort of way, one could say that *prajñā* has two facets. One relates to the knowledge of the Spirit in its aloofness, the transcendental knowledge of the transcendent; the other relates to the knowledge of the Spirit in relation to the world, the transcendental knowledge of the phenomenal, the knowledge of the world in relation to the Spirit.

There is a knowledge of the Spirit like the above which can only be described in riddles but spiritual knowledge has other facets and other ways of describing it which involve no puns, no puzzles but like all spiritual knowledge only a soul-insight. 'A man reaps what he sows', is one of such deep soul-insights. The Gita gives us many such truths, everyone a whole universe in itself. The Gita tells us that a man is what his *śraddhā* is, or what his deep thoughts and desires are; that on the spiritual path, there is neither transgression nor wasted effort; that men and Gods live in mutual interchange; that those who eat of the remains of *yajña* are freed from all sins; that those who eat for themselves verily eat sin; that the unreal has no true existence and the Real never ceases to be; that death is a renewal and a man takes on new bodies as he takes on new clothes. The examples could be multiplied. Each of these truths could be meditated upon and lead to soul's liberation.

The Ultimate Reality is beyond all words, beyond all thoughts, it cannot be described. In a sense, it is true of all knowledge. Communication is possible only of shared experiences. Colour cannot be described to a person who is born blind. Besides this incapacity, one is also speechless out of reverence, out of awe; one does not speak out of deference to the rules of the place. Silence is the rule here and any speech is so incongruent, so out of the place.

Those who know do not speak; those who speak do not know. The Ultimate Reality cannot be described, yet it has inspired throughout the ages lofty eloquence. Sages have used different images and used different modes and methods to point to this

Reality though however inadequately. In the Upanishads, Yājñavalkya and other sages used the negative mode of expressing it: *neti, neti,* Not this, Not this.

The spirit of the method is very well brought out in *Masnavi* by Rumi in a story form. A minstrel was singing before a Turkish chief. The refrain of the song was: I know not, I know not. "Whether you are moon or idol, I know not. What thing you desire of me, I know not. What service I shall bring you, I know not. Whether to keep silence or express Thee in words, I know not," thus went on the mystic song. This got on the nerves of the Turkish chief and he shouted at the minstrel. "If I were to ask you, rascal, 'Where do you come from', you will probably answer, 'Not from Balkh, not from Herat, not from Baghdad, not from Mosul, not from Shiraz.' Why can't you just say from where you came and be done with it. Similarly, if I were to ask you, 'What did you have for your breakfast', you will reply, 'Not wine, not kabab, not wurst, not lentils.' Why cannot you tell me what you did eat and no more." The minstrel answered, "Because my theme is very abstruse. Affirmation eludes you until you negate. I speak in negative, that you might catch a whiff of affirmation."

Besides the knowledge of the Self by the Self, there is also the Spirit's knowledge of the world as we have said above. This too is two-fold. The Spirit has two movements; one excludes and the other includes everything. In the *prajñā* relating to exclusion, life as lived is evanescent, painful, vain, alien. Man is merely a *nāma-rūpa,* a mind-body formation. He is a *skandha,* a concatenation, a meeting-point of various material and mental principles. He is *rūpa, vedanā, samjñā, samskāra, vijñāna.*

When this *prajñā* is developed, the desire-world falls completely from the soul. Sāmkhya and Buddhism have laid great stress on this aspect of *prajñā* and no worthwhile spiritual discipline can avoid it altogether. *Viśuddhi-mārga* admits that *prajñā* is of many kinds but elucidation of them all "will not serve the desired purpose and will also lead to unnecessary future confusion". Therefore, it discusses only that *prajñā* which "is related to the desired purpose", namely, the one which puts an end to the painfulness of existence and brings about *nirvāṇa*. With that purpose in view, it describes *prajñā* as "*vipaśynā*-knowledge of a purified mind". *Vipaśyanā*-knowledge is that view of the world which sees all things in their evanescence (*anitya*), in their painfulness (*duḥkha*), and in their phenomenality and otherness (*anātma*).

This knowledge can arise only in a purified mind and in its turn it is also a greatly purifying knowledge. *Dhammpada* says: When a man sees through *prajñā*, then all *saṁskāras* appear as transitory; then a man is freed from all *kleśas*. This is the Way (*mārga*), the Way of Purity (*viśuddhi-mārga*).

The world this *prajñā* gives may be dream-like and may create an eerie feeling but it has its own truth. At the level of *kāma-bhūmi*, the Spirit is a shadow cast by the world; at the level of the Spirit, it is the other way round. For people who enter the life of the Spirit, the world cannot have the same, old sense of reality, self-sufficiency and autonomy and being 'out there'. The new dream-like world has also its own functions in a Yoga of withdrawal — and withdrawal in some measure and sense is necessary for all Yogas. When one finds the world impermanent, vain, empty, without substance and reality, one is freed from the shackles of *saṁsāra*. And perhaps some find the emptiness of *saṁsāra* imaging the emptiness of *nirvāṇa*, a transcendental Emptiness upholding the transcendental emptiness of *saṁsāra*.

But the Spirit has also an inclusive movement which embraces the world. In this movement, the world is transfigured. One realises that the above-mentioned negation was for the sake of a higher affirmation, the emptying for a higher fulfilment. When the old desire-forms and the Ego-forms die, when the world reflected through those forms is no more, a new life, a new sensibility, a new world arises. New powers, new *indriyas* are born; devotion, worship and knowledge are born. The world is retrieved, rehabilitated, relinked with its source. One finds that the world is a habitation of the Divine and that at heart everything is an image of God, is God. He becomes a *yajatra*, a worshipper. Through his eyes, he sees only the auspicious, through his ears he hears only the auspicious. His life becomes a self-offering. He knows that life is not for pleasure and aggrandisement; on the other hand, it is a pledge and it has to be redeemed by a holy living.

So Spiritual knowledge does not necessarily mean turning away from the world; it is only turning away from its lower manifestations. On the other hand, when this knowledge arises, the world is transformed so much so that every relation and form becomes an image of God; every act becomes worship and homage.

By *prajñā* some people also mean, particularly the Jains, a state of all-knowingness, knowledge of all things past and present, obvious and hidden. That kind of knowledge is not ruled out but more strictly *prajñā* means 'Self-knowledge' and 'essential' knowledge of the world; which means there is a lot of knowledge which is not worth its name. Knowledge about all kinds of odds and ends is not spiritual knowledge. Knowing the world in its essence means knowing that we cannot store it or own it, that it is transient and illusory and unconscious; but 'essential' knowledge of the world also means, by an opposite movement, knowing that the world is the habitation and manifestation of God.

Prajñā is also not merely knowledge of the Spirit in its absolute or in its relational aspects, or knowledge of certain spiritual truths; it is also that knowledge which assigns a place to these truths in life. It is knowledge of *dharma;* it is wisdom of life. It is knowledge of limits and proportions. It is knowledge of how even a *dharma* becomes *adharma* through excess. For example, to eat to live is *dharma* but to live to eat is *adharma.* Even deep spiritual truths like compassion and courage can become evil through excesses. Freedom is a spiritual value but freedom without self-discipline is a misnomer. *Prajñā* is knowledge of *dharmas* in their various ramifications.

Prajñā is knowledge of 'truth' in each thing, its *dharma*, its essence and what upholds it. It is also the knowledge of these *dharmas* in their mutual relations. The concept of *dharma* is metaphysical as well as ethical. According to Buddhist Yoga, that which has the characteristic of knowing the self-nature of *dharma* is *prajñā*; its essential function is to destroy *moha* which veils the truth of a *dharma*.

The above discussion raises some important questions: for example, why is *prajñā* called knowledge when it is so different from ordinary knowledge? Is there a principle of continuity between them? Do they have some common quality? Does the ordinary faculty of *buddhi* image *prajñā* in some way? Also *prajñā* does not seem to hold the same premier position in several other spiritual cultures as it does here. In fact, more often than not they speak about knowledge and *buddhi* disparagingly. What accounts for this difference in approach?

When a spiritual truth is described as knowledge, the idea is to separate it from visions and images and even from the warmth and sweetness of emotions with which it is confused. Any intellect worth its name which has come out of the mire of desire has certain qualities which distinguishes it from other faculties and even exalts it above them: it has detachment, rigour, discipline, certitude, inexorability and universality which are important images of the Spirit. *Buddhi* deals not with moving images but with the universal and the essential in those images. This is one reason why the Ultimate Reality is considered as *prajñātmaka* or of the 'form of knowledge' or *Gnosis* in some spiritualities.

In every experience, there is immediate sense-knowledge and there is larger knowledge not contained in the immediate data of the senses. This knowledge is contributed by a deeper faculty of the mind called Reason or *buddhi* or Intellect or Thought. Thought illumines more than it sees or hears. This is a quality which thought shares with the knowledge of the Spirit which is even more direct and more essential. This is another reason why ultimate knowledge is likened to thought.

In Sāmkhya, thought has no independent power of self-illumination. In itself, it is *jaḍa,* inert, *anātma.* The power of self-illumination is borrowed from the Purusha which is the soul of thought and *buddhi* — that which one thinks not with thought but with which thought is thought. Though unconscious, *buddhi* is still nearest to the knowledge of the Purusha. At its purest, it has the power to reflect the Purusha as faithfully as possible in all its universality and transcendence. For this reason too, the two are spoken interchangeably.

This is the meaning of *buddhi* in Sāṁkhya — *chitta* in its state of utmost clarity and purity. But in the Upanishads, the word has also another meaning. Here, the purified mind is living, not dead; spirit, not matter. This mind works through various faculties equally pulsating with life, one of them being *buddhi* or *vijñāna*. *Vijñāna* brings out the universal in any spiritual knowledge.

According to this thought Divinity is one but it is capable of being experienced differently. The Upanishads speak of *annamaya purusha, prāṇamaya purusha, manomaya purusha, vijñānamaya purusha, ānandamaya purusha*. It is not that there are different Purushas to experience but the same Purusha is experienced differently at different levels. There is the experience of Divinity at the level of purified *manas*, but the same is also experienced at the level of *buddhi*. The two experiences have two different ethos. In the first, the experience is more particularised; in the second it puts on a more universal aspect. The distinction is important; its understanding will throw light on two different forms of spiritual experiences that we so often meet in different scriptures.

Manas particularizes; *buddhi* generalises. In the movement from *manas* to *buddhi*, spirituality rises from a spiritual experience to a spiritual truth. At the level of *manas*, the experience of Divinity is personalized and particularised; and so also the experiencer and the experience. God is a Father or a Master and the experiencer is a Son or a Slave and the relationship is filial or feudal. But the same experience at the level of *buddhi* has a different ethos.

For example, to feel a filial love for God, to be filled with his Sonship is spiritual experience. It is at the level of the personal and the particular. But to know that all are Sons in the same Fatherhood is spiritual truth. It takes place at the level of *buddhi* or *vijñāna*. It has a more universal visage.

Similarly, there could be a super-normal message at the level of *manas* — the purity of the message depending on the purity of the medium. But here the experience is personalized — a God or Angel communicating to a chosen prophet; the communication also being final if also not the first. But when this communication takes place on the level of *vijnāna*, it is not considered as a privilege of a particular person. Here seership is possible for all who attain to a certain level of purity; therefore, here there are no 'only' seers or saviours or the last prophets; here also it is not a God or Angel speaking through his chosen medium; rather it is knowledge and communication of the Self by the Self. Plato calls it the "communion of the soul with the unchanging".

Experience at the *manas*-level says: I am God or the Son of God or the Prophet of God; experience at the level of *vijñāna* says: *ātman* is *brahma*; thou art That; everyone is potentially God; that what is in you is also in the yonder Sun. *Manas*-experience says: I am the door. *Vijñāna* experience says: there are more doors than one imagines; that everyone is his own gate, his own light, his own salvation; that God resides in each indivisibly and that salvation already exists within each.

In Indian spirituality, *buddhi* or *vijñāna* is a definite and separate category. It exists just above the mental. True, this plane is not well developed in the human race as yet and people generally experience spiritual truths through the medium of a purified *manas*, which gives them truths of faith, joy, jubilation, truths of luminous forms, of a personalized God or Gods. These are great truths. But on the level of *vijñāna*, these truths are experienced differently. Here one rises from the vision of beautiful things to a vision of Beauty. Here one sees things under the category of universality, sees them *sub specie aeternitatis*.

One need not grade the two experiences but one should try to understand the difference between them. At the level of purified *manas,* there is faith, joy, sonship, prophethood, inspired utterances, luminous visions, chosen destinies, unique roles. It is like a young man in love who believes that he is the first and the last lover, that his beloved is the most beautiful in the world, that this love has not happened before and will not happen afterwards, that his ardour is unique and absolute. This feeling has a quality of innocence and health and there is a lot of colour and warmth in it. But there is another kind of seeing in man which is called wisdom to which these feelings look rather exaggerated and even endearingly foolish.

One of the greatest modes in which the soul knows is through universality, an important quality of *buddhi*. The truths of the Upanishads and the Gita have this quality in abundance. In the Upanishads, it is the message and not the messenger which is important. The message is presented in universal terms. It is no respecter of persons or place or time. These are *vijñāna*-truths.

Here, as we should easily realize, *buddhi* or *vijñāna* refers to a mode of knowledge which is direct, which is deep and which is universal. But there is also a lower manifestation of *buddhi*, a *buddhi* in its impure state. In this state, it is hardly an instrument of higher seeing; on the other hand, it is an instrument of lower passions and prejudices. In this perverse form, *buddhi* is contentious, argumentative, polemical, wordy, nihilist, sceptical. Its universality is false. It is even parasitic. It devitalises the truths of the *manas*-word. It tries to cut the protean and many-sided truths of life to its own limited and lifeless concepts and measures. It is this *buddhi* which is suspect in many spiritual systems. The corruption of the best is the worst. A perverse *buddhi* is the greatest enemy of spiritual life.

This objection to *buddhi* is welcome, for here the urge is self-correction and self-transcendence. But there are less wholesome sources of objection too. There are cults of faith which deny *buddhi*. Much of their faith is *rāgātmaka;* it is also credulous, superstitious and ignorant. It wants to believe rather than find out. It is *tāmasika*; it is also authoritarian. It tries to impose arbitrary beliefs which go against higher reason and therefore have to be supported by a lower *śrac'dhā. Prajñā* and *śraddhā* are kins but reason and faith make awkward companions. There was a time when faith denied reason; now in turn reason is denying faith.

Sometimes 'cunning' intelligence is compared to 'meek' piety.

But piety has not always been meek and many times it had all the cunning of intelligence. Because a perceptive *buddhi* shows how cunning a particular piety is, that piety retaliates by denying *buddhi*.

Sometimes mystics too have spoken against *buddhi*. They have contrasted the self-abandonment and 'madness' of love with the 'prudent' and 'calculating' intellect which is always counting costs and benefits, which cannot stake its all, which cannot love and labour without thoughts of any return.

This too does no more than rebuke lower *buddhi* which claims competence to pass judgements on spiritual truths and to direct and guide life. Life is not calculation; it consists in deepening, in self-giving, in self-consecration. Through the language of love, the mystics have spoken of this truth of the Spirit. They have spoken not merely of the 'self-abandonment' and 'madness' of love but also of love's *saṁyama, tyāga* and *prajñā* or its self-discipline, renunciation and wisdom.

Through the language of love, they also oppose a formal mode of worship and preach spontaneity and free self-giving in it. The Sufis also used this language to soften a prophetic view of life which was hide-bound, narrow and fanatic, which was devoid of love as well as reason, which threatened and promised, which was oppressive, joyless and harsh in judgement. The prophetic view was opposed to all colour, poetry and music in the soul. It believed in a God that had merely to be obeyed and served.

Fools and madmen have their rights. Partly the Sufis played that role in order to convey certain deeper truths of life which they could not safely do otherwise in an atmosphere where the spiritual base was narrow, direct spiritual investigation was frowned upon, faith was overvalued, and dissent was anathema.

In the Christian world too, a similar problem arose. The pietistic atmosphere was quite anti-intellect though not less jingoistic. Intellect could not safely demand freedom for itself; so it demanded and got freedom to be able to serve the Church. In this role, the intellect got exercised and was not altogether atrophied. When the circumstances took a more favourable turn, it could easily drop its apologetic role and function more naturally in keeping with its *dharma* which is to accept the discipline of facts, to analyse and evaluate justly, to deduce rationally and generalise judiciously.

Words have different meanings: one outer, lower and narrower; the other relatively inner, higher and broader. In their outer meanings, there is no conciliation; in their inner use no dichotomy. *Śraddhā* and *buddhi* in their deeper meanings are in happy accord and mutually fulfilling; in their lower meanings, they know no harmony.

Faith in its higher sense does not mean belief in arbitrary propositions but it is faith in the larger and deeper life of the soul; ingrained feeling of the deeper truths of life. It cannot be taught and propagated artificially from outside and one cannot be conditioned into it; it is self-born as in Nachiketa. It could be quickened by a pregnant Word, or by an infusion from above or by contact with a Teacher.

Similarly, in its higher sense, *buddhi* is not cerebration or cogitation or mentation or speculation or laborious reasoning; it is that purified state of mind in which it is capable of reflecting things as they are. It is capacity for seeing things in their universal and transcendental aspects. It is born of detachment. It comes when the world begins to fall from our eyes. So long as we make too much of the world and even of the next, this kind of seeing is not possible. It is born only in ungrudging, generous and awakened hearts, in minds that are broad and wide and deep and tranquil. It comes from seeing things not enthusiastically, not even ecstatically but dispassionately, discriminatingly and calmly. It consists in seeing things even dialectically, seeing in a given form its past as well as its future and even its opposite forms, seeing life in death and death in life against the background of immortality.

The lower *buddhi* opposes not only the truths of *śraddhā* and higher love but also the truths of the higher *buddhi*. Similarly, when one believes in propositions that are the products of a wordy mind, it involves double infringement. It violates higher reason as well as deeper *śraddhā*. The need is to develop a higher consciousness, in which both are purified and both have their due place and both become mutually enriching. The lower mind is incapable of understanding the deeper truths of the Spirit. It is like a salt-doll trying to fathom the sea. Yoga says that in order to fathom the ocean, one must in some sense become the ocean. No eye has seen the sun except by becoming sun-like.

Buddhi is the name of this sun-like state of mind. According to the Upanishads, its seat is 'heart'. In this state, the mind is massed consciousness, *prajñāna-ghana*. The Ultimate Reality is of the form of knowledge, *buddhi-svarūpa* and it is *buddhi-grāhya*, known by Intellect which is mind at its purest and most universal.

Section 3

Bhakti-Yoga

Chapter 3

Bhakti

Yoga has one special characteristic which distinguishes it from many other spiritual practices — it is *sukha-sādhanā*; it is founded on joy-cultivation. There are practices which are based on penance, forced denials and even self-laceration and self-torture but the spirit of Yoga is different. Its initial aim is to give the *sādhaka* the vision of a luminous form. When that happens, the mind is rested and pacified. It can make the rest of the journey in trust and confidence. The senses and the mind are fulfilled and they no longer revolt. One builds one's spiritual edifice in co-operation with one's senses and mind.

For achieving this end, Yoga makes use of several means. Yoga has found by experience that different men and women have different temperaments. Some are more reflective; others more ecstatic; some more devotional; some think more deeply; some act more purposefully; some feel more profoundly. The secret of success lies in making use of the dominant trait in man. Yoga teaches that a man should work in harmony with his deeper nature and not at variance with it.

Love is a great emotion and is universally found. When it is purified and directed towards holier things, it fills the *prāṇas* with a new thrill and throb. And when one has felt the touch of the Divine, one can never be the same again.

Temperament not merely defines the path of a *sādhaka* but probably it also determines to a great extent the way in which he conceives the highest reality. The Gita speaks of several paths and defines their goals in terms which are at least apparently very different. There is the Sāṁkhya Yoga, the Yoga of Knowledge which worships the Unmanifest. Here there is no Form to which the mind holds on to. And if a Form does arise, even a luminous Form, it is soon negated. It is a great path but a difficult one and by its nature cannot be a popular one. But there is also another path, the Path of Devotion which worships the Divine in His Form or one of His Forms and approaches Him with a loving heart. Arjuna asks Lord Krishna: Which Yoga is better, the one that worships the Unmanifest (*avyakta*) or the one which worships Thee in Thy human and divine form with devotion? Krishna replies that both are good but the difficulties of the first one are greater.

But though it is useful to make a distinction between the two Yogas, the two are not as watertight as some men suppose them to be. There is a lot in common between the two. Except in certain overtones, the ancient Bhakti-Yoga is very close to the Yoga of Knowledge. There is a time when *bhakti* is converted into knowledge of the heart and knowledge of the Supreme generates *bhakti* in the heart. And as the Bhakti Movement of the medieval times shows amply it is possible to love the *nirguṇa* as profoundly and deeply as the *saguṇa*.

Bhakti is founded on the feeling of love, reverence, adoration and trust. Spiritual love must be distinguished from the emotion of love which is merely its outer expression. It is a silent homage and worship offered by the heart to the indwelling truth of the heart, a truth which one may not be able to spell out but to which one is secretly drawn.

There is a man who denies, who disbelieves; but there is another who says yes to the truth of existence, who believes in the life of the Spirit, who has a secret faith in the moral order. This spirit of Yea which is opposed to the nihilistic spirit is called '*āstika buddhi*'. *Bhakti* is founded on *āstika buddhi*.

Another name for *āstika buddhi* is *śraddhā*, inadequately translated as faith. It is self-born. It is incipient knowledge of great things ahead. At the level of *śraddhā*, the knowledge is more of the nature of a feeling; but with spiritual development, this feeling deepens into seeing. One now knows what one had only deeply felt. The knowledge latent in *śraddhā* becomes manifest in *prajñā*.

The outer mind tells us that there is no other world than that of matter and mind and sensible qualities and logic. The evidence of the senses oppose the knowledge felt by *śraddhā* to be true. There are constant references to this opposition of reason and faith in spiritual literature. We are told to eschew reason and imbibe faith. In some spiritualities, reason is regarded as the voice of 'Satan'.

But we need not accept this view of reason. Reason too has its place. Disbelief when it is not compulsive works for intellectual integrity. It is a spur to a truer and more definitive knowledge. It also indicates that the soul will not rest in a mere feeling, in a mere presentiment. And like the excesses of reason, there are also excesses and deformities of faith. In the absence of the restraints of reason, these excesses of faith play havoc.

Indian Yoga recognises no such dichotomy. *Sāttvika* love deepens into *buddhi* and *sāttvika buddhi* generates love. There is no contradiction between them except at the lower levels when they are unregenerate. Love merely denies *saṁśaya*, the serpent advice of a nihilist mind which denies all higher truth. And a modest intellect has no difficulty in admitting that love has its insight, its secret wisdom, its own intuition, an instinct for things which are deeply our kin.

Some of the deepest truths of the Spirit can only be expressed in the language of love though this love should be distinguished from the ordinary feeling which goes under that name. There is so much beauty and holiness in the world that one is moved to tears with gratitude for them. These tears are different from the tears that we ordinarily know, the tears of bitterness, resentment, of thwarted ego. These are purifying tears; tears at the sight of beauty and holiness of the Beloved in the heart and tears at one's own unworthiness; tears of separation and tears of union; tears that melt the heart and the tears that flood the Being; tears that express the cry of the heart for heavenly things and its anguish and helplessness; tears of contrition and tears of forgiveness; tears at the sight of what we potentially are and what we have become. There are tears of the stabs and wounds of love. Love heals but it wounds first.

Love is a great spiritual force but in actual life it is mixed up with a good deal of lust and ego. In that form, it serves no spiritual purpose and in fact works for bondage rather than for liberation. It does not improve in quality even if this love is termed theological and turns to God rather than to fellow-men. The love is *rāgātmaka* and as a result also *dveshātmaka*. It loves in order to hate. It loves its deity and in order to prove that love, it hates the deities of others. Behind this love and hate is self-love, and the dark shadow of *avidyā*.

Most of the love that we find in the world belongs to this category. It loves in order to hate, affirms in order to deny. It is either *tāmasika* or *rājasika* and more often a combination of the two. *Tāmasika* love devours its object while *rājasika* love is restless and discontented.

Love has to be purified from all these qualities, from its selfishness, its foam, froth and effervescence. Only when love become *sāttvika*, it can become spiritually rewarding and can be used for higher spiritual purposes. In that form, it becomes unifying rather than divisive, liberating rather than narrowing. Now it turns from carnality to divinity. It goes beyond the confines of earthly love.

In this form, it enters into a love-play with the Lover in the heart. It is eager and shy at the same time; it waits expectantly, timidly; it passes through various stages of *māna* and *abhimāna*, of hopes balanced by fears, of despair and exaltation. These moods are purifying and they bring into the open all that lies within. All these movements, all these hopes and disappointments become *sāttvika*, become *aklishṭa*, become liberating. They no longer belong to the usual ebb and flow of the mind, to its dualities and ambivalences. They become part of a transcendental love-play. These become part of one love — one great love which burns up all lesser loves. This loves is one-pointed; it is undeviating; it is indifferent to all that does not pertain to the beloved. It finds fulfilment in her alone; it becomes an ever-burning flame which consumes all impurities and turns everything into gold.

Love, they say, is a means of *sādhanā*. In a way this is true but in a deeper sense love comes at the end of the *sādhanā* when the *sādhaka* has shed all *rāga* and *dvesha*. This idea is implied in the Gita. There love does not lead to *bhakti* but one becomes a *bhakta* when one has gone beyond the three *guṇas*, *guṇātita*, when one is established in equality, *samatva*. When one has shed his *rāga* and *dvesha* and *aham*, the world for him becomes beautiful and benign. The heart becomes peaceful, joyful, grateful, faithful and trustful. All the sense of alienation ceases; the mind becomes full of acceptance and it sees the face of the Divine in everything.

Though the emotion of love plays a great role, the ancient Bhakti-Yoga as we find it in the Gita is not wholly based on it. It includes *buddhi* and will and works too. At the base of all Hindu Yogic *sādhanā* including *bhakti*, there are two ruling sentiments: *ātma-bhāva* and *brahma-bhāva*, Self-possession and World-possession. These two never leave Indian spirituality whatever be the form of *sādhanā* and they have influenced all subsequent Bhakti Movement even when the emotion of love was receiving an increasingly greater emphasis on its hand. Kabir and Nanak were great *bhaktas* but their *bhakti* breathes the classical spirit. It is full of renunciation, *ātma-bhāva* and wisdom.

Bhakti is depicted in two different images: first in the image of rapture, intoxication, drunkenness, ecstasy and self-forgetfulness. But the *bhakti* of the Gita completely avoids this language. On the other hand, the devotee of the Gita bears no ill-will towards any being (*adveshṭā sarvabhūtānām*); he is friendly and compassionate (*maitrah, karuṇah*); he is without attachment (*nirmama*), without egoism (*nirahaṁkārah*), equanimous in pain and pleasure (*samaduhkhasukhah*), forgiving (*kshamī*); he is content, harmonious, self-controlled, resolute (*saṁtushṭah, yogī, yatātmā, dridha-niśchayah*) and one who has surrendered his mind and heart unto God (*mayyārpitamanobuddhih*).

Closely connected with the above are other differences. One type of Bhakti-Yoga speaks of the tears, trials and tribulations of the soul, its pangs of separation, the hopes and despairs of love;

the other type speaks of the state when hunger and thirst are assuaged, the heart is pacified, the search is over and one finds the face of God in everything. The language of the first is eager, tearful, ecstatic; of the second state tranquil and self-possessed. The two belong to two different temperaments but they also represent two states in a developing spiritual life. First the eyes burn with the desire to see God, the ears to hear Him, the body to embrace Him, the heart aches for His company. Then He appears assuaging all the thirst and hunger bringing the fulfilment of union. Love goes beyond ecstasy; it passes into *ātma*-surrender.

Whatever be their differences, we find the two *bhaktis* existing together at any particular period and even in the same individual. If the medieval times for which we have fuller records represent a continuing historical truth, then the two *bhaktis* must have existed side by side in earlier periods also. When we first meet ecstatic *bhakti* in Alvar saints and other saints of the medieval period, we find that it is already full-blown. Therefore, it must be having a hoary ancestry, existing side by side with the more self-possessive *bhakti*, the kind that we find in the Gita.

We find these differences within the Bhakti Movement because contrary to appearances, love is not a simple emotion. It is emotional as well as intellectual. It even enters the will. There are people who feel so much in order to do so little; on the other hand, there are people whose devotion is more effective, who serve without much emotional froth.

Even within the broader quality of love as emotion, its quality and direction differ. One love is more parental; another more fraternal; and yet another more conjugal. In the path of devotion, all these loves have been taken up, purified, idealized and transformed. One is God's servant (in missionary and proselytizing religions, the servant turns into a sergeant, a soldier and a salesman), his son, even his parent, his lover. One conceives of Him and loves Him as a master, or father or mother or child or friend, or lover. As a result of this *sādhanā*, different human relationships themselves are raised up and uplifted.

In its (*bhakti*'s) simplest form, God has been conceived and loved as a parent. As a father, God could be stern and commanding but he has really the heart of a mother. The mother is tender and forgiving. She feeds you, looks after you and anticipates all your demands. Sometimes her touch is rough but it is well meant. Sometimes she denies you things but it is to save you from harm. It is like a child wanting to play with fire while the mother stoutly disallows it.

Though you love God as mother but the mother is not dowdy. She is supremely beautiful. Her comeliness, youth and power are beyond compare. Yet her beauty is of a kind that does not excite lustful thoughts. It is a holy beauty. She inspires worship. Her form is full of kindness, benignness and affection. When one loves God as mother, he begins to look upon all women as mother. Lust is conquered.

But spiritual life is not all syrup and lollipop. It also consists in accepting the ugly and the hideous gracefully and gratefully and seeing the hand of God behind them. The Mother destroys as well as creates. The devotee learns to love this face of the Mother too. In this aspect, She is the great Kali who strikes terror in the heart of those who live in the illusion of Names and Forms; but to those who have gone beyond this illusion, she is supremely good and loveable. In India, saints like Ramaprasad and Ramakrishna have worshipped God as Mother and cherished this face of the Mother too and they reached the supreme goal of spiritual endeavour. Mother is *prasannarūpā* (of joyful mien) and *sundarī* (beautiful) but she is also *vidāruṇa* (terrible) and *krāntalokatraya* (Terror of the Three Worlds).

In the mystic tradition, God is also widely conceived as a Beloved. He is an embodiment of all charm and attraction. He incites love in you; he calls unto you. His image fills your ears. Everything reminds you of him but he himself is hid somewhere else. You see him even in your own reflection but he adroitly escapes your grasp. He entices you but he himself remains elusive. He appears, disappears, reappears. He plays hide and seek, fast and loose.

Vaishnavas of India have celebrated this divine love through the image of Radha and her companions for Krishna. Krishna is God; Radha or Gopis are individual souls. Krishna attracts. He makes Gopis do all kinds of indiscretions; he makes them leave their homes, their kith and kin; makes them face all sorts of gossips and scandals; makes them face scoldings of their parents and husbands; makes them wander all over. They look for him all around while he is hid in the corner of their heart.

Vaishnava poetry portrays the whole gamut of divine love, portrays all the sentiments that accompany love. It portrays the protestations and endearments of love, the vows taken and the promises broken, the quarrels and perjuries of love, the earnestness of the lover and the light-heartedness of the beloved. Krishna is a coquet, a trifler. He incites passion which he does not fulfil. Radha keeps the trust but Krishna fails to return. It leads to wounded pride, to solemn avowals, to cajoling and coaxing. Krishna is suave and smooth; Radha, the soul is trusting. Radha is faithful but fidelity is not Krishna's strong point. He is the inconstant one in love.

But he is full of beauty and charm. He is beautiful to behold, sweet to hear, and soothing to the touch. His presence fills Radha with thrill and rapture and his absence with pang and anguish. And yet Radha hugs to the very Form which teases and torments, which withdraws as soon as it is embraced.

Passing through these phases, love is purified. It acquires one flavour — surrender to Krishna, joy in the joy of Krishna. Through this journey, Radha imbibes Krishna, makes him her own, becomes his reflection, his image. The two become one and you can see the one in the other.

One realizes that Krishna's beauty is not all sweetness; it is a consuming fire. By one look, it destroys all evil, all impurity, all sin, all darkness. Separation was not imposed in a cruel spirit; it was a preparation for a deeper union. Nothing is more purifying than the fire of separation. It burns up all dross of desire and self-hood.

Krishna is also conceived and loved as a child. Vaishnava *sādhanā* sings of the antics and frolics of child-Krishna. In the Vaishnava *kīrtana* celebrating Yashoda's love for Krishna, one can see many mothers and grandmothers, remembering their own children at home, weeping tears of joy.

This *sādhanā* has a wide appeal for there is a parent in most of us and it takes little convincing to believe that our children are Gods. But the true test of this *sādhanā* comes when it purifies parental love and they begin to see Krishna in children even other than their own. In the present stage while parental love is a great asset and has a great biological and social value, it also works for narrowness, for pettiness, for social oppression, injustice and spiritual bondage. Parents' love for their children is generally ignorant and selfish. It is an extension of their ego. They treat their children as dolls, not as Gods. In most cases, it neither makes the parents nor the children better.

The children are victims of parents' unregenerate love. Instead of treating children as Gods, the parents play the God in relation to them. They want to make them and shape them in their own image. They want them to become heroes, great generals, scientists quite beyond their natural endowments. But when we love them as Krishna, we must regard them as coming from Krishna. They have their own truth of being, their own spark, their own God-given life. We must respect them for this life, for what God has planted in them and allow them to express the truth of this life.

When we love our children as Krishna, the first tendency of an unregenerate love is to exalt them above others. But this is not the practice of the Yogic love but of creaturely love, of ego, of pride and prejudice. To love a child is to become a child. It brings us closer to the influence of the Heavens. True love brings humility, abolishes distinctions. On the spiritual path, one has to be humbler than a child and grow in unity.

Ordinarily in their love of wives and children and other kith and kin, people forget Krishna. But the Vaishnavas have made even these love-objects into mediums and vehicles of God-remembrance. That which could be a hindrance becomes an aid. Ordinary, natural human relations are raised up, uplifted and made fulfilling.

The path of *bhakti* is a great path of *sādhanā* and there are temperaments for which this is the best and to which no other path will suit. And though it has its own ethos, it has deep affinities with all major *sādhanās* and Yogas including the traditional Dhyāna-Yoga. In fact, love and worship of God (*īśvara praṇidhāna*) is recognised as one of the best and quickest methods of spiritual knowledge (*pratyakchetanādhigama*) and for removing all obstacles of the path by Pātañjala Yoga. Can we express Bhakti-Yoga in the language of Dhyāna-Yoga? Do the developments in Bhakti-Yoga correspond in some ways with the stages and stations of Dhyāna-Yoga?

Bhakti brings concentration. One love drives out multiple loves. This brings intensity and faith. The thought of God itself is modified, purified. First, the love object is a mental image, something constructed out of imagination, out of subconscious suggestions, constructed out of faces we have loved and desired, or thrown up by our hopes and fears. But increasingly, the image becomes less material and more psychic. It becomes more sweet, more tender, more luminous and more joyful. From Krishna's face, we go over to his beauty, from *rūpa* to *rūpa-mādhurī*, from his thought (*bhāvanā*) to sentiment (*bhāva*) for him.

At this level, there is a lot of love and exchange of confidences. There is zeal and ardour, palpitation and rapture. There is even a kind of fusion and oneness, a spiritual marriage.

Then a still more consuming passion for Krishna takes over, a passion deep and tranquil. The *sādhaka* is no longer satisfied with His image or reflection or shadow however luminous. He wants Him alone. An emotional or sentimental attachment however sweet and joyful it may be to His image will no longer do; the *sādhaka* wants to be shaped in that image. All impurities are destroyed.

The distance between God and Soul is abolished and one sees God as the reality of one's own heart. The steps are clear. First, one seeks the beloved in the beautiful and the joyful; then one finds her in one's own heart. Then one realises that one is one's own beloved. The idea could also be put differently. One realizes that God is not only the Beloved; He is also the Lover; He is not only the Cherished, He is also the Cherisher. He alone is.

But some do not agree with this Krishna of Yoga seen in a trance or seen in one's heart alone. This is not sufficient for them. From the trance of Yoga, He must come into the waking consciousness; from His seat in the heart, He must come down into our eyes and ears. The ear must be able to hear Him, the eyes to see Him in an embodied form. He is seen in the *vigraha* on the altar that we worship; He is seen in the faces of men and women around; He is seen in the elements of Nature, in the Sun and the Stars and the Moon and the Fire and the Earth. He is everywhere seen with open eyes.

According to Vaishnavas, even after one is established in unity with God, the transcendental play does not cease. Even though the Soul and God become one, they still go on playing at being united and separated. The tears of separation and the joys of union do not cease. The *sādhaka* enters the eternal *Vrindāvana*.

Bhakti brings not only love but also wisdom and knowledge. The *bhakta* knows the nature of God; he acquires knowledge of His secret Names and Forms. He knows that God is one's own secret Self (*ātman*) and He is also the secret Self of all (*sarvātman*); that He is the Last Resort (*parāyaṇam*), the great Way (*mārga*), the Great Medicine (*mahaushadham*). He knows that whatever a devotee offers him in love whether it be a flower or a fruit or a leaf it is accepted by Him. He also knows that in whatever Form we worship Him, that worship goes to Him so long as the worship is sincere.

But *bhakti* is not all Yoga. It has its own ethos, its own emphases. In India, through *bhakti*, spiritual life received a new fertilizing force. The older Upanishadic truths received a new confirmation at the hands of innumerable saints, most of them drawn from people of humble origin. Spiritual life was renewed and received a new authenticity. There was a tendency to deny life under the influence of *māyāvāda* and *anātmavāda*. But under the influence of *bhakti*, the life of a householder was spiritually rehabilitated. There is a godhood in human relations, a godhood in parents, in children, in friends, in husbands and wives. To worship God in them is the perfection of all God-worship. Through *bhakti*, earthly life was raised up to heaven and the heaven was brought down to the earth.

Certain spiritual truths received a new emphasis in the Bhakti Movement. *Nāma-smaraṇa*, rememberance of God's name became the premier mode of *sādhanā*. "*Nāma* is the real incarnation of God in the Kaliyuga," says Sri Chaitanya Mahaprabhu. *Nāma-saṁkīrtana* entered the humblest cottage in the farthest corner. It was greatly enriching, spiritually speaking.

The role of Guru acquired a new importance. In many cases, even the distinction between God and Guru was lost. Not only God was the real Guru but according to some the Guru was the God. It was easy to miss the deeper spiritual truth of the statement and in many cases it bred a narrow sectarianism. The atmosphere has been replete with claims and counter-claims for one's own Guru.

The importance of serving Godly men was also greatly stressed. "A house in which there is no God-worship and no hospitality and service of men of renunciation is like a graveyard where dwell ghosts," says Kabir. Behind this observation lies a great idea. A family is more than a house, more than a husband and wife and children. It is an institution of Dharma. It is an invisible idea supported by a whole array of spiritual truths. The family is breaking because God-life is declining.

In the same spirit, there is a new emphasis on the need for cultivating the company of good men. Shun bad company; above all, shun those who are atheists, nihilists, deniers. The advice finds its classical expression in Tulsidas: "Shun those to whom Rama and Sita are not dear, even if they are close friends and relatives. Like Prahlada who gave up his father or Vibhishana who gave up his brother, or Bharat who gave up his mother, or Bali who gave up his Guru, or the damsels of Vraja who gave up their husbands."

A man is known by the company he keeps. But even more than that, he is shaped by it. Ordinary company men keep is one of the most debilitating thing. It is a most idle preoccupation. Through this one receives and imparts the poison of an unregenerate life. It produces spiritual darkness. A beginner should cultivate good company because it strengthens his resolve and avoid bad company because he is amenable to its bad influence. Spiritual life should be protected from this influence when it is weak. But when it acquires strength, it requires no such insulation. Bad people automatically lose their hold on the thoughts of a saintly person. He need not leave them; they leave him.

Other values stressed by Bhakti-Yoga are humility and compassion. One should be humbler than a straw, more forgiving than the Mother Earth. Compassion towards all creatures including animals and birds is a value which distinguishes religions of Indian origin from many other religions. In its more practical shape it expressed itself in a mass vegetarian movement, a phenomenon which we find missing elsewhere. Many religions teach mercy but it does not seem to extend to God's animal creation. True the God of Prophet Hosea "desired mercy, and not sacrifice, and the knowledge of God more than burnt offerings", but this note is unrepresentative of the spirit of the Bible old or new. Jesus overthrew the tables of the money-changers in the Temple, but there is no record that he felt the wails and tears of the animals that were sacrificed on a large scale in the Temple and preached against their slaughter.

They failed to evince the support of even St. Francis of Assisi who otherwise called them sentimentally brothers and sisters. One of his disciples cut off the foot of a swine. When the master of the swine reported the matter to St. Francis and in great rage called them "hypocrites, thieves and liars", the saint was greatly troubled and he rebuked the holy Brother for giving rise to "so great a scandal". So it is the scandal and not the cruelty of the act which moved St. Francis of Assisi. The holy Brother was of course unmoved by the complaint of the master of the swine "seeing that this pig, whose foot I cut off, is rather God's than his."

There were other values and other truths which the Bhakti Movement emphasized but we need not go into them here. In a way, none of these values were new but in the crucible of the

Bhakti Movement they combined to crystallise in a new form and give rise to a new ethos. And under the influence of many great *bhaktas* and *santas*, they acquired a new urgency, a new power. It made religion living for millions of people. *Bhakti* is now one of the greatest elements in Hindu religion. It has brought meaning, solace, sweetness, enrichment and a sense of direction into the lives of millions of people. *Bhakti* has penetrated into every nook and corner of India. This sentiment has informed all art-forms, poetry, sculpture and music, popular and classical. It has given India a unity which transcends regional, linguistic and political differences. This unity has stood many challenges and survived many historical upheavals.

The Bhakti Movement was also a great spiritual movement to which the humblest brought their contribution. Though like all great spiritual movements, it was aristocratic in one sense — in the sense that none unworthy could belong to it — in another sense it was very democratic. It was no exclusive preserve of any caste or class. In the development of Hinduism though Brahmins played a noble role, Hinduism has never been exclusively 'brahmanical'. It is particularly true of present-day Hinduism. It is the product of influences emanating from the humblest sources, and from most diverse circumstances. Kabir was a weaver; Raidas was a cobbler; Garibdas belonged to a Jat family; Sain was a barber; Guru Nanak's father was a petty official; Tukaram's father was a trader; Dadu was a *dhunia* (carder) according to some tradition; Krishnadas was born in a Kayastha family and so was Dharnidas; Sundardas belonged to a Vaishya family. Andala was a woman saint prefiguring almost by a thousand year two other women saints, Mira and Sahajo Bai. More recently we had Sri Ramakrishna who was an unlettered Brahmin. These are merely some of the more well-known names but they are part of a spirit which has informed all communities and all localities. Practically every village and caste has a tradition of its own saints. The cobbler community has been particularly rich in its saints. Even the father of Shri Jagjivan Ram was known as a *santa* to people immediately around him.

Most of these *bhaktas* and *santas* were not conscious of championing any particular religion, even the religion in which they were born; they were merely trying to live the life of the soul and were giving expression to its truths which in the process strengthened a culture conveniently called Hinduism.

Though without any such forethought, the Bhakti Movement did meet the challenge of the day and fulfilled the needs of its times. And understandably so. For the Movement had deep roots in the life of the people; therefore it could not be divorced from their lives. It came at a time when India lay prostrate before the Muslim invaders. It tried to tame their ferocity and fanaticism by the message of the fundamental unity of all religions, by preaching that different people worship the same God under different names. It was a difficult message for the fanatic mullahs, qazis and military generals — How could Allah be so faithless as to take on a name given by the infidels? But it could not go without influencing some princes like Akbar and Dara Shukoh and also strengthening the people in coping with their rulers. Some saints like [Samartha] Ramadas felt the shame and humiliation of the people to whom they belonged and gave a call to them to oppose oppression. The Santa-*mata* also helped in the creation of an indigenous Muslim Sufi movement which was larger in spirit and more accommodating than Prophetic Islam.

Bhakti is a great method of *sādhanā* and has greatly enriched the life of the people but it has not stopped some spiritual thinkers from pointing out its inadequacy too. They say that people who overcultivate *rasa* and *bhakti* fall a prey to people who cultivate power. It is true that *bhakti* was opposed in spirit to the Illusionism (*māyāvāda*) of Shankara and the *anātmavāda* of Buddhism, the two approaches which denied the world of *nāma-rūpa*, but it too brought its own brand of other-worldliness. It forgot this world in the beauty and *rasa* of the transcendental world.

As a method of *sādhanā* too, it tends to produce at least in lesser *sādhakas* a certain weakness, both of the mind as well as of the will. It makes them sentimental. It makes them superstitious and uncritical. By putting a premium on *śraddhā*, it neglects intellect.

It creates an atmosphere of credulity in which people claim all kinds of miracles for their teachers. Some *bhaktas* are cloyingly sweet and they give an impression of weakness.

Amorous *sādhanā* can breed effeminacy and therefore some people preach going to the Krishna of Kurukshetra rather than to the Krishna of Vrindavana. Similarly in the *sādhanā* of a child for God the Father or Mother, it is sometimes revolting to see some adults whining like children when at their age they should be producing them. In older spirituality there was no lack of love and worship of God as parents, but that spirituality produced characters like Shravana Kumar and Rama. But the new spirituality is sentimental. It makes babes out of adults. In the Vedic and Epic spirituality, there a certain heroic mould which accompanied all forms of *sādhanā*. *Sādhanā* was used for strengthening and enriching the life on the earth and for fulfilling its obligations. The new *sādhanā* is for purely transcendental ends.

Section 4

Buddhist Yoga

Chapter 4.1

Buddhistic *Sādhanā*

By Buddha's time, a split had occurred between body and mind, Nature and God, *saṃsāra* and *nirvāṇa*, This and That, Here and There, *idam* and *asau*.

Or, more truly, the split was not a new thing. The view that saw the two divided was equally ancient as the view that regarded them together. The two are two different dimensions of the soul, the two archetypes, and they approached the same problem from two angles. While the Upanishads represent one window-view, Sāṃkhya represents another. Buddhism represents the richest culmination of Sāṃkhya. While there is a good deal of Sāṃkhya in the Upanishads and the Gita too, it has been adapted there to a different weltanschauung or world-view.

The new view looks at the world from below as it were. It dispenses with all hypotheses about God and Self and Divinity. It will take nothing for granted. In an Upanishadic view, the world comes to us reflected as it were in a divine medium. The Buddhists want first to savour the world as it is without God. It is a heroic view and it is not an ordinary, empirical view. Ordinarily the world comes to us bathed in a thousand hopes and illusions. It is difficult to bear the touches of a nature bare of soothing disguises. This also needs a Yoga of a kind, a deepened sensibility, a superhuman strength.

And when we turn to the world with this resolve, what do we find? What is man without a Self, a principle of divinity in him? According to Buddhists and even many others who do not belong to their weltanchauung, such a man is a ghost inhabiting a shadow-world, a myth imagining itself to be real, a fleeting reflection on the screen of time, a successive blank in a deepening void. He feels, he thinks, he knows; but behind his feeling, thinking and knowing, there is no soul, no knower, no thinker, no feeler. His senses and mind are temporary formations and his body is a deserted, unoccupied tenement.

Though such a dummy and blank, yet he cannot be stamped out easily. He persists like a bad dream, like an indelible, inky mark. An illusion at heart, he weaves forms after forms which seem to endure, hold out even in their evanescence and transience. He seems to live through repeated deaths and, what he calls his life, is really an image of death.

Himself no more than an apparition, he follows a mirage which evades him constantly. A beggar with nothing but hunger and grasping for his assets, he is invited to a Barmecidal banquet which his greed will not allow him to recognise as such. Through his craving and grasping, he becomes his own tomb, getting more deeply buried, becomes his own fossil, daily becoming more body-like.

And though so rushed, his life is a mere goose-stepping. His life is a stream in a stagnant pool. The stream follows a fixed groove. It is governed by an iron-rule which knows no violation, no infringement, no relaxation. He is built out of the elements of his avarice, and covetousness and the citadel so built knows no dismantling. He cannot cheat or trick or evade his lot. That which is sown has to be reaped.

When man is conceived without reference to a spiritual transcendental principle, he becomes a mere *pudgala*, a fleeting shadow, a chance aggregate of elements, a concatenation. His world is empty in a deep sense. It has no moral and spiritual worth. Moral actions have no validity and from them accrues no merit. There is no principle of *yajña*; works, charity, self-discipline have no meaning. There is no law of karma, no law of causation. Everything is arbitrary.

Buddha is believed to have denied the Self and in a way he did. But he retained it in a disguised form. He talks a good deal of *śīla*, *samādhi*, *prajñā*, compassion, and *kuśala dharma*. In fact, they are central in his *sādhanā* and he seems to embody them in his person and life. In this sense, some of his contemporaries like Purna Kashyapa, Ajit Keshakambali, Prakrudha Katyayana and Makkhali Goshala were more logical. In their view of the world, they abstained not only from a spiritual principle but also from a moral principle. They had their differences but they all denied the moral efficacy of man's actions. Katyayana taught that there are seven elements, uncreated, unmoved. They give neither pain nor pleasure to any one. There is neither a killer nor his victim. If you throw a sword on any one, it merely falls in the intervening spaces that divide these elements. No body kills; no body is killed. Kashyapa taught that from killing or robbing or stealing accrues no demerit; and from truthful speech, self-discipline and works of charity no moral merit.* Makkhali Goshala did not deny the truth of suffering or man's liberation. He taught that suffering is uncaused and so is the release from it. Man is caught without any reason in the web of repeated births and is released with equal unreason after he has passed through these allotted births (only 1, 406, 600). Man cannot hurry his release by moral action, nor prolong it by his evil actions. He has no power, no strength, no choice, no help.

These views have their minor differences but they share a basic similarity. In these views, all inhabit a spiritual waste; things are separated from each other by spiritual spaces or gulf which nothing can bridge over, neither love, nor kindness, nor knowledge. Every thing happens without rhyme or reason, moral or logical. Everything is empty, alone, arbitrary, without any spiritual merit or efficacy. There is a chance coming together, but no togetherness, no sharing, no help, no hope. This is a meaningless world in which men play blindmen's buff or chase their own tail in a merry-go-round.

Buddha spoke very critically of these teachings and teachers. But they were not without a consistency of their own. Men who held these views were well-known teachers and great ascetics of their day. And their views were not ordinary, empirical, *chārvāka* or hedonist views; they were yogic views, views arising out of a

---

*There is a Vedantic rendering also of the doctrine but its context and intentions are entirely different. The *Brihadāraṇyaka Upanishad* says: This eternal greatness of a Brahman is not increased by deeds (*karma*), nor diminished.

deepened meditation. But it was a yoga which was viewing a world without a spiritual and even a moral background and Self. Without this background, there is a tendency to a depreciation and erosion of the world.

There is a good deal of this view in Buddhism and the Vedantic *māyavāda*. But it is hidden from the view by an equally great insistence on the spiritual and moral principles, on *brahma* or *nirvāṇa*. But a world without *brahma* and *nirvāṇa*, whether immanent or transcendent, is not unlike the world described by these teachers.

But some experience of this kind is an important element in a man's spiritual growth. Without this experience, the world continues to hold a fatal fascination for the soul.

Therefore every scripture, even a scripture like the Gita which promises unreservedly God's grace on His devotees, contains a good deal of this view. The Gita describes men living unregenerate life thus: "Held in bondage by a hundred hopes, and given over to lust and wrath, they strive to obtain by unlawful means hoards of wealth for sensual enjoyment. And bewildered by numerous thoughts and enmeshed in the web of delusion, addicted to the gratification of desire, they fall downwards into foul hell."

When our Gods fall, our world also falls. This is a recurring experience of Yogic *sādhanā*. But there is also another experience of equal importance: that unless this world falls, Gods are not born in the soul. But it is possible, at least, for a time, that an old world has died and a new one is not yet born. Our hunger for the higher Truth has to be equal to our distaste for the lower world. In a spiritual economy, this equation is generally maintained. The two impulses reinforce each other. The hunger for truth fills us with a new *vairāgya* or distaste for the world, and the *vairāgya* from the lower world awakens within the soul the memory of a greater life.

Chapter 4.2

Contrast between Upanishadic and Buddhistic *Sādhanās*

Though Upanishadic and Buddhistic *sādhanās* have an underlying unity, they also have important differences, differences of principles, practices, temper, outlook. We should become aware of these differences for in their own way they are important. Many of these differences arise because they are approaching the problem from two different directions — they are looking at the same coin but at its two different sides.

Before we discuss the subject further, we also want to make a clarification. The words Upanishadic and Buddhistic are used in a generic way, as names for two tendencies. In concrete *sādhanā*, the two have met again and again and there is a lot of the one in the other.

The Upanishadic *sādhanā* is the adoration of a purified heart which goes out in adoration to the farthest end of the world. It pours itself out. It sees in everything its own power and reality, the Reality of the Self. It sees Fire and in it it sees the power of the Godhead. It sings, '*agnimīḷe*'. Is '*īḷe*' from the same root as 'adore'?

Buddhist meditation is increasing detachment of the mind from all its forms and formations till what remains is so different from all that we have seen and known. There is no image left to describe it. Therefore, it has been called simply as *kaivalya*, Alone, or *svarūpa-sthiti* or merely *nirvāṇa*, a stage where all created forms have ceased.

In the Upanishadic *sādhanā*, one seeks the hidden self of all, the secret life behind everything. So the path of the *sādhanā* is illumined with that hope and light. The Buddhistic *sādhanā* makes sure that we shall not be satisfied with anything less than the Transcendent. It will not be satisfied with half-way houses however warm and sunlit.

On the path of Upanishadic *sādhanā*, there are many aids, and many prizes. There are Gods and luminous forms. The Buddhistic *sādhanā* says that these too have something of the illusory and the transient in them and we should not be satisfied with him.

All truth is grist to the Upanishadic *sādhanā*; all falsehood is poison to the Buddhistic *sādhanā*. Upanishadic *sādhanā* is in love with truth. Buddhism and Sāṁkhya are repelled by falsehood.

In the Upanishadic *sādhanā*, everything is a moving image of the eternity. In the lowly horse, it sees not only a reminder of a universal energy but an epitome of the whole universe. "The dawn is its head; the sun its eyes; the wind its breast; the universal fire its open mouth." In short, in the Upanishadic *sādhanā*, it sees the universal in the particular.

In the Buddhistic Yoga, the movement is different. In this approach, the tendency is to deny the universal. What is a particular object? In the Upanishadic approach, it is meeting-point of many universals; in the Buddhistic approach, it is a combination of different *dharmas*, odour, colour, sound, an uneasy and artificial combination of mere particulars. As a result, in the Buddhistic *sādhanā*, the object dissolves into its lower constituents; in the Upanishadic, it is linked with the intangible, impersonal, universal source from which it derives. In the Buddhistic *sādhanā*, the world and its objects dissolve, evaporate, come to nothing; in the Upanishadic *sādhanā*, they are rehabilitated, raised up. The earth rises up to meet the heavens.

Buddhistic *sādhanā* consists in escaping *duḥkha*; the Upanishadic *sādhanā* is a search for joy. The first seeks escape, escape from illusion, *māyā*; the other seeks truth. The first seeks escape from the touch of impurity; the other seeks the embrace of the pure.

The two emphases are obvious in the two literatures. Though Buddhism teaches the realization of *nirvāṇa*, there is little discussion of this state; on the other hand, there is a lot of discussion of what constitutes *duḥkha* and how to escape it. In the Upanishads, on the other hand, there is constant praise for the life of Self, of *brahma-sthiti*, but not much mention of the world of *duḥkha*.

Buddhism discusses the laws of becoming, of change, of rebirth, of movement in the *saṁsāra*. The Upanishads discuss the law of Being, of Self, of that which remains unchanged through all the changes, the immortal in the midst of the mortal.

The Upanishads speak of two birds on a tree of life. One of them eats the fruits; the other one merely looks on. Buddhism discusses the first bird, its joys and pain, its bondage and grief and the way for its liberation. The Upanishads discuss the second bird that grieves not, that merely looks on in freedom.

The two views are not peculiar to India but they represent two approaches and have a universal approach. The Greek teachers likened the world to a vanity fair, like a gathering at the Olympic Games (πανηγυρις). Of those who gather there, there are three classes; those who come to buy and sell; those who come to play and compete; and those who come to look on. Of them the last were the best. It is the Upanishadic bird on the tree who merely looks on. It is the theoretic (literally the life of a spectator) life which the Greek mystic taught.

In the Buddhist Yoga, we have lists of objects on which to meditate. In the Upanishads, there is no such list. All elements, all surrounding objects, all environing nature is good enough — the sun, the earth, the moon, the sky, the rivers, the mountains, the night, the dawn, the day — all were objects of contemplation.

The Buddhistic ideal is expressed in terms of *nirvāṇa*, *moksha*, *mukti* or what in the Greek world the Orphic Mystery religion called release or (λνοις). The Upanishadic ideal is *brahma-sthiti* or what Plato called 'Living with Gods'.

As we have said, we have used the two words Upanishadic and Buddhistic to convey two tendencies. But this is done at the expense of accuracy. In actual practice, the two tendencies go together. There is a good deal of Upanishadic *sādhanā* in

Buddhism and vice-versa. Similarly, there were developments in Buddhism which were close to Upanishadic approach and there were Upanishadic developments which were close to Buddhism. *Māyāvāda* which derives its authority from Upanishads was felt by many to be nothing but a name for Buddhism. Similarly, Mahayana, an offshoot of Buddhism, developed a stem of *sādhanā* and approach very close to those which derive from the Upanishads.

Chapter 4.3

Anātma

Anātma is a great concept which Buddha used in order to convey a deep spiritual truth which could not be conveyed otherwise. But in the hands of later *āchāryas*, that truth was lost and *anātma* survived as a mere dogma. It is now an article of faith in a codified theology, a creed rather than an experience of the soul.

Anātma originally meant that the things we live by and by which we lay so much store lack inner worth. All our pleasures and achievements have no intrinsic significance, no heart, no soul. They are transient, ephemeral. They are with you today and, without a warning, leave you tomorrow. They are like a kingdom obtained in a dream. They are blank, empty, nominal. They are all like a bubble, like a summer lightening, like a flash in the pan, like a will-o'-the-wisp. Not only our gold and pleasures but also our idealism and ideologies, our manners and accomplishments come to nothing. They dissolve in our very grasp; they slip through our fingers. They are a mirage.

Anātma does not mean absence of Self, it means the presence of Ego. It is there not only in our profanities, scoffing and desecrating; it is there also in our heaven-storming theologies, religious platitudes and righteous attitudinizing.

There is a good deal of cant, pious fraud, hidden carnality, unexpressed ill-will, sanctimonious hypocrisy, pretence and mask in our worship, piety, ideology. There is more religion in an honest doubt than in a tearful faith. There is more humility in the straight posture of an upright man than in the genuflections of a servile man. We must become aware of all these garbs and disguises.

It is also important to become aware of the domain of *anātma*. It is as wide as that of the *ātman* of the Upanishads. You go to the end of the world, *anātma* is there; you go to the end of the five Elements, the five senses, the five *praṇās*, the five *tanmātrās*; you go to the end of the mind and the intellect, and the Universals of the *buddhi*, you do not see the light of Consciousness. All is the play of Prakriti, Nature, its formations, combinations, mutations; all exchange and interchange of these formations, existing by a kind of barter and see-saw between themselves but never self-existent. All these formations, objects, senses, mind, reason are held together by a kind of mechanical energy. All is change, a process, a link. All have a derived existence. All are part of a mechanism; perhaps, a self-acting mechanism but still at heart mechanical. In none, there is Light of the Self.

Even our thoughts, most brilliant thoughts and intuitions are blind. They share a basic thoughtlessness, a deep nescience. There is a tendency to regard our thoughts, at least the more intelligent ones, and our idealism and more generous impulses as *ātman*. But if we look at them more closely, they are as blind as other formations. At least their intelligence and generosity derive from another source. And in most cases, they feed the forces of selfhood and the Ego shines through them.

The doctrine of *anātma* only means this that those who seek truth, significance, authenticity and reality in the life of the senses and even intellect, in getting and spending, in social warmth and ordinary give and take, in good manners and genteel behaviour, in Art and Speculation are in for disappointment. Buddha saw in all these *anātma*, their otherness, their externality.

Upanishads also say precisely the same thing but from another angle. They say that neither the sun, nor the moon, nor the stars have their own light. Their light is borrowed (*Kaṭhopanishad* 5.15). Like the Buddhists, Upanishads see no light and consciousness in the world which it can call its own. All its light, energy, truth, consciousness come from another source.

The Upanishads speak of a Reality which is beyond the ken of the mind; there the eye goes not; speech goes not, nor the mind (*Kenopanishad* 1.3). They speak of a world which is *a-prāṇa*, *a-manas*, without breath and without mind (*Muṇḍakopanishad* 2.1.2). In short, they speak of *brahma, nirvāṇa, ātman*. On the other hand, Buddha spoke little of *nirvāṇa* and *brahma* and took them for granted but spoke of *manas*, and *pudgala*, all that is not *nirvāṇa* or *brahma* or *ātman*. No wonder, their accounts differed. But they were speaking of the two sides of the same coin; therefore, there was also a basic unity between them. It is like a half-filled glass of water. One says it is half-filled; another says it is half-empty.

The two approaches view the problem from two different angles but both complementary. Looked at analytically, from below, a man is a formation, an aggregate, a *pudgala*, a *pañch-skandha*, a link in the chain of its own self-sustaining birth-cycle. Buddha says, snap this chain by right living and right meditation and right understanding; shed the false personalities of *nāma-rūpa* just as a serpent sheds its skin and find the fulfilment of *nirvāṇa*. This is the Buddhist way of describing man and his way of salvation.

But looked at intuitively from within as it were, man is a soul, a Self, an image of Gods. This is another side of the picture which the Upanishads stress. Not that they neglect the other side. They are not saying that you will find the Self in your ego, in your cravings, desires, feelings, knowing. On the other hand, they say, exceed them; by exceeding them, you would cross over the ocean of pain and death and enjoy immortality and Self.

Buddhistic method of *sādhanā* is the famous Upanishadic method of *neti, neti* (Not This, Not This). This too is *anātmā, duḥkha, aśuchi, anitya* (non-self, painful, impure, fickle). But the Upanishads also combine it with another method, the method of '*etadvaitat*' (This also is That). *This* is full; *That* is full. The fullness of *This* is derived from the fullness of *That*. All this is pervaded by God and this is to be enjoyed by renunciation.

There is a verse in the *Īśopnishad* which says:

Unmoving, it is swifter than the mind. The sense-powers (*devas*) reach it not. Speeding on before, past others running, it goes standing.

According to traditional interpretation, it means that there is a life which exceeds our actions, our thoughts, our speculations. This life surrounds us; we live in it; we move in it. And yet we cannot reach it; our senses cannot grasp it; our mind cannot comprehend it; our imagination cannot picture it; our voice cannot praise it. It outstrips us in every way.

But there could be another interpretation equally valid and enriching. The traditional interpretation is in terms of the Self but the verse could also be interpreted in the language of *anātma*. According to this interpretation, a man's little self is in all his desires and cravings, in all his thoughts and emotions and efforts. Let him go to the farthest limit of his mind and intellect, and the little self is already there. Let him go to the extreme of joys and tranquillities of the four initial meditations; let him even go to the extreme of the four infinities of the four *arūpa* meditations, the little self is even there. The domain of the *anātma* is as wide as the domain of the Upanishadic *ātman*. It is the *māyā* of a later-day spiritual thought who presides over the whole world of *nāma-rūpa*. This thought is beautiful expressed in a poem of Kabir:

1. माया महा ठगिनी हम जानी।
   निरगुण फाँस लिये कर डोले, बोले मधुरी बानी ॥

2. इक डाइन मेरे मन बसै। नित उठि मेरे जिय को डसै,
   या डाइन के लरिका पाँच। निस दिन मोहे नचावे नाच।

3. कबीर माया डाकिनी, सब किसहीं कौं खाई।
   दाँत उपाड़ौं पापणी, जे संतों नेड़ी जाई ॥

4. कबीर माया पापणी, फँद ले बैठी हाटि,
   सब जग लो फन्दै पड़्या, गया कबीरा काटि ॥

5. कबीर माया मोहिनी, मोहे जाण सुजाण।
   भागाँ ही छूटै नहीं, भरि भरि मारै बाण ॥

पद

माया तजूँ तजी नहीं जाई,
फिरि फिरि माया मोहि लपटाई ॥

माया आदर माया मांन, माया नहिं तहाँ ब्रह्म गियान ॥
माया रस माया कर जांन, माया कारनि तजै परान ॥
माया जप तप माया जोग, माया बाँधे सबही लोग ॥
माया जल थलि माया आकासि, माया व्यापि रहि चहुं पासि ॥
माया माता माया पिता, अति माया अस्तरी सुता ।
माया मारि करै व्यवहार, कहै कबीर मेरे राम आधार ॥

The two interpretations are complementary and give rise to two systems of *sādhanā* which go together. The two cooperate like the two wings of a bird or two blades of a scissors. The two *sādhanās* are termed the path of *avidyā* and *vidyā*, of *asambhūti* and *sambhūti*. One without the other leads as it were into a darkness, one deeper than the other. The path of *avidyā* or *asambhūti* demolishes false knowledge, false Gods, false idealizations — and falsity or *māyā* is as pervading as Truth. The path of *vidyā* and *sambhūti*, on the other hand, builds up and helps to see the visage and impulsion of Gods in everything we do and are. The former path helps to discover death and falsehood that lurk in every corner; the latter path helps us to see and enjoy the immortality and Truth of the Self in everything, the Light in the darkness. This is the combined method of conquering death through *avidyā*, or *vināśa* or *asambhūti* and enjoying immortality through *vidyā* and *sambhūti*.

For the students of the Upanishads, we want to stress the importance of *anātma* and *nirvāṇa* though the concepts got their extraordinary stress in Buddhist thought. They are two most beautiful and useful key-words and no other words could define as well as they — in so far as words can define at all — a most essential process of *sādhanā* and a most important attribute or Reality.

The fact is that unless a very living and urgent and overriding sense of the *anātma* takes hold of us at some stage or the other, we cannot advance very far on the spiritual path. *Anātmā* is a fundamental, leading element of the *sādhanā* and at one stage or another, it must become its corner-stone. Wherever we go, whether we turn right or left, upwards or downwards, inwards or outwards, there is nothing which abides, nothing which belongs to us, nothing which we can call our own. Everything has to be left behind, to be exceeded. If this sense of *anātma* is not strong, we shall get identified with luminous forms, with partial joys, sweetness, fervour, hopes, consolations, promises, graces, God, Gods and powers on the way.

Section 5

Gods

Chapter 5.1

Vedic Gods

In the Vedas, Gods are Beings to whom man brings the homage and adoration of his heart. He praises them, glorifies them, invokes them. Gods in turn respond to man's prayers and bestow on him all kinds of blessings, material and spiritual. When invoked, they come to his feasts and demand their share of the offerings. Nourished by him, they in turn nourish him, as the Gita tells us. Here we are taught a great spiritual truth, the truth of interchange between man and Gods. When man invokes Gods, they are born in his soul and raise him up to their own status. Through worship and adoration, man grows into their likeness. But if he withdraws his worship, they also withdraw from his view. It is in this sense that Gods die in atheistic and positivistic epochs. They withdraw more and more into their natural habitat, into 'heaven', or deeper and deeper in the cave of the heart; and man sees less and less of their presence in the working of his mind and heart.

But during Vedic days while they lasted, Gods were a living presence. The worshippers established a sense of deep intimacy, trust and affinity with them. Everything around was astir with divinity, instinct with life. The Fire was no ordinary fire, just to cook one's food and warm one's cold nights. He was a messenger between the worshipper and his Gods. He was a purifier who burnt everything false; his burning flame was a symbol of man's aspiration towards the Godhead. The Earth was not just sand, clod and mud. She was a veritable Mother on whose breasts we all feed. She was a psychic Reality. She was *ananta* (boundless), *vipula* (vast), *kshamā* (patient), *riju-hasta* (liberal handed).

But this kind of approach is possible only when man is in a state of innocence as it seems he was during the ancient Vedic days. During this time, it seems it was like waking up in the morning of creation with eyes full of wonder and the heart full of worship. The Gods are still in their handiwork and have not withdrawn. Their creations reveal and not conceal them. In this morning of creation, the songs are on the lips and the praise is in the heart and everything is soaked in divinity and Gods and men walk on the earth in fellowship. Gods are invited to men's feasts and they bring gifts and largesse with them.

But something snaps and that stage passes away. Something happens either to the Gods or their worshippers. Gods withdraw behind a veil and the veil is no more than man's desire, mind and selfhood as the wise men tell us.

Vedic Gods suffer deflation. And strangely enough, it is first at the hands of the Upanishadic sages through their teachings of *brahmavāda* and *ātmavāda*. Through this teaching, Gods lost their independent status. They were no longer entities but reflections, projections and powers of the Self. Without the power of *brahma*, Agni could not burn a straw, nor Vāyu move it. Gods work with borrowed power but they deludedly think it is their own. From fear of Him, Agni burns; from fear of Him, Sūrya shines; from fear of Him, the Vāyu, Indra and Death move. They all act with the power of *brahma* and ultimately dissolve into a featureless Brahma. And the joys of Gods are nothing compared to the joys of the knowers of *brahma*.

But in a way it was not real deflation. Rather, it was an attempt to bring out the unity of the spiritual life which in the Vedas was being expressed in a different way but the sense of which was getting lost. In the Vedas, the same Reality was worshipped as the most pre-eminent one under different names and symbols. But the surface mind has its own limitations and it was easy to regard those Gods and symbols as independent and different and even to regard them anthropologically. So the concept of the unity of spiritual life had to be salvaged; the concept of Gods had to be purified, deepened. Upanishads did no more than this. In the process, something was lost in the way of concreteness, freshness, vitality and poetry; and the concept of Gods tended to become abstract but the attempt itself was necessary.

The old, Vedic approach was possible so long as the soul did not lose its primeval innocence, its child-like quality, its intuitive way of 'feeling' and 'living' the world. But when the soul put on another attribute, when the intuitive heart receded and the thinking mind came to the fore, the old approach was bound to lose its effectiveness. So now the same idea had to be formulated and expressed in the language of the mind. But the formulation itself retained its experimental foundation and it never degenerated into mere logic and concept as it did later.

Upanishadic *ātmavāda* was an attempt to recover the old sense of intimacy with Gods but under new conditions when they had withdrawn from before the eyes of man behind a veil. Now they have withdrawn to the cave of one's heart and they have to be first met there. This meeting lacks nothing of old intimacy and intensity.

Later on, Yoga came. It was an attempt to discover methods and processes by which to enter the depths of the heart where Gods had retired under increasingly more difficult conditions.

In the *Mahābhārata*, we have a great, inner balance between all these forces. All the aspects are equally and fully stressed and brought out. We have here the Vedic intimacy with Gods; we have the highest form of *ātmavāda* without Gods being internalized; we have *brahmavāda* with Gods retaining their fullest status.

Here, they retain their fullest interest in their worshippers. They are nourished by the power of Truth which in turn they nourish in our souls. Consequently, they are inevitably there wherever there is a *yajña*. They are present in the assemblies of wise men where deeper truths of life and the Spirit are being declared; they are there invisibly watching a righteous battle where heroes fight for Dharma. When the sages go to the court of the Kaurauvas to dissuade Duryodhana from the path of unrighteousness, the Gods are there; they are there when Lord Krishna himself goes on a similar mission; they are there when Bhishma enunciates the truths of life from his death-bed in the battle-field; they are there when Lord Krishna shows his Celestial From: "Rudras, Vasus, Sādhyas, Ādityas, Asuras, Aśvins, Maruts, Ushampās, Gandharvas, Yakshas, Siddhas, all in wondering multitudes beholding that Form; all the great sages and the Perfect ones and Gods chanting in resounding songs the praise of Lord Krishna."

It is understandable. Truths of the soul, noble, words, heroic deeds — these are the raiments on which Gods feed and by which they are nourished. The Gods are called *somapā*, the drinkers of Soma. They drink of the Soma of truth and wisdom and by that they are strengthened and by that strength they increase their activity in our souls.

In the story of Satyavan-Savitri, Savitri follows the auspicious Lord of Death who is also the Lord of Dharma when he takes away the soul of her husband. No mortal can walk on this path but also no one can obstruct those who are steadfast in their Dharma. The great Lord of Death asks her to desist from following him and offers any boon except the life of her husband. Savitri herself asks for no boon but only enunciates some truth of the spirit. Her words are honey-sweet to his ears and they fill his soul with a melody. His joy overflowed in more boons and eventually the life of her husband was restored. Gods are rightly called *sompā*.

Gods reside in the hearts of pure men, in the arms of the heroes, in the prayers of the devotees, in the hospitality of the house-holders, in renunciation and in selfless service.

But in the course of time, the spirit of the *Mahābhārata* was lost. *Brahmavāda* of the Upanishads gave way to *māyāvāda* and their *ātmavāda* to *anātmavāda*. It may even be called degeneration but perhaps that is not the right word to use. The new doctrines were perhaps attempts at new adjustment with the new mentality of the age and new powers of the soul, which were strong in analysis and intellection but weak in synthesis and intuition and even weaker in *prāṇa-śakti*.

The seeds of *māyāvāda* were already there in *ātmavāda* and *brahmavāda*. The subsequent developments merely brought it out into the open. One cannot deny Gods without at the same time denying the world. The two are inextricably bound up.

Man's definition of his Gods is ultimately bound up with the definition of his own nature, ideals and world. A man is what his God is. If God is defined neither this nor that, neither a father nor a mother, neither a friend nor a foe, neither a lover nor a protector, then a worshipper meditating on those qualities tends to imbibe those qualities. If God is 'Nihil', a man also tends to become 'nihil'— I am using the word in its transcendental sense. When the *brahma* or *ātman* or Gods are made too transcendental and taken out too completely from the affairs of men and their world, the world loses its foundation and substance and becomes a work of an illusory power. The transcendental aspect of the Upanishadic view was receiving a too one-sided emphasis with the result that it was eroding the world, the Gods, the men.

So by the time of Buddha, the depreciation of Gods was gone very far indeed. Though in the Buddhist literature, there is a plethora of Gods but their powers and status are sharply curtailed. They no longer symbolise higher Truth, higher consciousness, higher puissance and are no longer objects of our worship and one gains little by worshipping them. Their function seems to be to appear and pay homage to Buddha from time to time, confirm his teachings, to be at his beck and call in general and be the cheer-boys of his teachings.

These Gods of new description were at the best celestial beings who lived a life of great pleasures. This view of Gods was in keeping with the doctrine of karma which was now being preached with a new emphasis. Those who sow in good deeds reap in greater enjoyments. They are born on a plane with greater claim to enjoyment and also for greater capacity for it. So in Buddhist, Jain and even a good deal of Hindu thought, Gods were only 'enjoying beings' born in *bhoga-yonis*. *Bhoga-yonis* are states or worlds in which one initiates no new fruit-bearing karma but enjoys past good actions and by enjoying their fruits exhausts them. Once those fruits are exhausted, one comes back to this earth again to work out his destiny. In this view, Gods are no powers to whom one could appeal for succour or to whom one could bring one's heart's worship.

Whatever their fall from an original pedestal, Gods in Buddhism were still great merit-forms and not desire-forms or Ego-forms as they tend to become in different religions. They were those who had in the past followed the path of virtue and lived a life of meditation before winning these God-worlds. And their new status does not make them lax and arbitrary and seek other goods. They may not be liberated yet, but they like serving those who are. And though their powers and joys might not have been equal to the powers and joys of an Arhata or a Buddha but they wanted to make things easy for him, for there was a spiritual merit in it.

They played a great role in the life of Buddha even when he had not become one. As a prince, he was protected by his father, the king, from all unseemly sights that might inspire in him thoughts of unworldliness. When Buddha went out occasionally on a tour of night-seeing, Gods first took the form of an old, decrepit man bent with age; later on, that of a sick, ailing man and then of a dead man being carried on a funeral bier. They also inspired, on these occasions, the charioteer to explain, against the express orders of the king, that every one who is born is subject to the domain of sickness, old age and death. Later on, when even as a prince Buddha went to a forest, a God appeared before him in the guise of an ascetic, introducing himself as a monk who was wandering in the search of the auspicious and the indestructible (*sivamakshayam param tat*) and trying to escape a world which was subject to flux (*jagati kshaya-dharmīke*). All this was done in order to awaken in Buddha the sleeping memories of the life of renunciation and search.

Again, at the time of Buddha's great austerities when he had given up all food, Gods entered his pores and nourished him. During Māra's onslaught on Buddha when at one stage they had a dialogue with one another, Goddess Earth bore witness to the truth of Buddha's declaration.* It was on the advice of Gods that the

---

*The curious thing is not that the Earth bore witness but that she was believed by Māra. It is more than can be said about modern Indian courts.

Māra turned away from Buddha, defeated and humiliated. During the weeks of his enlightenment, the serpent-God surrounded him with the seven folds of his body while his hood served as an umbrella to protect Buddha from the rain and the sunshine.

Buddha's renunciation and enlightenment were cosmic events for which the Gods had been preparing for aeons. They were waiting for a Buddha to come and set the wheel of Dharma in motion. This they did not as retainers and hosts of Buddha but as exalted beings who cared for Dharma. In this respect, they still retained something of the old dignity. In the old Hindu thought, as we find it in the Upanishads and the *Mahābhārata*, even the Gods, even Brahmā Himself, meditate, engage in *yajña*, in austerities, observe *yama* and *niyama*. Some of the names for Lord Śiva are *yoga*, *yama*, *niyama*, *dama*, *śama*. They do these things not because they expect anything to gain but because they are made of the very stuff of those attributes.

But the similarity between Hindu and Buddhist approaches stops here. Buddhists make the Gods bow too often to Buddha while he receives their homage as a matter of fact. Perhaps the Buddhist writers thought that if they made Buddha recognise the greatness of the Gods, it will take away something from his own. The *Mahābhārata* develops a different viewpoint. There the sages and Gods meet in great mutual welcome. They offer each other seats and homage. They do it because they see in each other the reflections of the same truth, the power of the Yoga, Dharma, Law. And this does not take away but adds to their stature.

Chapter 5.2

Ego-Gods

The Upanishads say that God chooses him whom he wills. This is true in a deep sense. It means that He is beyond our choices and preferences, our likes and dislikes and our conceptions of Him, our definitions of right and wrong, false and true.

But there is a sense in which we choose our own Gods. God made man in His own image. But man also made God in his image. Our God is what we are. If our hearts are pure, our Gods are also pure; and if our hearts are impure our Gods too are impure.

Gods have been worshipped as projections of the *ātman*, as names for the principles of Truth and purity in the soul, principles which they themselves implant in the soul. But there is also another angle from which they can be discussed — from the angle of the *anātma*, as projections of our desires and cunning. This is an important angle. This helps to purify our concept of Gods which is mostly a mixture of many things.

It is to be remembered that our discussion is a limited one and belongs to a particular context. Gods also represent another important side of our nature which is neither moral, nor immoral. Gods also personalise impersonal and universal traits and powers in the psyche. The soul does not seek merely to be good; it seeks a larger reconciliation and transformation. It is difficult to do justice to the number and variety of Gods as they embody different traits and needs of the psyche. Here we only touch the subject.

In most cases, men do not seek a God who will transform them. They are not dissatisfied with themselves; therefore they seek no self-transcendence. Therefore, they have no use for a God of

Truth, Knowledge, Wisdom and Justice, the qualities which are also the goods of the soul and to which it aspires secretly.

There are also not many who want a God who is a comforter in their sorrow, a strength in their weakness, a companion in the difficult journey of life, a leader and advisor in the moments of indecision, a support who blesses their labour and gives them support to be true to themselves and to those around, a teacher who helps them to be just and fair.

Most men want a God who humours them and gratifies them, who vindicates and justifies their wonted way of life, who sanctifies them in their own eyes and in those of their friends.

The first and perhaps one of the lowest conception of God arises when some people, particularly those placed in power and position, want a God who does not merely confirm and endorse them in their possessions but who would still grant them their yet unfulfilled ambitions. They want their kingdom to extend; they want war-booty, particularly in the form of gold and young girls; they want their enemies to be slain and humbled.

If this God wants blood-sacrifice, animal or human, well, there is plenty of it at the beck and call of these chiefs. There is a class of priests who are prepared for a consideration to be the inter-mediaries between this God and his votaries.

There is a good deal of God-worship at this level everywhere. And it is not all straight, frank give and take, business — sacrifices and oblations for benefits received. It is generally accompanied by a whole system of psychological props and religious supports — piety, worship and thanks-giving for God, the Bountiful.

In the theologically-minded people, the idea of self-interest gets disguised. They want nothing for themselves. All is for the greater glory of God Himself. Therefore, is it too much to expect God to bless their labours? They expect God to march at the head of their armies in their crusades or expect him to be their Vicar-General in their missionary work amongst the black, brown and yellow barbarians. Any empire is an incidental result of their toil which is purely missionary. They have been God's aggressive salesmen, and surely no one should envy them these little prizes and commission.

Then there are people who are oppressed, who are weak, who suffer for no apparent failure on their part. Many of them go to God not for succor and redress but for justice and even revenge. And most religions have provided for this need also. There is a system of compensatory justice, the institutions of Hell and Heaven. The oppressors of the earth go to Hell while the oppressed enjoy posthumously the pleasures of Heaven. And there is also the promise that the meek shall inherit the earth.

But this alone will not do for the theologians. To the moral question of oppression, they have also added the metaphysical dimension of beliefs. Surely believers and non-believers cannot be treated at par. While as believers we expect our rewards, the non-believers should also not get away scot-free. So it is paradise for the believers and a hell for the non-believers, infidels, heathens, pagans and heretics. It is one of the greatest pleasures of some of the greatest saints of Christianity to watch the heathens being cooked in the fires of hell.*

While we want mercy for ourselves, we want justice for others with a secret expectation in some corner of our mind that God would judge them harshly and even temper his justice with vengeance. In fact, there is no need for God to judge for we have already judged His opponents for Him. His task is now merely to execute this judgement. Let them now be consigned to the fires of the hell and let the sight give unconcealed pleasure to the eyes of the righteous. This is an important strain of certain religious books particularly of those in which the prophetic trait predominates. While these books invoke God's mercy on the believers with great intensity, they invoke Allah's curses on the non-believers with the same passion and insistence. A mere heaven for the righteous without a hell for the unrighteous will be quite an outrage for the pious.

Modern states some of which are equally doctrinaire but in a secular way have no room and no patience for a future hell. They

---

*St. Augustine, for instance.

consign their non-believers and heretics and heathens to prison-cells and slave labour camps.

In the few examples we have given above, we can see how Ego-Gods originate. If a man follows simple joys and pleasures and accomplishments and securities of life, it is only natural. It is even a form of worship. Security, *yogakshema*, is one of the life-goods God promises to his devotees. Similarly, if a man avoids suffering, that too is natural. God himself is called *duḥkha-śoka-paritrāṇa*, a shelter from pain and sorrow. But when our desires become inordinate, when they ride rough-shod over others, when in our suffering we do not want its redress but revenge, then we become denatured and Ego-Gods take birth.

But Ego-Gods come fully into their own when our desires take on moral and theological disguises. When the Ego uses a higher principle for a lower satisfaction, the truth itself is perverted and Ego-Gods are born. We worship these Ego-Gods when we worship the lower in the higher.

When a man gives for the sake of ostentation, when he gives in the expectation of a return, when he gives with contempt, with condescension, when his left hand knows what his right hand has done, he worships Ego-Gods.

When a man prays or fasts for the reputation of it, he is praying to Ego-Gods and fasting to feed Ego-Gods. When he goes to a temple of God without first reconciling with his neighbour, his worship is received by Ego-Gods.

When a man's knowledge is for self-exhibition and self-aggrandisement and when it takes undue advantage of the ignorant, the knowledge is in vain and its merit goes to the Ego-Gods.

When we use moral truths not for self-improvement but for finding fault with our brother, we worship Ego-Gods.

Faith, conscience, celibacy, service, compassion, pity, love, *yama*, *niyama*, *yoga*, all are spiritual truths but all can be adapted to the fulfilment of Ego.

Conscience, they say, is the inner voice of God. But it can become Ego's instrument in self-torture in which it takes a secret pleasure. There was so much self-congratulation in the words of

Job's friends who had gone to him for consoling him in his sorrow.

Ego is very clever. It could derive strength both from being bad as well as being good. Being bad may not agree with its self-image, therefore it castigates it and feels moral about it. But when one is good, the Ego could derive another kind of pleasure, the pleasure of self-satisfaction, the pleasure of being good, its pride and superiority. It is good to be good but not good enough from a spiritual angle. One has to be selfless.

There can be so much self-indulgence in renunciation. We renounce because we feel that what is given to us is so much less than our share, so much less than we deserved. Renunciation is a form of protest.

Love which should be a form of self-giving becomes an instrument of self-imposition, an instrument of greedy demand. There can be so much luxury in sympathetic tears, so much ego in sorrow. Some observe religious poverty but they wear it like a badge. Some withdraw from the world because behind their withdrawal is a secret complaint that the world was not made for them but instead they were made for the world.

Because of the amount of mixture of half-truths, because of the quality of the rationalization they involve, Ego-Gods abound in the most unsuspected places — in the preachings of the moralists and the theologies of the theologians and the philosophies of the philosophers. They support an individual ego and sometimes a tribal ego and in turn are supported by them.

An Ego-God is bad enough but when he is codified in a theology, when he is officially adopted, he becomes worse. Ego-Gods arise from laws which have a universal operation but they have a personal equation and personal expression. They arise as a result of different pulls in the psyche of an individual. But when that problem is solved through purification and transcendence, those Gods also dissolve. But by becoming a part of an official, spiritual pantheon they acquire a new social dimension and acquire a new foothold in the individual psyche.

Perhaps, the original impulse of the theologians was well-intentioned. Seeing that man is subject to so many pulls and is likely to err in so many ways and give birth to so many false Gods on the way, they thought of helping him by having a close look on different versions of God and choose the best one and give it to him for his guidance. Thus they constructed a best possible version of God out of the experiences of the best persons or out of the experience of a person they knew to be the best and gave it to the laity for worship.

But the problem is not as simple as that. Firstly, the official version acquires its own vested interests. The official version has its officials who have their own interests to defend.

Secondly, the official version does not save a seeker from the errors of his mind. But what happens is that it replaces the errors of the individual with the errors of the officials.

Thirdly, whatever the version of God, official or non-official, it has yet to pass through the individual mind which remains there in all its intractability. The fact is that there is no short-cut to God-life. Ready-made definitions of God are no substitute to *sādhanā*.

Fourthly, the official version of God however exalted it may be intellectually may not conform to the experience of the saints out of which it is supposed to be constructed, nor to the psychic needs of those whom it is meant to help.

Let us take a concrete experience of many people on the spiritual path. Some of them have a high sense of inadequacy of this life; they also feel that their own efforts are in vain and that all doors are shut and they depend entirely on a saving grace. They see the effulgent light above and the depth of a darkness below and they find the gulf unbridgeable. Some power other than their own could alone save them from this fallen state. And it breeds in them a sense of resignation and surrender to a higher will. Many mystics have followed this path or rather have been led to this path inevitably by the compulsion of their own psyche.

Out of this experience, Christians have constructed certain doctrines like the Original Sin and Christ the Only Saviour. How they necessarily follow from this experience is difficult to say. In any case, other nations have done as well, spiritually speaking, without deriving the same doctrines. From the same experience other Christian sects have also derived some other supplementary doctrines like Predestination and Justification by Faith alone. In one rendering of this doctrine given by Luther himself, the worse you are the better it is for your faith. "Be a sinner and rejoice in Christ, who is the conqueror of sin, death and the world," he said. Many outside the Christian fold would regard these doctrines as preposterous and even within the Christian fold, they occasioned a good deal of argument and blood-bath in their own time.

Now we take up the next point. While they can hardly be fairly derived from the experiences of the saints, they may also not conform to the psychic needs of the seekers. Take Original Sin. It is hard on people who do not have a developed sense of sin. Therefore, under the influence of this dogma, many Christians feel uncomfortable when they do not feel sinful. Others overcultivate it, though it is hardly possible to do that in the Christian sense. They feel most soulful when they feel most sinful.

This has led to another institution called Confession with all its exaggerations. Confession has a kernel of truth. It is good if we can unburden our soul. It has a cleansing effect. But there is also a type of mind which can be called confessional. There is such a joy in confessing. Some confess to more sins than they have committed. The mind is very clever. It soon learns to extract pleasure and even profit out of its confessions. Women learnt to convey their love for the priest by confessing before them their love for their paramours. Confessions were a kind of love-letters to the priests.

Some people realised that the more they confessed, the more they rose in the estimation of their priests and fellow-man. There is a story very popular in the medieval ages written by Giovanni Boccaccio which depicts a hardened criminal who, even in his death-bed, could not help calculating the advantages of a good confession and made such a show of his contrition and confessed so superbly that he died in the odour of sanctity.

St. Teresa found that "there was more of self-love than desire of penance" in some sorrows.

There are scores of sects and groups at present which have turned confession by its individual members to great advantage. These sects have always some members who could be given the title of heroes or stakhanovites of confession. They tell the audience how terrible they were in the past, how they used to beat their mothers and cheat their comrades before they came to the sect to which they now belong or to the teacher who wrought this wonderful conversion in them. Now the whole of that past is left behind and now thanks to the teacher with whom they are now they have become models of virtue for the others to follow.

St. Augustine belonged to this type of confessionals. He made his confessions with great stage-effect and there was more persecution than piety in his confessions.

Chapter 5.3

One God of Theology

From a spiritual point of view, there is no sufficient reason for the religious feuds and competition that have been so great a part of human history. There is worship and seeking in the soul and in some at some stage, they become strong and they take to a more active spiritual search. Also people begin with different motives and they are at different stages of their search, but where is the reason for feud and competition?

The fact is that besides an upward pull, there is also a downward pull as we have seen. There is tendency for all spiritual seeking to get mixed up with lower motives. Truths also get instituitionalised and acquire interests of a different kind. In the passage of time, they also tend to lose their innerness and get externalized. They need renewal from time to time.

Also generally speaking, men do not go to Gods for a higher life but to seek justification for their wonted way of life, or seek to push their interests more actively. In human affairs, egos fight in the name of their Ego-Gods. Ego-Gods are projections which our desires and thoughts throw up constantly in self-justification.

Religious controversies have covered quite a range and it seems any alibi has been good enough for them. But there we shall take up only one controversy and that too briefly which centres round 'One God' and 'Many Gods'. Another facet of this theme is 'our True God' and 'their False Gods'.

'One God' has been the bee-in-the-bonnet of the religions of Semitic origin. It gets repeated emphasis in the Old Testament but there it is still not couched in theological terms. There it is simply assumed that the God the Jewish tribe worshipped was the true one and the Gods of other tribes were false. The Old Testament speaks of the Gods of the foreigners with soulful contempt as 'errors', or 'terrors', 'nothings' and even as 'dung', 'shames', abominations'. We do not have the records but we can safely assume that the sentiment was heartily reciprocated and the other tribes had similar epithets to describe the Jewish God. The rival Moabites had their 'one' God in Chemosh and the Ammonites in Milkom and so also the Hittites, Hivites and others. And also all of them thought that they were the 'chosen people' of their respective Gods.

These foreign Gods were also not 'abominations' as the Old Testament calls them. They incarnated great qualities and were capable of inspiring those qualities in their worshippers. For this we have the testimony of the Old Testament itself. It contains accounts of many saints who are of non-Jewish origin, persons like Noah and Job of superhuman qualities. Whatever Gods they worshipped, those must have been of great qualities.

By the time of Jesus, many changes had taken place in the Jewish world. It was no longer small and insular. It was open to all kinds of influences both from the East as well as the West. It had come into contact with Buddhism, from which, it is believed, it borrowed some of its ideas and monastic institutions. The Greek influence from the West also had a great fertilizing effect on its ideas. Politically, it had lost its freedom and belonged to the Roman Empire. This had created in the Jewish people its own despair and hopes.

Jesus belonged to this environment. Like many other Jews, he believed that there was 'one' God and even that "salvation belonged to the Jews".* But he was one of those who must experience spiritual truths in their person. He was invaded by a sense of holy presence which he simply called his Father. In the Gospel part of the New Testament, there is no controversy about One God and Many Gods, between Theism and Polytheism, between True God and False Gods. Jesus had no relish for intellectual, theological controversies. His simple message to the

---

*Bible, New Testament, John, 4.22.

people is to love their God with all their heart and to do unto others what they would like others to do unto themselves. The attempt was to bring a measure of inwardness into their worship.

But as we proceed from the Gospels to the Acts, we find a spiritual deterioration. There is less of direct experience and more of faith, less simplicity and more rhetoric. The atmosphere is more sentimental, more controversial. The emphasis is not on One God or even God but on Jesus Christ, on One Mediator. Christ replaces God. "There is one God, and one Mediator between God and men, the man Jesus Christ." To this two more mediators would be added in course of time: the Church and Virgin Mary. One God, one Mediator One Church, One Book, that was the motto of the people who were to overwhelm Europe in the coming centuries.

With the introduction and triumph of Pauline Christianity, a new element came into religious culture, a passionate narrowness, a fanatic faith, a doctrinaire intellectuality, a sanctimonious piety. As soon as Christianity became a state religion, old temples were destroyed, idols demolished, the practice of old religions banned. The suppression was systematic and sustained. Old Gods were not only dethroned but their very memory was stamped out.

Thanks to sustained, doctrinaire work, polytheism became a dirty word and even now when very few dirty words remain, polytheism is regarded to be a more primitive and less developed stage of religious consciousness.

Monotheism got another reinforcement in the rise of Islam. If anything, it was even more trenchant in its monotheism, and as intolerant. Christians used preachers and used force to facilitate an argument. Islam thought that argument was redundant and preached through conquest.

Though the two religions have a common source and share a common intolerance of the heathens and infidels, still they are no comfort to each other. In the beginning of its career, Islam met Christianity often enough in the battle-field; it destroyed the Christian empire in the West Asian countries and in North Africa. Now in our own times, with new riches and influence, Islam is becoming a threat to the Christian influence in Africa.

But considered doctrinally, through the two combined effects, Islamic and Christian, God became singular in number and masculine in gender. That it was not so always is attested by the whole history of religion. In its intuitive stage when religious truths have not become intellectual propositions, we find that religious consciousness has conceived of the deity in many different ways, as a single, or dual, or triune, or multiple principle; as one or many; as masculine, feminine or neuter.

For example, the very word 'God' was neuter in its original Teutonic home. But when this word was adopted by Christianity after the Teutons became Christians, the word became masculine. The word 'Allah' has a similar history. It is considered plural in origin by many scholars. Allah which means 'the god' derives from *ilah* which is plural. The Biblical 'Elohim' which is a name of the Jewish God is regarded a still further plural of *ilah*. So Elohim is doubly plural, a plural of a plural.

It is believed that Al-lāh (Allah) which is masculine had a feminine counterpart in Al-lāt, a goddess which is mentioned in the Quran. Al-lāt means no more than 'the Goddess', as Al-lāh means 'the God'. But Al-lāh was retained and Al-lāt was discarded. Was it because of a preference for the masculine principle over the feminine one?

Similarly, the Quran mentions another Goddess Al-Uzza which means 'the Mighty'. The feminine principle was pushed out but its masculine form was retained in Al-Aziz, one of the names of Allah. Again, was it because of a masculine predilection in a primarily patriarchal society? But this explanation will not do because they (Goddesses) were doing very well in that society before the advent of Muhammad. In fact, it is said that all the deities of the Meccans were feminine except Allah. They were regarded as the daughters of Allah. But Muhammad silenced his followers by arguing that how could God beget daughters which Arabs themselves were ashamed to do. Was it male chauvinism of the Prophet or his followers? More likely of the former.

The explanation of the deity as singular and masculine may have social causes and may have also social effects, some of them even good but the issue is different. Does it add to the psychic content? Does it make the spiritual content richer? And does it justify all the crusades, forced conversions, a systematic denial of God's revelation in other ways, vandalism, a billion-dollar industry of propaganda?

How is God the Father a superior concept spiritually than God the Mother? In some ways, and at least for some, the second may even be superior. Similarly, to express the deity in terms of a feminine principle may be more suitable for certain psyches and it may express certain intimacies better than a masculine understanding of the deity. Psychologists tell us that a man is both male as well as a female. He must derive these contents from a being or source which is both male and female. And many spiritual traditions in the world have done it.

Similarly, from a psychic point of view, a monotheistic approach is no better than a polytheistic one. In fact, a pluralistic approach conveys certain psychic truths better than a unitary approach. It introduces a principle of variety and choice and freedom which is good for human personality. It also makes allowance for variety of human nature, and variety of psychic needs.

If we look at history, it would be difficult to maintain that the doctrine of One God has represented a deeper mystic seeing. More often it has been an ideology, a rallying point, a slogan representing a bid for power, a spirit of domination.

But it has an appeal of its own. Its first ally is in the human intellect. There is an ingrained love of unity in the intellect though its unity is reductionist. The One God approach has also a certain usefulness. When Nature puts forth a larger human grouping, it supports it with a new deity which replaces older ones of the subgroups which now constitute the new collectivity.

Sometimes, One God approach is necessary to simplify spiritual life. The Gods may multiply to an extent that it becomes difficult to cope with them. They have to be brought to a manageable number. But it must be said that Christians and Muslims faced no such problem. Christianity inherited one God idea from its predecessor, the Jews. Similarly, the Meccans had only a limited number of Gods. If at all the problem belonged to their neighbours and they should have been left alone to solve it for themselves. But, perhaps, we must worry about a speck in the eye of a brother when we have a board in our own. This is our idea of brotherhood. But they took it upon themselves to solve their problem for them which they did by destroying their gods and lending them their own.

Again, sometimes it happens that a people forget the inner unity between their Gods and in such cases, the idea of one God is a most rough and ready sort of method of restoring that unity. If one God idea has a spiritual motive, it is this: it is a groping attempt to arrive at a principle of unity in the world and the Self. It is a mask of the Truth which Vedas declare as 'One Reality which the wise call by many names'. Upanishads say that 'All this is Brahma', or 'All this is inhabited by the Lord'.

One God is an outer sense of the idea of One Reality. In this sense, God is a unit, not a unity, a unit superior to and truer than other units. Unfortunately, it is in this sense that the doctrine has been accepted by its votaries. And in this sense, it has been a fertile source of religious fanaticism and bigotry.

Generally speaking, it is the prophets, reformers and men of action who have accepted this doctrine — for perhaps their mission was to create a well-knit nation out of loose tribal confederations — and not the mystics. Some one spoke of God being one in the presence of Eckhart; the saint snubbed him and said, "You prattle too much about God."

In the Muslim world, the word for the concept of One God is *tauḥīd*. As usual, the Muslim mystics did not quarrel with the utterances of Muhammad but tried to give them a deeper meaning. Al-Ghazzali, a theologian but also a mystic, who tried to reconcile Sufism with Prophetic Islam taught that the doctrine has four layers of meaning. The deepest layer of meaning consists in self-annihilation, in being able to see God in everything. When this happens, a man "sees the God everywhere. Multiplicity is not seen by him. This is the highest stage of *tauḥīd*." At this stage of *tauḥīd*, "one sees nothing besides the essence of God". He exhorts his followers to "know the One, look at the One, talk of Him alone, seek Him alone, eat of Him alone and like Him alone, and see nothing besides God in all affairs, and whatever you witness, consider it to be His manifestation".

How close to the Vedanta and how much different from that spirit of Islam which has carried fire and sword to distant lands in the name of One True Allah and destroyed local temples and places of worship and forcibly converted people.

This rendering of *tauḥīd* means that there is only God, Brahma, and no world and no Gods of Ego and desire and success that the worldlings worship. Al-Ghazzali is giving expression to this idea when he says, "If one repeats the Kalima — *la ilāha illā 'llāhu* (There is no god but Allah), and yet cherishes the love of the world, his repetition of Kalima is false."

One God means 'love of God alone'; and denial of multiple Gods means denial of love for the things of the world. This sense of *tauḥīd* is also brought out in the Bible, when Jesus is taken out to the peak of a mountain and shown the world and the nations in all their glory and offered sovereignty over them, but Jesus replied, "The scriptures say, Worship only the Lord God and obey only Him."

That this deeper meaning of *tauḥīd* fails to prevail is easy to understand. The prophetic rendering may not be deep but it is closer to human mind and emotions. It provides a ready rallying point. It easily divides people into friends and foes, the faithful and the infidels, a division easy to understand and quite heart-warming.

Also it is easier to understand God in terms of self-assertion than in terms of self-annihilation of which Al-Ghazzali speaks. It is difficult to conceive of a God as an indwelling spirit, seated in the heart of every person; but it is easier to conceive of him sitting in his heaven and speaking to his followers through an accredited and legated person, his beloved Son or his Messenger. It is difficult to conceive of God as 'One Reality which the wise call by many names', or to 'see His essence in everything' but it is easier to think of him as a powerful potentate out on a crusade humbling his rivals who pretend to his throne. Semitic religions claim that their God is a Person. Probably, yes. But in practice, He is only an anthrop, a man but of very huge proportions. There was a book "Estimation of the Heights" which was once very popular with the Jews. It gave the measurements of the different members and limbs of God, his eyes, ears, lips, beard etc. It also declared: "Blessed is he who knows these measurements, for he has a share in the world to come."

History shows one very interesting point: that countries like Egypt, Babylonia, Greece, Rome, China, India, where there was a multiplicity of Gods, were relatively free from large-scale religious persecution. There might have been other evils — superstitions, coarseness, illiberalism — but not mass-scale religious persecution. That is a phenomenon bequeathed to the world by Semitic religions. Is there something in these religions which promotes intolerance?

I think, it is their doctrine of One True God. It fills them with self-righteousness. This has inspired them not only to persecute heathens and infidels but has also not made them overindulgent towards their own dissentient sects. Heresy-hunting has been pretty cruel.

In order to guard against religious intolerance, we should modify our approach: we should purify our worship rather than impose our definition of the deity. If the quality of our worship is pure, it would be received by a deity who is equally pure. Otherwise, it goes to feed the Asuras, the Ego-Gods.

In the spiritual realm, there are two categories: God and your neighbour. And correspondingly there are two ways of looking at them: you could look at God through the neighbour or the neighbour through your God. In the first approach, you will think that if your neighbour has the same needs and constitution and impulses as you have, then his God in whatever way he is worshipped and by whatever name he is called must mean the

166 / MEDITATIONS

same to him as your God means to you. In short, it means that if your neighbour is as good as you are, so must be his God as good as yours.

But if you look at your neighbour through your God then it leads entirely to a different outlook. Then you say that if your God is good enough for you, it should be good enough for your neighbour too; and if he is not worshipping the same God in the same way, he must be worshipping a Devil and he qualifies for liquidation and conversion.

The first approach promotes tolerance though it gives plurality of Gods and varieties of modes in worship. The other approach gives One God and one mode of worship but breeds intolerance. Here one idea tries to generalize itself through conquest and calls itself the truly one, the truly universal.

There is a Bible called "The Greatest in Love" which has been sent to millions of homes in India free. Its language has been modernized but it has lost nothing in fanaticism. In fact, the more bigoted portions are underlined. Among the several pictures it contains, there is one of American Indian boys and girls. It is accompanied by three captions which we give here.

"They have retained their identity. A separate nation within a nation. The American Indian.

"Yet all are the same before God. There is only one way for all men to be accepted by God.

"And we can all be saved in the same way by coming to Christ, no matter who we are."

This is what the Christian churches mean by their claim to universality, by equality of all before God. It means denial of other ways, denial of different ways of intuiting the deity, and denial of different ways of approaching him.

In the long history of Christendom, there have been lots of controversies, many of them lethal ones, on all kinds of points mostly more subtle than substantial, but there was never a dispute about the superiority of Christianity and inferiority of other religions. All were agreed on this point. All believed that non-

Christian nations lived in spiritual darkness and they should be shown the true path of salvation.

Similarly, even during recent centuries, hundreds of thousands of missionaries must have gone out to heathen lands. Many of them were great teachers and scholars and men of great industry and curiosity. They learnt native languages, customs, wrote works of grammar and translated important texts of native religions but it is seldom that they thought they too could learn a few things from the religions of the natives in religious matters. It was very rare if any one thought that the Eastern spiritual wisdom was as great as their own. The least of the missionaries was prepared to teach the best of the orientals so far as religious truth was concerned. Such is the smug self-satisfaction of Christianity.

The recognition and respect for Eastern wisdom and religions came from nominal Christians, from great humanists and universalists like Voltaire and from men of reason and science who form quite an influential section of the Western society today. An average, simple Westerner is also more open to appeal of thoughts from different countries. There is even a wind of change amongst deeply religious Christians, particularly those who are not connected with the missionary activities. All this is a welcome development and it is in keeping with the spirit of the age which demands universality and breaking down of the barriers of prejudice and insularity.

Chapter 5.4

God-Experience at the Levels
of *Manas* and *Vijñāna*

We have said that *prāṇa*, *manas*, *buddhi* are instruments of the soul. It is veiled by them but it is also revealed by them. They obscure it but through them it also rediscovers itself and expresses itself. We have seen how the soul is obscured by its instruments; we have also said that the purpose of different *sādhanās* and Yogas is to purify them. We shall now say something about how soul-knowledge or God-knowledge is expressed through them.

Probably, we aim at the same God but we establish our contact differently. This happens because of two reasons. Firstly, because we have different assortments of these instruments. They are differently distributed amongst us and they bring with them their own motive and impulsion and characteristics. Some react to the suffering of the world, others to its flux, some to its otherness, some to its mechanicalness. Some react emotionally, others intellectually. Some seek a principle of purity in their actions and motives, others seek a principle of delight in things and in themselves, and yet others seek a principle of knowledge of things and the Self. These differences arise partly because of the difference in the instruments which an individual has at his disposal.

Also when a contact is established with the soul, its outer expression is defined by the instrument through which it is expressed. As we have seen, these instruments have their own colour and flavour which they impart to different soul-expressions.

For example, let us see God-experience as it is expressed in different scriptures. The difference does not arise merely because one experience could be deeper than the other, but we are here mainly speaking of the difference that arises because of the difference in the medium through which that experience is expressed.

As we have seen, the tendency of the *manas* is to particularise while that of *vijñāna* is to universalise. So when you experience God at the *manas* level, you experience him as a Father or as a Mother, or as a Beloved. But at the *vijñāna* level, the experience comes to you as Fatherhood or Motherhood of God. At the *manas* level, God is my father, my mother; at the level of *vijñāna*, he is the father of all, mother of all. At this level you experience the divinity in its attribute of fatherhood and motherhood. At the level of *manas*, you see God in a personal relationship; you see your mother, your father. At the level of *vijñāna*, you see the mother of the Universe of which you are a part.

It is not that the *vijñāna*-experience is diluted, only it is more tranquil. And it is not that the *vijñāna*-experience of God is more impersonal and that of the *manas* level more personal. Rather it is more personalized and the relationship too is more particularized. On the *vijñāna* level too the relationship is very deep and intimate. Nothing could be more intimate than to realize God as the very Self of the Universe. At the level of *manas*, it is a personalized relationship between a personalized God and the person of the devotee. At the *vijñāna* level, it is a tranquil realization.

Can we illustrate it from an example, borrowed from a more familiar field? If *manas* were to 'know' the Gravitation, it will feel it as the earth attracting an apple. On the other hand, *buddhi* will know it as a law, as a principle of things.

It is not that there are different Gods to experience but it is the same God experienced differently at different levels and reflected differently through different mediums. When God is experienced through a predominantly sense-mind, it has sensuous qualities of form, colour and sound. If animals have a God,* there is no doubt that they must be experiencing him differently.

---

*Walt Whitman says they have and a great one too. "They do not sweat and whine about their condition. They do not lie awake in the dark and weep for their sin. Not one is dissatisfied, not one is demented with the mania of owning things. Not one kneels to another, nor to his kind that lived thousands of years ago, not one is respectable or unhappy over the whole earth." *Song of myself.*

The God of the scriptures of the religions of the Semitic origin is predominantly a *manas*-God. In the Bible, there is such a constant reference to the eyes and ears and hands of God and he is seeing and hearing and grasping and walking so often that it has troubled many theologians and they have tried to explain those references away. There is also no doubt that in some cases at least, the God-experience is of a more intellectual kind but the language and the expression used is of the sensuous type. Yet, in spite of this, these scriptures retain a uniqueness of their own which can only be explained by the fact that their God is *manas*-God.

On the other hand, the God of more mystic and Upanishadic tradition is predominantly *vijñāna*-God, even when, sometimes, sensuous imagery is used. For illustration, take the Upanishads. There the flavour is different. Firstly, the name for the object of pursuit is not God but Brahman and Atman which savour of *vijñāna*. Secondly, God does not see and hear here. It is not that God's power of seeing and hearing are denied. But the idea is expressed differently. 'It' is not that which is seen by the eyes or heard by the ears but it is that by which the Eyes see and by which the Ears hear. "That which is unexpressed by speech but with which speech is expressed, that which is not thought by thought but by which thought is thought, which sees not with the eyes but with which one sees the eyes," declares the *Kenophishad*.

This distinction will also explain the difference between the teachers in the Upanishads and the teachers in the Bible and the Quran. In the Upanishads, the teachers are seers of a truth; in the Bible and the Quran they are carriers of a message. In the Upanishads, they are seers; in the latter tradition, they are prophets.

Following from the above, one finds another difference. In the Upanishads, one finds the names of many teachers, some of them of the highest attainment and realizations. But they do not occupy the centre of the stage. Their name is mentioned once and then they retire from the stage; it is now the teaching that takes over, the message speaks. In the Upanishadic literature, it will be difficult to find an 'I' being used by the teachers. In the Biblical literature, the atmosphere is different. The messenger occupies the centre of the stage. The message becomes a personal matter of the messenger. He must push it, promote it in all ways. The teacher in the Upanishads is a *vijñāna*-teacher; in the Bible he is a *manas*-teacher.

It is also for this reason that we know so little about the life, circumstances and moods of the Upanishadic teachers. The current explanation offered is that because the Indian soul is ahistorical. I think the explanation is true though it is meant in a deprecatory sense and though it is part of a larger explanation. There is something in the soul itself which seeks ahistoricity. Some souls seek *vijñāna*-truths which by nature do not have liveliness and colour of the *manas*-truths.

This is true even on a more mental plane. For example, you may know all about Newton, the bench, the tree and the falling apple and it may have its appeal to a certain part of the mind but it will not satisfy man's more abstract intelligence.

We again repeat that it is not a question of superiority and inferiority. It is a question of trying to understand different expressions of God as they come to us reflected in different mediums and channels of the mind. In man, there is a good deal of the vital, sensous and mental element which must find fulfilment in God and a good deal of soul-life must express itself through this element.

And it is a vital expression, an enriching expression, a life-giving expression. And it is not only one of the purest but also the most popular. No nation or race can do without it and there must be a constant effort to purify this expression.

But a more mystic bent in the same nation has also given us another tradition, a tradition of a *vijñāna*-God, and *vijñāna*-teaching. And yet the two traditions are part of the same truth, the truth of establishing a most authentic relationship with the Brahman, with God, with Self, a relationship which is in keeping with a man's mental, moral and intellectual assets, a relationship in which he will feel most at home. Sometimes, under the impression that a *manas*-God is superior to *vijñāna*-God, there are people of great intelligence trying to be men of faith, trying to believe in a particularized, personalized God, and also vice versa. But this does not help. Men of *buddhi* should try to seek a God of *vijñāna* though for a time the path may lie through a God of faith and if *buddhi* is not pure one may arrive at a God of theology rather than of *vijñāna*.

St. Augustine was a man of great intellect trying to be a man of faith. And apparently he succeeded. But only apparently. For his intellect had no universality; it was contentious and it sought a faith, a passionate cause, a *casus belli* which he found. It sought the joy of self-abasement before a new God and the thrill of its skilful employment in demolishing old Gods.

Section 6

Human Psychology
vis-à-vis
Spiritual Seeking

Chapter 6.1

Pleasure and Pain

There are two kinds of people. One kind is self-centered — all their concerns, their pain and pleasure revolve round themselves. On the one hand, while they will not see a beam in their own eyes but espy a mote in the eyes of a brother, on the other hand, they will make a mountain out of their little suffering and think little of the pain of others however great. Even if they had a pin-prick, they would think it was the end of the world. On the other hand, even if there was a holocaust around, only that part which affects them personally will move them; about the rest they feel unconcerned.

But there are also people of a different kind though a small minority. They think little of their own losses and profits — in fact, they are hardly conscious of them. But anybody else's suffering, even if he were a total stranger, becomes their own suffering. They may not have the means and intelligence to remove that suffering but they suffer by a kind of sympathetic participation.

Generally, a man is an amalgam of these two tendencies, the self-regarding one being more predominant. But even the most hardened ones cannot do without some elements of sympathy — they will shrink like dry wood. Sympathy has a life-value; its total lack spells death.

On the other hand, if a person had more thoughts of other than of himself, he would really have a different kind of personality though apparently he looks like the rest. He really embodies a certain kind of universality and inhabits a different kind of world.

Such persons are freaks or probably pointers to a future development. But for the kind of individuality Nature has yet evolved and in the kind of world we live, certain amount of insensitivity to the pain and pleasures of others is inevitable and biologically necessary. It is a necessary part of the half-evolved state in which our individuality has grown. We hear the stories of saints on whose bodies were found the marks of blows inflicted on other men and animals. With that kind of sympathy and participative life, how many would live for any length of time in this world full of knocks and whippings dealt not by Nature but by fellow-men? If we could enter into the pain of even animals, corn and vegetables, we could not even eat and drink. And what is true of pain is actually true of joy. If everyone's joy became our own we should burst and die of it.

So a certain kind of insensitivity to the joys and sorrows of others has a certain survival-value and is a necessary concomitant of the earth-consciousness in which we live. But those who see in their heart a different possibility and in whom has awakened a seeking for a larger consciousness, this insensitivity will not do. It is irksome to them and it appears to be a denial of their deeper truth of life. Fortunately, as we grow in consciousness and our sympathies widen, we also develop a mind and body vehicle of a subtler material appropriate to the new level of consciousness, capable of holding and expressing the larger and more participative life of the soul — its greater joys and sorrows.

Meanwhile, the body and mind vehicle is good enough for the joys and sorrows of an ego-centered mentality. Most of these joys and sorrows originate in what the Buddhists call *sparśa*, or contact of the mind with things. They arise when "the senses move among their objects", to put it in the language of the Gita. These contacts are always accompanied by pleasure and pain and we want either to repeat or to avoid them. The attraction for pleasure develops into a desire, a hankering, a coveting, a grasping. Aversion develops into resentment, ill-will, wrath. Thus they weave a destiny around us and we are caught in their web. We sow the seeds of desire and reap the harvest of repeated births and deaths.

Beyond these joys and sorrows arising out of *sparśa* are those which originate in the Ego which are even more raw. Our contact with the world is partial and indirect, established through the five senses. So we know the joys for what they are worth of seeing and hearing, tasting, touching etc. But there are even inferior joys than these — the pleasure people derive from ill-will, from dominating, from inflicting pain and indignities on others, the pleasure of power, of despotising, tyrannising, of dictating and controlling, of censuring and hurting, pleasure of bragging and boasting. There are also more sophisticated pleasures of attitudinizing, of playing the wise, the humble, the pious, the helpful. There is also a malicious pleasure which derives from the pain of others.

The same with our pain. It is equally raw. The pain that Nature and ill-health inflict on us is only a fraction of the pain that fellow-men inflict and that too is nothing compared to the pain that a man's own ego inflicts. In the *Mahābhārata*, there is a story which tells us of a hundred ways of feeling miserable. There are not as many ways of feeling cheerful. We feel miserable because our advice is not heeded; because our worth is not recognized; because while obviously we have the talent others have the success; because while we help others, others do not help themselves; because everywhere there is the rule of the mediocrity while talented ones like us are passed over; because while we deserved more and were capable of more, we were just ignored, set aside; because people are plotting, conspiring to topple us down; because our friends do not praise us enough — why, many of them behave even worse than the enemies. For all these and other sundry causes, a man can feel miserable.

A man feels pain not only in his pain but more fundamentally in the pleasure of others. Behind our pain, there is a deep-seated ill-will, *dvesha,* wrath.

Besides being raw and unregenerate we notice another quality of pain and pleasure at this level: that they are more of the nature of pain than of pleasure. If we ponder deeply, then we find that even our pleasures at heart are woven with pain. They are born in pain and lead to pain. They are painful in their roots as well as fruits, painful in their ancestry and painful in their progeny. In the language of the Pātañjala Yoga, they are painful in three ways; they are painful in their results, painful in their very satisfaction;

and they leave behind latent tendencies which cause future misery.

While pleasures use their bait, we have little capacity for them. At the end, they leave us exhausted with our regrets. In the very midst of enjoyment, we know that those pleasures are ephemeral and will not last long. We also know that just at that very moment, others are having more of the same pleasures — and what could be more sorrowful than that?

Eventually, the pleasures are gone, the capacity for pleasures is gone. Only a painful memory remains, a nostalgia for good old days that one knows will never come back again. Everything is gone except a grouse, a lament, a regret, a painful memory, a hankering, an unquenched thirst, a proclivity to repeat those pleasures woven with pain. Sages tell us that this proclivity gives rise to repeated births and deaths. When the present body falls, the seed of hankering creates another body. The law operates with the inevitability of doom, with the inexorable fiat of a destiny. Of this tree of life, old and new, nescience and hankering are the roots, attraction and aversion are its trunk, pleasures stolen from pain are its branches and buds, pains, regrets, lamentation, envy are its blossoms and bitter fruits.

We have spoken above of only unregenerate pain and pleasure, pain and pleasure of people who are self-centered. These affections are fruits of a lower level of consciousness and they, in turn, keep a man bound to that level. But not all pain and pleasure are of that kind. There is also a variety which is liberating and spiritually rewarding.

Suffering is an important dimension of man. There is something lacking in a man who has not known suffering. His life is unauthentic. He has not gone into the depths of his being nor has he felt the touch of the Real. Suffering is more than an unpleasant sensation. It is a knock of reality. There is a kind of suffering which reflects in some strange way the pain and anguish of existence itself. Suffering is more than a feeling; it is the secret language of a greater life. It has not merely to be borne with patience, it has also to be understood in all its transcendence.

The very first thing to be understood about suffering is that it is not necessarily a penalty for undesirable actions done in the past. It could be so but that is only one way of looking at things and one aspect of the problems. There is also another angle and another aspect. According to this angle, suffering is meant to help man in his onward progress.

Pain helps man at every step. In the very beginning of his moral and spiritual life, it purifies his pleasure and gives him a measure of self-control. If man was capable of pursuing pleasures alone, his life and pleasures would continue to be coarse. He would continue seeking pleasures of an unregenerate, half-awakened consciousness. It is the intervention of pain which makes him seek a different kind of pleasure, a pleasure untouched by pain. It also makes him seek a principle which is more than that of pleasure, a principle of the good, *śreyas*. It also teaches him a measure of self-control. He learns not to pursue pleasure too precipitately for it is intervened by pain and he also learns to bear pain which is inevitable. Thus pain becomes the foundation of a new moral and spiritual consciousness.

It is also pain in us that awakens us to the pain of others and therefore to others. Those who lead a life of pleasure are hardly awake to others or even to themselves. There is no motive, no challenge. Of course, pain by itself could teach nothing if there was no supporting higher consciousness. Without this consciousness, it would only be a brute, animal pain borne dumbly and inflicted thoughtlessly. But given that consciousness, suffering is a great activating force, a great catalyst, a great opener.

Some etymologists derive the word 'agony' from a Sanskrit verbal root '*ag*', to drive, to impel, move, from which we have also the English word 'agent', and according to some even the Sanskrit word '*agni*', fire. So agony is not just a passive feeling; it is a great driving power, an activator, a quickener and an agent of a spiritual consciousness. It burns up all the false that surrounds the soul and quickens it and awakes it.

Even in Buddhism where suffering is generally passively

conceived and is only one of the twelve terms of the law of 'Dependent Origination' (which describes how man is caught in the wheel of rebirth, how one term binds a man to the next, equally mechanical), there is however one place where the role of suffering as a liberating force is acknowledged. In *Saṁyutta Nikāya*, we meet a different law of 'Dependent Origination', which works for liberation. In this, suffering does not lead to *jarā-maraṇa*, old age and death, as it does elsewhere; on the other hand, it leads to faith and starts a new cycle. "Becoming is causally associated with grasping, birth (*jāti*) with becoming, sorrow with birth, faith with sorrow, joy with faith, rapture with joy, serenity with rapture, happiness with serenity, concentration with happiness, the knowledge and vision into things as they really are, passion-lessness (*virāga*) with disenchantment, liberation with passion-lessness, knowledge of extinction (of intoxicants, *āsavas*) with liberation" (2.3 of *Saṁyutta Nikāya*, C.A.F. Rhys Davids and F.L. Woodward.)

It should be kept in mind that *duḥkha* or suffering in Indian thought is not merely psychological but is ontological. It has a metaphysical, transcendental connotation. It is not personal *duḥkha* but a name of a quality of that unregenerate life which has to be exceeded. It is name of a life conceived without a spiritual dimension, without God. The Gita calls this life 'the abode of suffering', *duḥkhālayam*. In that suffering of man which is spiritually significant, this 'world-woe' forms its heart. It works in him as a feeling rather than as a fully-formed thought or knowledge. It becomes knowledge only when one spurred by suffering takes to a life of self-reflection and self-understanding. Meanwhile, there is a vale of tears and a dark night of the soul.

The Gita tells us that there are four kinds of people who take to God-life. Of them, the afflicted (*ārta*) are the very first ones. The rest in their order are the seekers of knowledge (*jijñāsu*), the seekers of truth as it is (*arthārthī*), and the seekers of wisdom (*jñānī*).

The Gita's division can also be put in the language of the four Aryan Truths of the Buddhists.

The first impulse to the path of Yoga is sorrow as the Gita says. Sorrow is also the first great spiritual realization according to Buddhists. But from the first, he must go over to the next truth. He must become a *jijñāsu*. He must realize that sorrow is not without a cause. It is not accidental, nor uncaused, nor unmerited, nor without antecedents as some of the contemporaries of Lord Buddha preached. The experience of sorrow is a great help but by itself it is not enough. Simply because a man suffers, does not lead him to spiritual enlightenment. The second step must follow. He must become a truth-seeker.

Then the third step comes. One becomes an *arthārthī*, a seeker of the path of liberation, a path which leads to the extinction of all suffering. He must realize that this path exists, that there is end to suffering. With the fourth step, he becomes a *jñānī*. The eyes of wisdom open up; he knows the path that leads to the end of sorrow.

Like sorrow, happiness too can be liberating though in certain spiritual traditions it is a suspect. They emphasise more the role of guilt, confession, expiation, self-immolation, conflict and crisis. There are people who feel a certain sense of psychological depth and emotional richness in tears and the more mournful they are, the more spiritual they feel.

True, there is a level of happiness which just like sorrow is very shallow. The Gita says that there are three kinds of happiness or *sukha*. The lowest one is *tāmasika*. It accompanies a life which is predominantly animal, which is ruled by the law of sleep, indolence, thoughtlessness, *nidrālasyapramādottham*. It is a life of strong passions and possession. The second level is *rājasika* in which senses follow their objects for their immediate pleasure without regard to the fact that it may be deleterious in its future results. The third one is *sāttvika* which is also the best. Here a man follows what is good rather than what is merely pleasant — the path of *śreyas* distinguished from the path of the *preyas* of which the *Kaṭhopnishad* speaks.

Buddhists also tells us that joys have many qualities and many depths. Not mentioning the bliss of the state of *nirvāṇa*, which is happiness of the liberated ones, there is also a liberating joy which belongs to lower states. There is '*kāma-sukha*', joys that belong to the sensuous sphere, and there is '*dhyāna-sukha*', joys that belongs to different stages of *dhyāna* or meditation.

Of the *kāma-sukha* itself, there are two varieties. One variety is demeaning, animalizing. It refers to the lustful, hateful, wicked life whose fruits are bitter. But the other variety refers to the happiness of a life lived in virtue, truthfulness, detachment, contentment. This happiness is ennobling and it prepares one for the joys of a meditative life. In fact, no one can enter the meditation-sphere unless one has lived a self-controlled life. In Buddhist thought, *dhyāna* comes from an inner-satisfaction of a life nobly lived and of a virtuous ideal of life well followed. If this self-satisfaction is not there and the mind is full of regrets, concentration is not possible.

Here is a point of difference between this approach and the approach of some neo-teachers. The new approach says, Have no regrets whatever be your life and ideal. The old approach said, Have a life and ideal noble enough to cause no regrets.

The next are joys of the four stages of *dhyāna* of which we shall only notice here a few characteristics without going very much into them. With every stage, these joys grow in power, intensity, purity and tranquility. Increasingly, they bathe you, swathe you, soak you, interpenetrate you, flood you. They also become increasingly more inner, more mental. We must also notice another quality of their's which is relevant to the discussion here. They are self-liberating, self-transcending. The joy of a particular stage itself reveals its own inadequacy, points to a still deeper joy of a purer quality of the next stage. Here it is unlike the pleasures of the lower state of consciousness where their coarseness and inadequacy are brought out, as we have seen, by the intervention of the principle of pain. But here, *sukha* itself has the seeds of self-liberation from its lower versions.

There is also another very striking point here. While Buddhism so much emphasizes the Aryan Truth of *duḥkha*, its *sādhanā* is mostly s*ukha-sādhanā*; its Yoga or spiritual discipline involves the practice and cultivation of *sukha*, of joy. There is no anguish here, except in the background. The path itself is joyous till it leads to the bliss of *nirvāṇa* when everything again is regenerated, reconciled, made whole.

As one moves to these peaks, one finds that the fountain source of one's joy is one's own self. Satisfaction does not derive from contact with things but comes wholly from within. Of course, nobody is a stranger here and everybody is a part of oneself. A man feels the joy of communion, the joy that others are just there and we are their comrades. And since he does not want to become anything different from what he is, he feels the joy of just *being*. He is established in his Self, *ātmanishṭha*; he takes delight in his Self, *ātmarāma*. One knows suffering no more.

It is only in certain forms of Vaishnavas *sādhanā* that the suffering is not totally abolished. The pang of separation does not dissolve in the joy of union. The two are retained in a Reality which is both, in which Krishna himself becomes Radha in order to relish and be relished by his own otherness.

Morality

What is morality? It is difficult to be precise about it because one definition could be contradicted by another and also because the same action could be done with different motives and there are different ways and even motives for looking at the same thing and action. But these difficulties are only logical. In real life, moral actions are quite recognizable though not precisely measurable and may even fail to conform to outer moral criterions. Moral life is a most important part of human life though it is found badly and some say even inextricably mixed up with lower motives.

Though morality is such an important fact and principle of human life and growth but if we look within us a little more closely we find that a good deal of our psychic life is amoral. For example, a pleasure in the pursuit of its fulfilment is amoral. It may be held in self-control or check but only if it is frustrated by circumstances or there is a greater pleasure to pursue. But in themselves pleasures know no other law than the law of their self-satisfaction.

Pleasure and pain are fundamental to human nature and according to psychologists even the first, rudimentary sensations have pleasurable and painful tones. A man's instinct is to seek the pleasurable and avoid the painful and at this level it is also a *good*. The psychological theory of hedonism provides the first theory of morals also. The moral is that which brings pleasure and avoids pain. Thus by avoiding pain, it follows its good by keeping away from such objects as fire, etc. Through pain and pleasure, Nature provides, at least, in initial stages, a rough and ready criterion of what is good and what is bad. The criterion is automatic in its working on a faculty like reason which is not yet developed and which is also not sure and certain in its working.

But reality is not a cornucopia. It may fail to supply satisfaction to many of man's pleasures. Also one man's pleasure may be another man's pain. Therefore, the society approves some pleasures and disapproves of others. But to an individual wedded to the pursuit of his pleasures the social penalties are merely additional pains which he should avoid. So the law of his moral action is still to pursue pleasure but without being found out.

This does not always work and the society too has a few tricks up in its sleeves. It demands a more voluntary submission from the individual. Social approval and disapproval become internalized in the individual in the form of a Conscience. Conscience is society's policeman posted in the very mind of man.

These theories about the child and the Conscience are not deep enough and they do not have the right ring and they convey the ethos of a materialist outlook. The child is not a devil in pursuit of its carnal pleasures; it has a natural trust in and affection for the parents and it imbibes and absorbs from them a good deal including elements of social ethics. The parents too are not scheming against their children and they try to give them the best they know. Similarly, a Conscience is more than an internalized constable. It is an element of higher life.

All this is true. A child's pleasures are innocent. Their pursuit becomes pernicious only later on in the grown-up people when they do it without scruples and without regard to others. We may also accept the above theory of the Conscience for a limited purpose however inadequate it is. For it brings out an important point into the forefront: there are many people who know no other Conscience except the one which approves and disapproves on behalf of the society. It is not always bad and sometimes it also helps. But it means that a deeper law of wider sympathy and mutual life and inner purity has not awakened in them yet.

When this deeper law is not awakened, Conscience is not merely a voice of the society, it is also the voice of one's self-regarding impulses whose task in the pursuit of their pleasure is to appear correct to others and even to oneself. This gives birth to a good deal of rationalization open and concealed, a good deal of sanctimonious hypocrisy, pious fraud, tongue in cheek talks. It is to this mixture in morality we referred to in the beginning of the chapter.

The Conscience is not merely a voice of our desire, it also learns to take pleasures in its own hardness and morbidities. It gnaws at the heart for its good as well as for its evil. It becomes an instrument of our ego.

It is very purifying to become aware of the lower side of one's nature without its masks. If one learns to look more closely into one's impulses, motives and desires and ambitions, one will find that they are very self-regarding. They have a remarkable single-mindedness and they pursue their aims without scruples, regrets or remorse. They are in one sense blind but they have a prudence and cleverness of their own. They can wait for their opportunity. They know when they can get their fulfilment. Meanwhile they stay patient and resist exposure. They can put on masks. For example, give aggression a chance and it would operate with perfect self-justification, with the clearest Conscience. But if it knows that it would be opposed and would meet a check, it could look perfectly innocuous, appear an embodiment of a perfect Christian charity. It would appear unthinkable and most unfair to link the idea of an aggressive intent with so charitable and peaceable a disposition.

Grosser forms of dispositions are easy to tame. A man will find it beneath his dignity to indulge in too open forms of avarice, robbery and violence. They do not agree with his self-image. But when the same impulses put on masks, come disguised in principles they are more difficult to control and even to detect.

Here at this level, morality is not for self-improvement but for preaching, for finding faults with others. When we say that a certain man's actions are bad, what we generally means is that he should not do unto us what we shall like to do unto him.

Indian thought has approached the problem in a somewhat different way. Though one meets the highest morality in the Upanishads and the Gita but there is not a single 'thou shalt' and 'thou shalt not' in them. They discuss the problem psychologically, in terms of levels of consciousness and their growth, in terms of a widening vision and the release of *prāṇa-śakti* form its present state of self-limitation.

The fact is that every level of consciousness has its own corresponding morality and Conscience. A deluded and unregenerate consciousness has a deluded morality, probably a clever but yet unregenerate morality. Therefore, morality cannot be taught in the ordinary sense of the term; and morality does not consist in certain rules of conduct given by certain superior beings or even by certain chosen Incarnations or Messengers which can now be prescribed for the laity and followed by them under the supervision of the priests and the theologians. Every stage has its own morality and its own capacity for further morality. One can not buy one's morality ready-made; one has to imbibe it, absorb it organically as the plants absorb sunshine and water; one has to grow into a different person; one's centre of consciousness and motivation has to change. One has to grow into a greater vision and power and capacity for a greater morality.

Fortunately, this is possible. For morality is not God's commandments but is the very imperative of the soul, its inner urge and its ultimate fulfilment. In fact, when illumined by the soul, every impulse wants to shed its lower expression and wants to come into its own. The *prāṇa* wants to give up its desire and restlessness and the *manas* wants to give up its impotent rage, anger and debilitating prejudice. In a man seeking a lower expression for its impulses, there is automatically a sense of dissatisfaction, deviation and unfulfilment. On the other hand, when one does or desires something which is in keeping with the inner purity of the soul, one feels a sense of authenticity and fulfilment and rejuvenation. He feels expanded, feels as if something has been added to him.

By becoming increasingly aware of this inner guidance and identifying oneself with it, one strengthens it. In fact, one should practise self-awareness. One should learn to watch oneself without approval and disapproval. This helps in many ways. There are many things which work furtively, but when we become aware of them, when they come into the light of the consciousness, they lose their power. As we grow in the power of self-awareness, we shall also be able to recognize many positive factors in our inner life which are ordinarily crowded out off the stage by more clamouring and grosser ones and therefore not seen at all. The practice of self-awareness helps the growth of a 'spectator' consciousness which is a great spiritual power in moulding life. It cuts at the very root of the life of attachment.

One could also start from another angle, from below as it were. In the very midst of the kind of life a man leads, he should build up an aspiration for a life of purity and keep the vision of a higher life before him. In this way, sooner or later, the soul-principle will come to the fore and take up the guidance of life. That will spare many griefs and pitfalls.

There is a tendency these days to express the ethical in terms of the uncomfortable. Morality is associated with guilt and temptation and expiation. It is not unusual to see some people struggling to be moral but in the process becoming morbid and aggressive. But true morality comes when there is "delight in things honourable", as Plato defines virtue.

Life of an individual is enmeshed in desires and egohood. To come out of it is painful. Therefore, an initial struggle cannot be ruled out altogether but its rigour can be softened by exercising understanding rather then a stubborn self-will. There is tendency to fight it out with one's nature, to grapple with one's individual impulses and temptations. The path is a rocky one even wnen in some cases it succeeds. Moreover, it is no path to offer to those one loves.

The larger teachings therefore suggest a more understanding path. They say it is not a question of individual impulses and overcoming them. These impulses or their like, in one form or another, inevitably belong to a particular level of consciousness. A higher consciousness will automatically give a higher morality. For this change, we need to establish the rule of worship, service, desirelessness, and equal-mindedness in our heart. And as their domination increases, a new power and vision, a new sympathy and fellow-feeling, a new self-transcendence would be born in the soul and the character of the morality and Conscience would also change. The older motives would not do and they would fall along with their masks and pretentions. The truth of an inner discrimination would replace an outer rule of conduct. A hidden soul would take charge of our lives, a soul whose very life is purity, who by nature is *rita-bhuj* (nourished by truth), whose very attributes are dedication, service, justice and fairness.

Chapter 6.3

Love: Human and Divine

Some have turbulent passions, red-hot, volcanic. Sex is generally violent and some have more than a moderate share. Spiritual culture has taken notice of this fact. It has tried to tame it, moderate it, sublimate it through different methods. Some methods or rather stages involve denial; others preach exhaustion through indulgence; and yet others provide regulatory channels. In most cases, it is a combination of different methods. The problem is not considered as a mere moral question or as a matter of simple do's and don'ts but is treated psychologically.

When love is concupiscence, a pure physical hunger, appetite, voracity, a form of insatiety, rapacity and aggrandisement, it means the animal life is very strong and the spiritual life is not yet for such a man.

But there is also an ardour and zeal, warmth and solicitude in the heart which has a libidinal expression and which manifests itself, on human level, in sexual attraction. Yet behind this attraction is a longing and yearning for a more intangible reality, for a deeper union, self-abandonment and self-giving. The human beauty, youth and comeliness awaken memories of a beauty that never languishes, of grace and comeliness which is not of this earth, of a youth, bloom and form which never fade. The love for this beauty has found expression in the best of poetry and other art-forms.

So the love which has merely a physical expression and does not awaken deeper memories and longings is spiritually speaking not significant though that may still have its use for the continuation of the race and for the health of the individual.

LOVE: HUMAN AND DIVINE / 191

In a man ordinarily we have both the components. But it is the presence of the spiritual element that makes even physical love fulfilling. The qualities of tenderness, gentleness, sympathy, self-sacrifice are the soul of physical love. As love deepens and becomes more purified, the sensuous accidents become increasingly less important. The bodies disappear and the souls alone remain. Love becomes an act of adoration and worship of the Divine. The Vaishnavites have emphasized this aspect.

The Dharmashastras make use of these two elements in yet another way. They join two persons in a sacrament of marriage, in a venture of dharma, where they meet in mutually fulfilling obligations to support the fabric of society and the cycle of life. The relation is sober and of deep attachment. The partners are taught to live in loyalty, truthfulness and never-failing companionship. The approach is even more difficult than that of the Vaishnavites. This is a large question and it is no place for discussing it. But it may be said that this relationship should grow out of the fullness of the spirit. A forced partnership will help no one. The old ideal also does not agree with the facts of life as they are with the contemporary world. In the West, there is already a marital crisis. Its leaders will have to find new adjustments, new ideals. In any case, the old ideal will have to withdraw for the time being to the cave of the heart — where all Gods and ideals withdraw when the circumstances are not propitious.

We have spoken of the two elements in love; the physical and the spiritual. But the problem is how to know the one from the other. Reflective people know that desires is capable of throwing up a lot of verbalization which looks like the spiritual. Shakespeare tells us that men's love resides "not truly in their hearts but in their eyes", and that at "lovers' perjuries, they say, Jove laughs". When the blood is hot, vows and protestations come too readily to the tongue. We know the sophism, bathos, farce, jargons, rhapsody and extravagance of romantic love. When baulked, it feeds on that denial and, if the talent is also there, it bursts into poetry and gives us pictures of Helen and Beatrice and

Juliet, of a "face that launched a thousand ships", and of a "beauty too rich for use for earth too dear". But if fulfilled, it turns away in revulsion.

It seems love prospers more in separation than in union. Henry VIII, waited for many years for the hand of Anne Boleyn, fought the mightiest man of Europe, namely the Pope, and in the process gave England its present religion, but even less then the same number of months of union with the lady of his love bored him and she was eventually beheaded. Leila-Majnu and Sheerin-Farhad are classics of love and many mystics draw their images from those stories but one can only speculate how the stories would have ended if the heroes were united with their beloveds.

Unfulfilled love can become a great force, a great actor, a great liar. It is bound up with the Ego, with its will to power , to achieve, to conquer. It feeds on what is denied to it. In the language of the Indian Yoga, it is *ragātmaka*, that is, its soul is attraction which goes hand in hand with aversion. It is bipolar, *dvandvātmaka*. What attracts also repels. In a good deal of human love, there is curiosity, will to make new conquests. When that is achieved, interest is lost and boredom comes. Behind this love is self-love, self-will. In this love, we are in love with an image thrown up by our mind, thrown up by unfulfilled desire, an image of half-forgotten memories of faces that have excited our fun or fancy or love which has remained unrequited. Sometimes it is not even that but only love of an animal in heat but of an animal who has imagination and ideas in which he can live for a long time.

There is another consideration. In the past, the poetry and feeling of separation in love was used spiritually for deepening, uplifting and sublimating it. In India and Persia and in the Troubadours of Italy and Spain a good deal of the best and most fulfilling poetry centres round this theme. But in the modern age, particularly in the West, this feeling is increasingly becoming less meaningful and its capacity to be put to any sublimating use is strictly limited. Marriage is postponed but not sex. Love is also less focussed today than it used to be. If one affair does not lead to an early result, there is already a second one at hand. So there is no time left for any conflict between desire and its fulfilment, no time left for sublimation and also no need for it, no time left for the feeling of separation and denial to flower into a single-minded yearning of the soul. There is also no time left for Christian heroism, time for fighting with temptation and perfecting one's moral nature.

It is true that it has its positive side too. In this quick fulfilment, one is also saved from the less savoury manifestations of frustrated love, its jealousies and morbidities, its devils of Laudon, its false sentimentalities.

There are also people who believe that the problem with the world is not too much sex but too little of it. They say that men must recover their frankness and spontaneity in sex. This works for health.

An Austrian even in his early youth felt the contrast between a Christian sense of guilt which accompanies sex in his own tradition and the glad acceptance of it by the Hindus. This even brought him to India and he spent a few years here. After he felt he had graduated sufficiently in the new spirit, he went back and settled in America to teach the new gospel to America. After the sexual explosion of the sixties in America and Europe, how much is there left for him to teach is difficult to say.

Today, there is not only a psychotherapy of sex which has a wide acceptance but there is also a 'yoga of sex' which is just making a beginning though it claims a hoary ancestry in the Indian Tantras, in the temples of Khajuraho and Konarka. Its message is: illumination through copulation.

This is a large question and we cannot go into its various facets here. But we must say that compliments to India paid by some of its admirers for its approach to sex are undeserved. It is true that in India in a particular period there were certain tantric practices in which the physical motif played more than a symbolic role. It is also true that in the treatment of the subject of sex, there was no hush, and no morbidity but it must also be admitted that there was the highest emphasis on *brahmacharya*. But to the Indian teachers, *brahmacharya* was not a sentiment but a science and their approach to the problem was not athletic but understanding. *Brahmacharya* was also not forced celibacy but a growth into higher life. And at no stage a burden was placed on a man for which he was not prepared. At a particular stage when sexual urge was also strong, men and women were expected to live as householders supporting the fabric of society. Priests in India were expected to live exemplary lives but they were always householders. It is only monks who voluntarily chose that kind of life who lived as celibates. But even here, in the life devoted to a most intense spiritual discipline and spiritual search, the teachers lived as householders in forests. It was a Brahmanic tradition equally respected by those who like Buddha followed a different one, the Shramanic tradition.

For these reasons, Hinduism was spared those morbidities and extravagances and excesses connected with enforced celibacy. On the other hand, in many other cultures, the excesses of celibacy have been as disastrous as the excesses of profligacy. In Europe, there was a time when peasants and other common people preferred a married monk to a celibate one.

There can be obsessive chastity but there can also be obsessive indulgence. In animals, sexual urge is regulated by nature. It has its reason and season. And probably in primitive societies also, there is some kind of natural rhythm. But in the modern commercial societies of today, the urge is continually stimulated for it is a source of great profit. In totalitarian societies it is a way of forgetting fear and insecurity in the warmth of a bed. It could be an interesting research to study the relative sex-behaviour of a people under the stimulation of advertisements and those under the stress of fear.

Furthermore, love uninformed by a spiritual principle becomes even worse. It becomes an expression of antipathy, aversion, self-hatred; it becomes spiteful and malicious. Its fruits are boredom, self-estrangement. It tries to fill a vacuum with something equally empty. After an onslaught of temporary rage, paroxysm and convulsions, one again lapses into listlessness, ennui and self-loathing.

This is the picture that emerges if we look at human love from its own angle but if we give it a perspective, lend it a spiritual dimension, view it from the vantage point of divine love, the picture completely changes. In fact, if one reflects on the problem a little more deeply one finds that earthly love is not as real as it appears at first sight. It deals with "a secondary phenomenon" which an "ordinary lover adores", as Ibn al-Arabi, a Sufi of the Middle Ages says. The real lover loves the Real, And in all his love for the secondary phenomena, he loves the one truly beloved of his heart.

So any worthwhile human love is a symbol and image of the divine love though sometimes it is expressed in physical terms. And at a certain stage, it has its necessity and usefulness also. At this stage one denies it also at one's own cost. But even at this stage, it embodies the attributes of soul-love in its truer form and awakens the memory of the delights of a soul-union. As that memory awakens, the physical expressions, acts, and symbols become inadequate. More psychic symbols are needed which can express the tenderness and love of the soul more fully, more adequately.

Putting it a little differently, we can say that the human heart is an ocean. Its emotions are more than surface froth and foams. They are deep. They cannot be satisfied by ordinary forms of beauty and comeliness and bed-chamber love. They must have an appropriate object, an object as great and as deep and as high as the love in the heart. Soul's love needs an infinite sky in which it can properly navigate, wider postures than earthly objects can supply. It needs a Transcendental Form, a Beauty and Comeliness which can fill the eyes and heart of the soul, a Beloved who can receive all that the soul can give. Here in this love, all the fever, fervour, excitement, over-wrought emotionalism, ecstasy cease and only a certitude of fulfilment and union remains.

In India, Krishna embodies this transcendental form and is the heart of a good deal of the *sādhanā* of devotion. But this form has been worshipped under other names too. Different saint-poets have used different forms for expressing the soul's love for God.

Kabir and Nanak have worshipped even the Formless and it did not make their love less focussed, less concentrated. Mira sang of her love for Krishna with such simplicity and directness that in her songs millions have found a voice and echo of their own God-yearning. Chandidas celebrates the divine love by singing the love of Radha and Krishna. His poetry is one of the best in India's devotional literature. In his poems, he celebrates soul's love for God, its yearnings, its pangs of separation, its ecstasy of union, its tenderness, sweetness, self-surrender with a matchless purity of feeling and diction.

Section 7

Semitic Religions
versus
Hindu Dharma

Chapter 7.1

Religious Tolerance*

I begin this discussion by referring to the name of the organisation under whose auspices we are meeting, namely the "International Association for Religious Freedom". I believe that an organisation like this fulfils a great need of the hour. Today, religious freedom is threatened in many countries in one form or another. But the most flagrant examples are the Communist countries. In these countries, there is a systematic attempt to destroy not only religious liberty but most other liberties and all expressions of religion. It is most unfortunate. Let us hope that the rulers of these countries will realize their mistake, and reverse the process. Religion is not an opiate of the people; on the other hand, it represents a very important dimension of life and is one of the noblest expressions of the Spirit. Religion brings a fulfilment for which there is no other substitute. To suppress religion is to maim the life of a people.

But religious intolerance is no monopoly of Communism. It is unfortunate but true that religious intolerance has been practised by religions themselves. There have been crusades; there have been religious versions of the "wars of liberation" practised by modern Communist states; there has been heresy-hunting, bitter and bloody and often accompanied by mob violence and official persecuting. In some cases, there was even genocide, a whole people decimated. In many cases, there was a systematic vandalism, and a systematic and continuing persecution of local

---

*Talk delivered at a Seminar on Religious Freedom, New Delhi, 11 July 1978.

cultures and religions till not even their memory remained. In fact, intolerance has been such a common and important part of these religions that Communism too is regarded as a religion on that account by some thinkers.

But thank God, today, people of Europe and America have won the battle for religious freedom, and for the right to worship in their own ways. This right, this freedom, this tolerance towards others is a great value and it has been won at a great sacrifice.

The story of the triumph of religious freedom is an interesting one. One aspect of religious freedom was freedom from all religions. Religions had committed such excesses that religion itself lost caste with many thinking people. Religion generated hostility in many people which still subsists in many secular movements including Communism. Another feature of this newly won religious freedom is the triumph of Reason. Faith had denied reason too long and now Reason, in its triumphant hour, was denying faith. Europe's rational movement became anti-religion and if we look at the development we shall understand why. When a great truth of life is denied, as reason was denied by faith, it sets up certain opposite movements. Let us remember that Reason came as a liberating force from the shackles of a narrow faith though it need not deny faith its due place in the new circumstances.

A third feature of the triumph of religious tolerance in Europe was that the scene of religious excesses in Europe shifted to other continents. Whether they were Catholics or Protestants, Jesuits or Methodists or Baptists, they turned to the countries of Asia, Africa and America. They might have differed and debated bitterly amongst themselves on subtle points of theology, which to the outsiders made no sense, but they all agreed that these new continents were benighted and they needed Christian enlightenment. In spreading this light, as they saw it, they used all kinds of methods — force, fraud, persuasion, trade, social service. In this new work, the white man's burden, the energy of Europe found a new outlet.

We do not fully comprehend the causes of the rise and fall of nations and cultures. According to Hindu way of looking, nations and cultures, like individuals, have their destinies and appointed time. The European spirit at that time was resurgent. It was making new discoveries and new conquests. It was a spirit which had affected equally the trader, the soldier, the clergyman. They all combined and opened up new continents for Europe. The sword, the ledger, the Gospel were for many years partners and they thrived in unison. They had superior guns and for quite some time we all, the conquerors and the conquered, believed that they also had a superior religion.

In India itself, their work was full of mischief. I have read the records of those times. One would have supposed that the men of God of Europe would be in a better position to appreciate the working of the Holy Ghost in India. But unfortunately, it was not so. In fact, the European priest and missionary was more contemptuous of Indian religion and culture than the European administrator or trader. Carey and Wilberforce wanted the Home Government to use force for the conversion of the heathens in India.

But we should not complain. In spite of several negative features there was also a good deal to learn for us from this new contact. Imperialism had its bad side but it was not established by men of straw. Many of the new rulers were men of great qualities. They had intelligence, dedication, organising skill, capacity for sustained and purposive work. They were men of great *tapas* from which we in India could all learn.

Secondly, the initial contacts between nations and cultures are not always fraternal though a fraternity is created out of those unhappy contacts in due course of time. God fulfils himself in many ways. The Europeans came as conquerors and as teachers. In the beginning, the relationship was unequal but time has corrected some of the old imbalances and we can all now be brothers in a world that has become physically one for the first time. The Western conquest opened up Asia to the Europeans but by the same token, Europe too was opened up to Asia. The old self-sufficiency of Europe is now broken and only the very narrow-minded and self-assured Europeans feel comfortable in the role of world teachers. The best minds of Europe have a humbler view of themselves and they feel they can also learn a few things from the spiritual heritage of the East and especially of India.

Hindus have their full quota of faults; they have their own pride and prejudices, but there is one quality of Hinduism which has attracted the attention of many outsiders and thinkers, that is, a spirit of tolerance in Hinduism, its pluralistic views of religions, the absence of crusades and organized missions to convert people. Take the *Encyclopaedia of Religions and Ethics*. Most of it is written by Christian theologians and has a distinct Christian bias. In fact, it could be called a part of Christian Apologetics. It discusses concepts like Charity, Love, Chastity, Pity, Truth, Purity. In all, Christianity comes out at the top and Hinduism is not even a poor second. But only when it comes to the discussion of 'religious persecution', that Hinduism scores over other religions by the absence of this phenomenon. This is a point which is of utmost interest to a Seminar which is discussing religious tolerance, and to an Association which stands for promoting religious freedom. This is a vast subject and a proper discussion of it will involve going into the whole ethos of Hinduism but this cannot obviously be done here. I shall therefore here refer to only one or two basic points.

The absence of religious intolerance in Hinduism is not incidental. It has grown out of the way in which Hinduism has viewed the world and looked at fellow-men and intuited the divine.

What is this view which may be called the theological base of Hindu tolerance if I may use this expression in this context? Expressed simply, it means that in Hinduism all symbols signify the same Reality. This is an insight which the Hindus have stressed again and again from ancient times. The Vedas, the most ancient scripture of the Aryan race declare that it is the "same

Reality which the wise call by many names". The *Atharvaveda* says: He is Aryamā; He is Varuṇa; He is Rudra; He is the Great Garuḍa; He is Agni; He is Sūrya; He is the great Yama.

This doctrine means that the world is a symbol, an image, a manifestation of God. By worshipping any one of His symbols and images, we worship Him. In its practical aspect, the doctrine is a plea for religious tolerance. It says that the symbols are not worth all the slaughter that has been perpetrated in their names.

The doctrine further says that in every one there is a soul; and wherever there is a soul, there is a seeking; and wherever there is a true seeking and a sincere worship, there is God. So this insight is against those exclusive claims which some religions make of knowing the "only, true God". Why should you know the true God? Are you better than your neighbour in qualities of the mind and the heart? Is your worship truer and more sincere than his? In this way of looking at things, it is not the definitions of God that matter, it is the truth and sincerity and intensity of the seeking and the worship. God is known to those who worship Him sincerely. He is no respecter of denominations.

God has made man in His image; but man too makes God in his image. He makes a little God out of his ambitions, desires and interest; then he sets him up on a pedestal and worships him; and he also forces others in worshipping him. And this he says is for the greater glory of God and for magnifying Him. But this is really for his own glory and for his own aggrandisement.

So the Hindus believe in the plurality of symbols and stress the importance of the truth of seeking. To these they add another insight that people have different natures, different dispositions, different degrees of preparedness. Their starting points are different, their capacities, talents and desires are different. Therefore, do not look for one mode and one medium in people's worship. Make allowance for their variety and respect that variety.

This attitude means that different peoples and different races have their own presiding genius, their own talents and their own *svadharma*. They worship the best when they worship through their *svadharma*. Therefore, we should imbibe an attitude of mind which believes that those who are not with us are not against us and those are truly with us who are truly with themselves. We should not play the big brother in relation to others.

In a garden different plants, trees and fruits have their own seasons, their own rhythms and own requirements. They have their own allotted share of sunshine, air and water and grow to their potential size. The gardener does not try to prescribe one season or one rhythm and one pace for all of them. He tries to serve them according to their own requirements. And that is enough. If he imposed his ideas on them, he should destroy them. Only in service according to laws of Nature and our potentiality, there is colour and variety, life and nourishment for us all.

When we go out converting people and imposing our beliefs and patterns on them, we show lack of faith in God. In fact, we deny God in others.

The spiritual life is a pilgrimage which is joined by different persons, coming from different directions, along different routes, passing through different terrains, using different modes of sensibilities and bringing with them for offering their different life-experiences. They sing and praise Him in different idioms, using different images, metaphors and symbols. The wise say: Do not fight about the symbols and images; look behind at the heart which is one.

The Hindu psyche has been shaped by such religious teachings and intuition which strengthened the roots of religious tolerance amongst the Hindus. Religious tolerance and religious freedom are great liberal and humanist truths but they have their roots in a still deeper truth of the Spirit and the Self. I have tried to present the Hindu point of view in this matter.

I hope this is enough for the time being.

Thank you.

Chapter 7.2

'Liberal' Christianity

There is some kind of inbuilt bigotry in Christian theology. It may put a little more piety and prayer into those who are influenced by it, but it could also make them more harsh in judging other peoples' religions. The practice of Christianity may make a man better in some respects but it does little to widen his sympathies and to open him up to the larger spiritual wealth of different peoples and cultures.

But the world has been considerably changing during the last two hundred years. A wave of rationalism and humanism has been flooding Europe. It has made Christian theology with its exclusive claims look pretentious. It has also fostered a new spirit of universalism and liberalism and a new awareness of a wider human family.

This new spirit has not left the Christian theologians entirely untouched. In the past, they saw in other religions nothing but the Devil at work and it cost them little pangs of conscience to send the best and wisest of their men to the Hell. But in the new intellectual and humanist climate, this will not do. For one reason because the Christian Devil and Hell have lost their terror. For another reason because their old pretentions have become laughable. In the new context, they must appear to be more modest, more tolerant even if they are not so at heart.

So there is a new theology under construction. It does not regard other religions as handiworks of the Devil. On the other hand, it says that there is a natural religious impulse that has been at work throughout history and throughout the world and this natural religion has its own validity. But, it finds its culmination and fulfilment in the revealed religion of Christianity. It also wants to find a place in its schema for Pagan sages and saints and even for non-Christian saintly men like Noe mentioned in the Bible. It cannot yet send them to Heaven but it also does not unceremoniously send them to Hell.

One such 'liberal' theologian is Cardinal Jean Danielou who recently died. Let us see what he says in his *Holy Pagans*.

Danielou admits that "there are men who did not know Christ either because they lived before Him or because knowledge of Him did not come their way, and yet were saved; and some of these too were saints". But that is all. For he hastens to add: "They were not saved by the religions to which they belonged; for Buddha does not save, Zoroaster does not save, nor does Mohomet. If they were saved, then it is because they were saved by Christ who alone saves, who alone sanctifies. Again, if they were saved, it is because they already belonged to the Church for there is no salvation outside the Church."

Donielou finds that Abel, Henoch, Daniel, Noe, Job, Melchisdech, Lot, the queen of Saba, are some of the non-Christian saints and even non-Biblical saints mentioned in the Bible. Abel was anterior to Abraham; and so were Henoch and Noe. Lot was a relative of Abraham but was not a party to the Covenant. Daniel was a Phoenician and Job an Idumean, the queen of Saba was a princess of Saba (South Arabia).

Jean Danielou concedes that these too were saints and that holiness is possible outside the Christian fold though that holiness "must always be inferior to Christian holiness". But "none the less, the fact remains that holiness of that sort is possible".

There are three levels of this holiness, the Pagan holiness being the lowest. God's will "is expressed on the Christian plane by the law of the Gospel, on the Jewish plane by the Mosaic law, on the cosmic plane by the law of conscience".

At the lowest level, "holiness within the sphere of the cosmic religion consists in a response to the call of God made known by conscience".

Man's religion has progressed from the natural or cosmic to the Jewish, to the Christian. "All Christian liturgy — Easter,

Pentecost, Christmas — have at the back of their Christian significance, a Jewish significance; and behind the latter there is a cosmic significance."

"The glory which shines from the face of Jesus Christ overshadows, as St. Paul tells us, that which shone from the face of Moses. In like manner, the glory shining from the face of Moses overshadows that which shone from the face of Noe."

This three-level development is evident in all spheres touching on religious life. For example, on the lowest level, there is a cosmic temple. The house of God is the whole Cosmos, Heaven His tent and the Earth His footstool. In Old Testament, this primitive atmosphere still continues. Abraham has that *parrhesia* with God — that freedom of speech which in ancient Greece was the right of a free citizen.

This gave way to the Temple of Moses. The establishment of the Tabernacle, whose ultimate form is the Temple, is the fundamental mission entrusted by God to Moses. The Covenant was Abraham's mission, the Temple that of Moses. Uptil now, God was everywhere but from the time of Moses till the death of Christ when a still higher stage begins, the Temple is the dwelling in which the glory of Yahweh abides. Upto Moses, sacrifice could be offered to God anywhere. But after that, only those sacrifices were pleasing to God that were offered in the Tabernacle. "Ye shall utterly destroy all the places, wherein the nations which ye shall possess served their gods, upon the high mountains, and upon the hills, and under every green tree."

In a divine plan, we are assured by Cardinal Danielou, this was a necessary stage, for the great danger was polytheism; the singleness of the sanctuary was as it were, the sign of the Oneness of God.

Thus a second great step was taken. The religion of Sinai fixed a gulf between God and man. No longer Yahweh talked on easy terms with the patriarchs. Henceforth He dwells in the secrecy of the Holy of Holies. Separating man from God marks an advance for it draws attention to two things: First to God's transcendence, His incomprehensibility, that He is wholly Other. No easy-going anthropomorphism any longer. Secondly, to man's sinfulness, his essentially fallen nature. Without this, the next third step was not possible.

In the next stage, the abode of Yahweh is no longer the Temple, but the Manhood of Jesus. "The glory of the Lord dwelt in the Temple until the coming of the Incarnation. But from that day it began to dwell in Jesus. The divine Presence is no longer to be found in an enclosure of stone, it dwells in Jesus Himself. With Him the Mosaic order comes to an end." There is a qualitative leap as the Marxists would love to call it, for Jesus is not just "a higher kind of Moses. Moses and Temple are figures but Jesus is the reality."

From this to the Temple of the Church was a most natural and easy step. In fact, it was no new step at all. It is a mode of saying the same thing. "It is the Manhood of Jesus that is the Temple of the New Law but this Manhood must be taken as a whole, that is today, it is the Mystical body in its entirety; this is the complete and final Temple. The dwelling of God is this Christian community whose Head is in the Heaven."

There are variations but the above is the essential theme of many new 'liberal' theologians. There is one de Lubac who says about the same things in his book *Catholicism*. We give a few illustrative pieces:

"Outside Christianity humanity can doubtless be raised in an exceptional manner to certain spiritual heights, but the topmost summit is never reached, and there is the risk of being the farther off from it by mistaking for it some other outlying peak.

"There is some essential factor missing from every religious 'invention' that is not a following of Christ. There is something lacking, for example, in Buddhist charity; it is not Christian charity. Something is lacking in the spirituality of great Hindu mystics; it is not the spirituality of St. John of the Cross. Outside Christianity nothing attains its end, towards which, unknowingly, all human desires, all human endeavours, are in movement: the embrace of God in Christ."

If this is true, then his conclusion is a fair one: "So long as the Church does not extend and penetrate to the whole humanity, so as to give to it the form of Christ, She cannot rest."

F.H. Hilard in his *Man in Eastern Religions* finds that to the question what is man, the Christian answer is the best. According to Christians "man is to be understood as primarily a person and not a mere manifestation". In this view man is "an individual", while the others "Hinduism, Buddhism and Taoism, agree in thinking of man primarily as an aspect of ultimate Reality".

Nicholas Bardyaev, in his *Spirit and Reality* says: "Theosis makes man Divine, while at the same time preserving his human nature. Thus instead of human personality being annihilated, it is made in the image of God and the Divine Trinity. The mystery of the personality is intimately related to that of freedom and love. Love and charity can flourish only if there are personal relationships. Monistic identity excludes love as well as freedom. Man is not identical with the cosmos and with God; man is a microcosm and a microtheosis."

Again, he says, "In Hindu and Platonic mysticism everything is diametrically opposed to the dialogical and dramatic relationship between man and God, between one personality and another. Spirituality is interpreted as being opposed to personality and therefore as independent of love, human freedom, and a relation between the plural and the one. The mystical way is that of Gnosis rather than of Eros." According to him, Hindu spirituality "is an austere and unloving mysticism. The absence of love is explained by the fact that this mysticism is unconscious of personality; it is concerned with abdicating rather than preserving the personality."

Evelyn Underhill, the well-known author of the book *Mysticism*, too seems to share this schema. She says: "In Christianity, the natural mysticism which like natural religion is latent in humanity, and at a certain point of development breaks out in every race, came to itself; and attributing for the first time true and distinct personality to its Object, brought into focus the confused and unconditioned God which Neoplatonism had constructed from the abstract concepts of philosophy blended with the intuitions of Indian ecstatics, and made the basis of its meditations on the Real."

She repeats the same sentiment at another place. After making the statement that a mystic is "willing to use the map of the community in which he finds himself", which means that mystical experience is compatible with different theologies about it, she continues to add that "we are bound to allow as a historical fact that mysticism, so far, has found its best map in Christianity", and that "the Christian atmosphere is the one in which the individual mystic has most often been able to develop his genius in a sane and fruitful way".

In India too, there is a group of Christian theologians working in the direction of 'liberalism'. It has become noticeable after India's independence. While Christian money and missions continue to work by and large in their old style (see *Report of the Christian Missionary Activities Enquiry Committee Madhya Pradesh*),* there is a group of Christian theologians who want an encounter with Hinduism on a different plane.

Here their greatest difficulty is the rival slogan that is fashionable amongst Hindu intellectuals that all teachers preach more or less the same things and that different religions are just different paths to the same goal. The problem of these new 'liberal' Christian theologians is how to salvage their religion from this demolishing, equalizing slogan. So they preach that every religion is *unique* and that we should all meet in our individual richness in a fruitful dialogue. While secretly hoping that this dialogue would prove that they are unique in a superior way, they invite us all to this encounter. And this should be welcome.

Some of them have taken Indian names, and live in Indian style and put on Indian dress. Some of them have even donned the habits of Indian sannyasins. The motives are mixed. Some may be

*It has been reprinted as *Vindicated By Time: The Neogi Committee Report on Christian Missionary Activities*, Voice of India, New Delhi, 1999.

following St. Paul's practice "to become all things to all men, by all means to win over some of them" (1 Cor 9.22); others because they find this style more informal and under Indian conditions more comfortable; others in order to understand and enter into the Hindu psyche better.

Dr. Jacques-Albert Cuttat, the Swiss Ambassador, poses the problem and invites us to this dialogue. He says in his *The Spiritual Dialogue of East and West*: "The West inclines to exclusivism, the East to syncretism. The view that salvation is only possible within the visible Church — a view expressly rejected by the Catholic Church — has been sustained by missionaries and eminent theologians, even today; such blindness for the spiritual riches of the East, for its mystical depth and intuition of the transparence of the cosmos to higher Realities, always implies a blindness for some basic aspects of Christianity itself. The East is tempted by the opposite extreme, syncretism; it consists in wrongly equating biblical values with Eastern religious categories. Such universalism is undoubtedly more tolerant, less 'violent' than Western Exclusivism, but equally blind to the specific inner visage of Christianity and the other biblical spiritualities."

While we are on this subject, we should not forget to mention the late Fr. J. Monchanin who assumed the name of Swami Parama Arubi Anandam and who lived in Tiruchirapalli District in a place to which he gave the name of Saccidananda Ashram. From these Sanskrit names, one should not think that he had become a Hindu. As the editors of his papers say, "his mission here was not so much to become fully an Indian or to realize in himself the final synthesis of West and East as to bring to India in a pure form, yet with a remarkable sympathy and understanding, the riches of a Christian soul". He himself defines his mission in these terms: "I have come to India for no other purpose than to awaken in a few souls the desire (the passion) to raise up a Christian India. I think the problem is of the same magnitude as the Christianisation, in former times, of Greece (the hellenisation of Christendom modelled on the forms of Greek sensibility, thought and spiritual experience). It will take centuries, sacrificed lives, and we shall perhaps die before seeing any realisations. A Christian India, completely Indian and completely Christian, may be and will be something so wonderful; to prepare it from afar, the sacrifice of our lives is not too much to ask."

Just two years before his death in 1957, he was writing: "I believe more and more in 'exchange'. India must give the West a keener sense of the eternal, of the primacy of Being over Becoming, and receive, in turn, from the West a more concrete sense of the temporal, of becoming, of the person, of love (of which India alas! Knows so little)."

We give more or less in his own language what he means by this dialogue. He sees in India spiritual goods which cannot be there for nothing. They are preparations and they point to her Christianization. He says:

"India has received from the Almighty an uncommon gift, an unquenchable thirst for whatever is spiritual. From the Vedic and Upanishadic times, a countless host of her sons have been great seekers of God. Centuries after centuries there arose seers and poets, singing the joys and sorrows of a soul in quest of the One, philosophers reminding every man of the supremacy of contemplation: upward and inward movements through knowledge to the ultimate.

"Communion with Him and liberation from whatever hinders that realisation, was for them the unique goal.

"Hundreds and thousands of men and women have consecrated themselves entirely to that end.... We may rightly think that such a marvellous seed was not planted in vain by God in the Indian soul. Unfortunately, Indian wisdom is tainted with erroneous tendencies and looks as if it has not yet found its own equilibrium. So was Greek wisdom before Greece humbly received the Paschal message of the Risen Christ. Man, outside the unique Revelation and the unique Church, is always and everywhere unable to sift truth from falsehood, good from evil.

"But once Christianised, Greece rejected her ancestral errors; so also, confident in the indefectible guidance of the Church, we hope that India, once baptized to the fullness of her body and soul, will reject her pantheistic tendencies and, discover in the splendours of the Holy Ghost the true mysticism..."

He hopes that "India cannot be alien to this process of assimilation by Christianity and transformation into it". But "should India fail in that task, we cannot understand, humanly speaking, how the mystical body of Christ could reach its quantitative and qualitative fullness in His eschatological Advent".

"Is not the message she has to deliver to the world similar to the message of the ancient Greece? Therefore the Christianisation of Indian civilization is to all intents and purposes a historical undertaking comparable to the Christianisation of Greece."

Hindus may have certain spiritual qualities like a sense of the holy in abundance, but the Church has the Truth in its possession. Therefore, "India has to receive humbly from the Church the sound and basic principles of true contemplation. The genuine Christian contemplation is built on the unshakable foundation of revealed truths concerning God and man and their mutual relations."

On another occasion, he says, "In that mystery, Hinduism (and specially advaita) must die to rise up again Christian. Any theory which does not take fully into account this necessity constitutes a lack of loyalty both to Christianity — which we cannot mutilate from its essence — and to Hinduism from which we cannot hide its fundamental error and its essential divergence from Christianity.

"Meanwhile, our task is to keep all doors open, to wait with patience and theological hope for the hour of the advent of India into the Church, in order to realize the fullness of the Church and the fullness of India. In this age-long vigil, let us remember — that love can enter where intellect must bide at the door."

The account of this attempt will gain in fullness if we mention a Colloquy which was held in Almora in April, 1961. It was attended among others by representatives of Christian institutions like Saccidananda Ashram, Kulithalai; Asirvanam, Kenkeri;

Senehsadan, Poona; Santi Bhavan, Calcutta; Vrindavan, Kottagiri; Jyotiniketan, Kareli. It was also attended by Dr. Cuttat, the Swiss Ambassador, whom we have already mentioned. The account of this Colloquy is given in a small paper named 'Indian Interiority and Christian Theology".

All these are people who advocate a dialogue with Hindu India on a deeper level. Let us look at this paper to find out what kind of mind they bring to this dialogue.

They believe that "Christianity as the one revealed religion for all men, cannot be lacking in any truth necessary for the salvation of man; it has the guarantee of the Divine testimony".

Their procedure is not to denounce Hinduism forthright. On the other hand, they take different categories of Hindu thinking and "after exhausting all the positive points that Hinduism provides as solutions proceed to show that Christianity gives the fuller and ultimate solution to those and all other problems".

Discussing the nature of this dialogue, they say that "the intention is not to inquire whether Hinduism has some positive values which are wanting in Christianity", for that is not possible believing as they do in Christianity as "the true revealed religion for all humanity". But they are prepared to look at certain particular values intensely realized by the Hindu sages which may direct "the Christian back to his own religion, in which he finds the same values more naturally embedded". "Hinduism as a natural religion does not exclude the possibility of such a deepening of interiority." Let us remember that this modesty in a Christian missionary that he can learn something however unimportant from Pagans is no small change.

The Colloquy proceeds to discuss some of the categories of Hindu religious thinking. One such category is Teacher-Disciple or *guru-śishya* relationship. After discussing it, it finds that "the only person in whom the positive values of the Hindu Guru are best verified is Christ". After discussing the Hindu concept of history, it finds that "the positive values found in the Indian history have their full meaning and natural setting in the Christian concept of history". It also discusses Yoga, its positive as well as negative aspects. While dangers and negative aspects are avoided, the positive aspects of Hindu Yoga "find their natural setting and full meaning in Christianity. Non-dualism and dualism, Yoga absolutism and Bhakti personalism, Sankara and Ramanuja, are in different ways related to Christianity. The Christian worships the Absolute of Sankara with the devotion of Ramanuja."

Hindu symbolism and idol worship has some positive points but the dangers are far greater. "The fundamental defect of Hindu idol worship is that it is purely a human attempt to so to say transubstantiate the material things into the divine without a prior incarnation, namely without a divine guarantee which assumes the human symbol into the divine economy of self-communication to man. Man cannot by his own powers raise himself to the divine level, which far transcends him. Hence the Hindu conviction that when the priest recites the prayers over the idol it becomes inhabited by the deity is a gratuitous assumption and hence superstitious."

But it is different with Christian symbolism. For example, "the Eucharist marks the culmination of human symbolism. In it the food of man is turned into the body and blood of God. There man's attempt to transubstantiate the material world into the divine is wonderfully realized — the Eucharist may be taken as a summary and completion of all human endeavour to grasp the divine Reality in human symbols. Hence it should form the converging point of all religious cult."

Hindu *bhakti* too has more demerits than merits. Its chief defects are that (1) "the notion of love itself is not perfect"; that (2) there is no integration between knowledge and love and one has to choose between them; and that (3) it lacks a "perfect concept of alterity; there is also no proper concept of sin".

But still, the *bhakti* of a Hindu could really be a "preparation for the final confrontation with the personal God who manifests Himself in the Christian Revelation".

Discussing *jñāna-mārga*, it finds that the Hindu doctrine of *advaita* is irreconcilable with the Christian doctrine of Trinity, but even that could become a step to the understanding of the doctrine of the three persons in one. How? First by opposing polytheism. Secondly by its strong metaphysical bias for unity: "Only against the background of the unique and absolute Reality of God can the doctrine of the Trinity and the immortal personality of man be properly understood. God in His providence insisted on the strictest monotheism, and uncompromisingly exterminated all tendency to polytheism in the chosen people in the Old Testament, before revealing against the background of that monotheism the Trinity of Persons in that one God, in the New Testament. Hence the Advaita with its strong metaphysical basis can be a proper *preparatio evangelica* for an understanding of the Christian message."

Once it is admitted that Christianity is the uniquely true religion, the summit towards which all religions are advancing, the 'liberal' theologians will not mind conceding certain subordinate spiritual qualities and attributes and values to these religions. In this expansive mood, they generously admit that some European Christians "have felt the wealth of India's religious past". The deep interiority which India has inculcated has even "led some of them to deepen their own Christian interiority". Some of them have been "struck by the vision of the spirit of poverty preached by Christ, [but] so fully and cheerfully practised by millions in India. The religious outlook in which everything of every event is looked upon as a work of God, a manifestation of the divine, has impressed many. Many have noted with admiration the so to say natural "aptitude for deep prayer and the contemplation of divine things which Indians manifest".

When the Pope came to India a few years ago, he praised India's deep spirituality. But it is in the above context that this praise should be understood. The praise conceals as well as reveals a good deal. It conceals the fact that the aim remains the same: Christianizing, proselytizing. But the approach, the methods of achieving this goal are to be modified.

In the past, believing Christians like Carey and Wilberforce were telling the rulers at home this: "The natives live in the sin and superstition and darkness of paganism. Surely God has not given us their charge, the empire for nothing. He wants us to bring them to the light of the Gospel, to convert them to Christianity." But the rulers were, it seems, less convinced about the benefits of Christianity to their subjects. But in their situation they could not also oppose this laudable object too directly. So they preferred a more equivocal approach. They counter-argued like this: "You are very true in your judgement of the natives. But precisely because they are superstitious, we must go slow with them and their religion; otherwise, it would become a law and order problem and we may lose the Empire altogether." This attitude saved India from the worst ravages of Christian missionaries.

But now political equation has changed and above all ideas have changed. The pretentious claims of the Church jar on the ears and they do not make it particularly popular even with its own flock. So a new, 'liberal' theology is in the offing, which is trying to give up the old method of forthright denunciation, and taking to the new method of a partial praise, a grudging and sometimes even generous appreciation of the values of other religions.

While praising Hindus, these new theologians are also saying more or less openly or *sotto voce* something like this: "You are fine. We find in your country a deep-seated pursuit of things spiritual. But God has not planted these seeds, has not done all these things for nothing. If he knows His own mind as well as we do, He must have been preparing you for Christianity, for receiving our truth, for becoming as good as we are."

Jesus had said: Ask, and it shall be given you; seek, and you shall find; knock, and it shall be opened unto you.

But the neo-theologians are telling us something like this: While Hindus asked, God gave it to the Christians; while the Hindus sought, the Christians found; while Hindus knocked, it was opened unto the Christians.

This is the great trinitarian mystery that these theologians teach. Though they use recondite and long-winded words and clothe them in the language of faith and fervour, we may be excused if we find in them nothing but a process of self-deception and self-congratulation.

Self-hypnosis or intensification of a particular idea is no faith and is inimical to a truly spiritual impulse. It may have its value in the initial stage and may help in steadying a wandering mind, but as we advance, its guidance becomes insufficient and even misleading. There we need a measure of liberation.

And for this liberation, we need not go the Vedanta or any high-flown language of the philosophers. What we need is a certain freedom from fixed ideas and images, freedom from obsessive roles of spreading the Gospel, a certain measure of modesty, a certain charity to see God's truth in different peoples and different nations.

For acquiring this asset, a 'dialogue' is no great help. Unless the mind is purified, a dialogue at heart remains a monologue. True to its etymology (from *legein*, to speak), a dialogue tends to be talking, pronouncing, declaring, seldom listening.

And yet the principle of growth is listening, self-listening, listening to the inner truth, listening to the inner voice of reason. But the mind fails to listen because it is already full of chatter. It is arguing, proving, disproving, all the time. In order to listen, it must grow into an inner silence.

When this capacity for self-listening develops, one may decide for himself whether he still wants to find clever reasons for what he knows to be false; whether he would like to be loyal to his inner seeing, inner voice and reason or he would still like to cling to some theology however hoary it is, or to some pet idea or image or role however dear and sweet these might have been. Learning takes place not in a dialogue where both the parties speak but in a place and situation where one speaks and the other listens. In other words, it takes place in a relationship which is frankly tailored for that purpose — where there is a teacher able to teach and a pupil eager to learn. But in a situation where both the parties are teachers or regard themselves so, there is very little learning.

If the new theologians feel that they have something to learn from India in the way of deepening their own interiority or such other things, this is a laudable object and this much should be good enough. Why must they insist that the Hindus must also learn form them in return? Leave that to the Hindus to decide. If they do not want to learn, the loss is entirely theirs. Let them wallow in their insularity.

The fact is that people learn on a deeper level than they think and formulate. They learn very little when they meet with that express purpose or rather meet to teach in the name of learning. But when they meet without preconceived notions, without a set purpose, on human level, with good will and friendship, they leave behind ideas, memories, influences which are picked up in ways unknown even to ourselves.

I personally believe that India has much to learn from the Western culture but, I am afraid, very little from Western Christianity. This is no paradox. Let us remember that West's culture is larger than its Christianity. In fact, a good deal of the best in its culture took place because it repudiated its Christianity and went back to its more classical sources or responded to its own inner impulses more readily than to its religion's disabling dogmas. The West had to wage a heroic and noble battle to free reason from the shackles of its religion's dictas and from its ideological tribalism.

And while we appreciate the eagerness of the new theologians to teach, a more cautions and critical approach may like to review what Christianity taught in the past. After all, the new theology is not so new as it would like to believe, at least in defining its aims.

Christianity has been the advance-guard and the hand-maid of Western imperialism during the last several centuries. The "white man's burden" of civilizing the world was only a diluted version of the Church's God-given mission of bringing light and salvation to a benighted and sinful world.

Wherever Christianity went, it carried fire and sword and destruction, particularly in the American and African continents. The local cultures were completely destroyed, sometimes more completely than a deluge might have done. And after the missionaries had tought the natives about the Sin, the Devil, the One God, and His only begotten Son, the first things the natives developed was a dim view of their ancestors — that they were benighted and that they are now deservedly in hell. They lost a sense of their roots, the capacity to be nourished by them. The natives lost their body as well as their souls. Now most of these countries have regained their political freedom but they have not recovered their souls.

Chapter 7.3

A Letter to a Sufi

6B/3, Poorvi Marg,
New Delhi – 5,
14th August, 1958.

My dear Respected Sufiji,

Your kind post-card. You will excuse me for answering you in English as this will facilitate my expression.

Your letter not only seeks to correct me on certain points regarding Islamic theology but makes mention of those that are different in your characteristic way. You will excuse me for saying that I have never shared your estimate of Hinduism. I have generally found it most artificial and external and argumentative and arbitrary. And it is difficult to argue with you because you have already made up your mind about most of Hinduism and Hindu scriptures. For example, you say: "As far as the Upanishads are concerned I have mostly gone through such of them as are available in Urdu and English." On the basis of such reading which must be extensive you found in your "analysis of Upanishads", that according to Hinduism "the highest stage is that of absolute unconsciousness". Well! But according to *Māṇḍūkya Upanishad* where the "deep-sleep state" is described, it is defined as "unified", a "cognition-mass", "whose mouth is thought", "cognitional, Lord of all, source of all, inner controller, all knowing".

But you assert that it is a state of "absolute unconsciousness". What can I say except that great scriptures yield their meaning when we go to them as humble pupils with love and aspiration, and not with a view to judge and denounce.

Again in your letter you say that "the Quran has strictly prohibited the use of words like mother, father, son, wife etc. for remembering *khudā*... These words degrade the image of *khudā*, and lead a man towards idolatry."

This is precisely what I said in my article that the Muslim approach to God is not as wide and comprehensive even when it claims to believe in a "Personal God" as the Hindu one. I believe that if God could be your "*hākim*" (master), he could be your father and mother and lover too. It does not bring down the concept of God, but makes it intimate and 'soulful'. It also ennobles man's relationship with those around him, ennobles his duty, his passions. Where God is missing from those relationships, they tend to be purely utilitarian, and beastly.

At another point you make a distinction between "worship" (*ibādat*) and "prayer" (*dua'*), Hindus being "bereft of prayer altogether or almost altogether", to put it in your own words. I believe this distinction to be more theological than real. Worship as well as prayer have different connotations according to the stage of the aspirant. In its more outward and undeveloped form, worship is more like begging and asking and demanding but as it deepens, it is more akin to self-surrender, to being a channel of God's light and will.

You define prayer (*dua'*) as asking God for one's human perfection (*insāniyat kī takmīl*) and mukti (*ākhirat ki nijāt*). Well! I shall put it differently. I shall not say "one's human perfection", but the "realization of one's inner divinity", which easily and naturally includes the former. Being what has been called pantheist, I do not believe that man is only animal and rational, but is divine too.

Further, you say in your letter that "Truly speaking, the philosophy of karma has closed for the Hindus all ways of begging everything from *khudā*. This philosophy describes the cycle of karma in such a manner as to eliminate from the very beginning, the issue of *khudā's* domain."

To put it or see it this way could be satisfactory to a debating intellect but is hardly worthy of an inner mind. I could easily retort that the preponderance of prayer and reliance on God's attribute of mercifulness has made the question of one's karma or actions or the purity of motives superfluous in Islam, but I shall refrain from doing that in spite of the fact that the line of argument would be quite after your style. Not only there is karma in Hinduism, but there is a good deal of karma in Islam. In religions of Semitic origins, we have a 'theory' of karma more rigid and iron-cast. They have angels preparing every moment a sort of Doomsday book of an individual, who has been given one life alone for eternal damnation or eternal reward. Where is the room in this theory for any mercy or grace? All for the day of judgment when God will judge and punish and reward, though you say that God as judge is against "the fundamental view-point of Islam"; I do not see how.

On the other hand, while the Muslim theory of karma is so rigid and arbitrary, the Hindu theory of karma is seeped through with hope, mercy and grace. These things are woven through its very texture. Besides this, in Hinduism the law of karma has been subordinated to the law of God's grace and God's infinity and power. In the realm of Spirit, human karma and God's authority do not contradict.

It seems any stick is good enough for beating the opponent. Hinduism has been accused on the one hand of a transcendental actionlessness, even of amorality; on the other hand, it has been accused of such a system of ethics and theory of action which makes God superfluous altogether. Of course, as far as you are concerned, you have contempt for every Hindu approach to Spirit or to action. In your own words, in Hinduism "moral and spiritual values and all religious truths have secondary place".

Again you say in your letter: "It does not appear to me that Islam has described Hinduism as atheism. It does describe such isms as idolatry (which in fact they are), but does not call them atheism."

Well I shall not discuss the Muslim scholars. When I wrote those lines on those pages, I had more specifically you in mind. According to you, in your own words, Hindu spiritual highlights are (1) "a united nation of animals" and (2) "a system of anarchy of thousands of castes and groups born of a belief in thousands of male and female deities". Any comment is unnecessary. Certainly you won't call it a state of belief. Similarly, more than once you have called *śrī mūrtis* (you call them idols) stalks and stones and Hindus worshipping these stones.

Certainly you would not give these practices and *superstitions* the status of theism or any worthwhile beliefs.

Well, I consider all those beliefs wicked which teach eating animals for no better reason than theological. If man is the superior creation of God, then he should protect His other creatures instead of eating them up. Look into the eyes of a cow or a goat, and you will recognize a friend, a fellow-creature, our life sustaining them all.

So far as "idol-worship" is concerned, I am for it and I believe that Islamic iconoclasm except for a few exceptions where it did have some spiritual significance, was the language of Islamic greed, conquest and self-aggrandisement.

Mūrti-worship was found good enough by persons like Sri Chaitanya Mahaprabhu, Sri Shankaracharya and Sri Rama-krishna, saints of the highest order to any one except those completely overcome by a partisan spirit or theological passions.

In Hinduism while we have the highest and most rigorous kind of *advaita* which denies all partial manifestations of the One or That, we also have another conception where God permeates all, infuses all, stands behind all, surrounds all. This is called pantheism by the theologians of the Semitic religions. I find that mystic experience of all saints, where they are not under pressure to conform to an officially established orthodoxy or dogma, confirms this experience of Hinduism.

The above difference explains many other differences. For orthodox Islam, everything seems to deny God, mislead man, take him to the path of *kufr* or infidelity. For Hinduism, given pre-liminary purity of body and mind, everything expresses God, is a vehicle, a channel of God, leads man to God. Forms lead him to the Formless; names to the Nameless. For official Islam a temple or a *mūrti* are prison-houses of God, but for Hinduism they are His channels.

In an important sense, I think Muslims are the worst idolators. They seem to think that God does not lie in man's soul and his aspirations; that is why an image would come in the way of man's realization of God. Hindus do not believe that. Iconoclasm is only an aspect, a corollary of the whole Semitic approach to religion. To them, it appears, God and Soul were not there, or at least were quite hidden before the advent of Christ or Muhammad. God and Soul came into being, "true" or "perfect" religion came into being or they became operative only after their respective prophets appeared. They believe only in that much past of religion and prophethood which prepared the way for their own particular one. And, of course, after their appearance, further and future prophethood or religious outflowering became superfluous. Hinduism is no believer or worshipper at the shrine of this historicity. It too worships only the "eternal" in the "temporal". That is why, its truth and religion, it calls eternal. For truths or religions which are born in time will also disappear and die away in due course of time.

Now that I am about the subject, I may say also another thing. In your pamphlet, 'Will Hindu India Listen', you have made much of castes and creeds in Hinduism. In fact, in Hinduism you have seen nothing but "the fascist like system of Aryanism", and "Brahmanism". Besides the fact that the scholarship of this attack is European and was unknown to Islam before the work of Western and Christian scholars, I do not agree with you in spite of certain unhappy and oppressive features of the caste system. To me this is not the whole and sole of Hinduism. I also believe that true fascism comes from exclusive philosophies and exclusive claims to truth and perfection such as you advance for Islam in your writings. I also believe that distinctions (those that lead to oppression, not those that lead to autonomy and *svadharma*) based on sociological and economic factors are bad. But the most dangerous are the ones that are based on official theologies and dogmas, that divide humanity in terms of the "believers" and the "unbelievers", the "elect" and the "damned". They are dangerous because they not only mutilate the bodies of men (as is clear from the Muslim record of mass murders, mass conversions) but because they mutilate the truth itself. The only unity they understand is the unity of conformity to certain wooden intellectual dogmas, and not the unity of participation of self-growing souls in a Godward voyage.

In the Hindu perception, "Every form of the faith leads to salvation", in your own words; but in this truth, you have found nothing but "a faint-hearted tolerating people and desperate pacifists". In it you have also found nothing but "anarchy". The only useful end to which this perception could be put to is, as you have suggested in your pamphlet, for Hindus to become Muslims. In another publication of yours, you say that "you see no future for Hindus except of becoming Muslims". This conversion will also not contradict their basic faith because they believe that "every faith leads to salvation". What sophistic argument!

You would not mind my saying all that I have said. You will, I hope, not mind my not joining you in your wholesale condemnation of Hinduism. In your writings I have never seen a single sentence which sees any good in Hinduism. I trust you will not mind my telling you that I believe that Hinduism is a great religion, a mighty religion, a great guide, teacher and friend.

I may also say that I do not feel as enthusiastic as you do about Mohammedanism, particularly Mohammedanism of your interpretation. But I have respect for Islamic Sufism, particularly that branch of it which broke through the Muslim intellectuality and orthodoxy. I have no use for officially established dogmas. But even then I shall not quarrel with those who find those Muslim dogmas helpful to themselves. I hope you would not regard this as usual Hindu "faint-heartedness".

With kindest regards,

Yours sincerely,
sd.
Ram Swarup

Chapter 7.4

Religion and Society

Yoga is merely a more intense concern with spiritual life. But what is spiritual life itself? Has it merely to do with some sort of personal excellence? Or, has it also a larger social significance? Can the truths learnt from the science of the Spirit and the Yoga be applied to a better understanding of the society and even in changing it — for the new demand is not only for a new interpretation but also for a change?

The modern psyche has various characteristics. It is socially concerned; it is active, enthusiastic, optimistic, technocratic; it is impatient and even angry with the old order and hopeful of bringing about a new one. To this psyche, the age-old questions, the questions of life, death, resurrection and salvation with which traditional religions have grappled, are secondary and even irrelevant. The new psyche demands that the religions too must conform to this urgency and requirement.

This demand is excessive but it has a kernal of truth and a historical validity. In religions too narrowly conceived, it is possible to forget the man in a theological preoccupation with Gods. Religious doctrines become more important than the fate and welfare of man. Preoccupation with the miracles of the saints can lead to the neglect of the common man. An excessive belief in divine ordinances leads to a devaluation of human effort. An excessive other-worldliness leads to the neglect of the world. Today, we know many cults of the body which deny the Spirit; but for many, many centuries we were ruled by various cults of the Spirit which denied the body. A tooth-brush was considered Devil's contrivance and the bath was killed during the medieval ages over a greater part of Europe. An unbalanced emphasis on faith led to the neglect of intelligence and *prajñā*.

There is also another unsavoury aspect of religion. In theory religion is regarded as a concern for man's higher good but in practice, it has not always been so. Many times it has nourished forces of obscurantism, superstition and fanaticism. Some religions had more of an ideology and less of a spiritual culture in them. They played high politics and were themselves great imperial powers. Some were frankly religions of the sword but others used a more sanctimonious language. They were hand in glove with feudal and other oppressive forces. European Imperialism and European Christianity were twins. It is difficult to say whether the flag followed the cross or the cross followed the flag.

As a result, Gods lost their moral authority and their priests also suffered in the estimation of many sensitive people. The concept of religion itself became a suspect. Some thinkers came and opposed the claims and assumptions of their religions and dethroned their Gods. They tried to place man again at the centre of things. They said that man is the measure of all things and that religion is made for man and not man for religion. It was a liberating thought. In itself it was no more than a repetition of an old spiritual teaching that the Sabbath was made for man and not man for the Sabbath, but it was so long neglected and so well-forgotten that when it was again resurrected it came with the force of a new revelation. Great truths have to be seen and lived and revealed again and again.

Nearer home, Hinduism never developed any considerable theocracy and was therefore saved from many of those undesirable influences which go with power. It was more of a spiritual culture than a system of power; and even in its worst days, it remained closer to its inner spiritual function and vocation and was not burdened with extraneous considerations like proselytizing. Its spiritual ethos was shaped not by the priests or ecclesiastical officials but by the seers and sannyasins who gave up all privileges, all position in any hierarchy secular or sacerdotal. There was a priestly class but its function was to attend to the performance of various religious and semi-religious rites; it exercised little spiritual influence — that was wielded by God-men, by *rishis*, *munis*, monks, *bhikshus*, *bhaktas*.

But even this religion was not immune from the coarsening and narrowing influences of times. In some of its later developments, it neglected the social dimension. It became increasingly individualistic. Personal liberation or *moksha* became an over-riding value to the exclusion of all other ends of life. It also became monkish. The life of a house-holder was devalued. The terrestrial life became irrelevant. An other-worldly outlook took over. Not only spirituality became individualistic and exclusive, it also suffered in quality. Even Yoga was increasingly conceived in terms of breathing exercises, trance-techniques and experiences of unusual visions and sounds. It got preoccupied with certain vows and practices like fasting, with certain modes of life and rules of worship, and with secondary virtues, *anuvratas*. These have their own importance at their own level but in less vigilant souls they can become substitutes for the larger life and vision of the Spirit.

While freely admitting all this, religion need not however give up its identity and be led by the social activists. Religion has its own legitimate field and characteristic approach. The problems of life and death, of the quality and depth of life, of truth and harmony and immortality, of reconciliation and regeneration are the deepest problems. A man who rises up to the reflective level naturally begins to seek out the meaning and purpose of life. From darkness, he turns to seek light, from death to immortality, from false being to true being. He simply cannot shirk this innate search, this natural development. Therefore, while ready to restore a neglected emphasis on the social dimension, religion need not accept wholesale social answers. For those solutions and answers are themselves partial and even motivated. Social concern is only a part of the motive of a social activist. Another motive is that he is wanting to run away from himself, his fuller self which he does not understand, from the deeper questions of life and death. Probably, he is nor yet ready for a deeper self-inquiry.

In a deeper religious perspective, the soul is both individual as

well as social; God and the neighbour are the facets of the same
category. In a deep sense the service of the neighbour is the
service of God; and those who serve God begin to see a new
dimension in the neighbour. In fact, the highest truths of life can
be expressed anthropologically as well as theologically, in
humanist as well as in religious terms, in the language of the
brotherhood of man as well as the fatherhood of God. Confucius
expressed the highest truths of religion in filial and fraternal and
even in political terms. "Those who have loved and served their
parents and fellowmen — it is immaterial for them whether they
have engaged in meditation, *japa* and austerities or not, whether
they have gone on pilgrimage or not, whether they have
performed the ordained *yajñas* or not. They are already arrived"
— that is the idea of a beautiful Hindi hymn.

But while it is perfectly legitimate to use one term in order to
show it also contains the truth of the other too; in practice, most
religious philosophers use both the terms for the sake of clarity
and unambiguity and in order to bring out their mutually enriching
roles. Plato's ideal man in his relation to other men "will do what is
just and in relation to the Gods he will do what is holy and he who
does what is just and holy must be just and holy". The 'gentleman'
of Mencius, the great Confucian sage, "is not ashamed to face
Heaven above, and below he is not ashamed to face man".

So true spirituality has no quarrel with the view which centres
round man. The differences comes up when different schools
begin to tell us what they understand by the word 'man'. Many
times, we use the same word while meaning widely different
things. In such cases, any agreement is seeming.

In modern sociological thinking, man is a psycho-physical
being, a body-mind conglomerate. In spiritual thinking, he is also
a Spirit. In this way of thinking, there is no opposition between the
individual and the social facets because the two are reconciled in
the life of the Spirit, are expressions of the same underlying
reality. But if there was no Spirit and no deeper unity then the two
could not be reconciled. Different individuals must stand in a

relationship of opposition to another. Any accord between them must be in response to some passing passions and interests and must be by its very nature temporary. This, in fact, is the dominant view of modern Sociology.

But by adding or using the term 'Spirit', we solve no fundamental problem and bridge no great gulf. We merely change the phraseology and shift the ground. Our essential understanding is not deepened and we can carry the same old controversies round a new word and even add a few new ones peculiar to the new word.

In this regard, Yoga offers us a distinct insight. It says it makes no difference what words we use but how deep we go into their meanings. Here the fundamental thing is not words but the level of consciousness from which they emanate. Whatever words we may use, a particular level of consciousness imparts its own quality and meaning to them. Linking up this insight with the problem under discussion, we may say that consciousness at every level has a private as well as a public face, but the two are in a deeper sense no different. Both share the quality of that level of consciousness. A self-centered consciousness is concerned with itself whether it engages in private or what it calls public work. It cannot rise above that level. It cannot be lofty socially when it is low and mean privately. So the opposition is not between the individual and the social but between an unregenerate and an evolved consciousness, between an outward, surface view and a deeper, inward look.

Not only modern sociologists but also traditional religions use their words in pretty outward senses. For example, the injunction 'Love thy God and love thy neighbours' is a formula which in a mantra-form contains all the truths of Yoga, all the essence of *samādhi*; but an outward mind understands the two terms, God and neighbour, in its own way. In mystic tradition, God is a *Spirit* and even popular religions use this expression frequently. But a little reflection will show that their God even at his best is no more than a luminous form (*rūpa*), or equivalent of an agreeable feeling (*vedanā*), or an exalted state of mind (*saṁskāra*). It is only the Upanishadic and mystic traditions which understand God as a

Mind or Nous and even something which is beyond Mind, which is *asamprajñāta,* which is *asaṁjñā,* which is No-Mind, which is Silence, which is *nirvāṇa,* which is Brahma, which is Purusha, a Person.

The True Neighbour

The same is true of the word 'neighbour'. A good deal of modern, smart thinking regards him frankly as a nuisance; but traditional religions still continue to think of him somewhat more sentimentally, expansively and even benevolently. But even this view is not good enough for a Yogic seeing; it is too superficial and outward. As a surface view of God has led to warring revelations, to aggressive wars against the infidels, so has an insufficiently deep view of the neighbour made man become his brother's keeper; it has led to the white man's burden, to the God-given mission of Christianizing the world.

The concept of 'neighbour' contains the quality of the consciousness from which it emanates. The 'other' is an image of the 'I'. The 'neighbour', the 'thou' cannot have a connotation greater than the 'I'.

Realising that the outer mind cannot follow deeper truths adequately, the more reflective spiritual traditions have stressed the importance of Self-understanding. They tell us not to be content with outer phraseology but to go behind it. They say, Know Thyself. But his self is not the unregenerate 'I'; it is the image of God.

If one knows himself, then all knowledge — the knowledge of Gods as well as the neighbour — will come to him. "A man who knows his nature will know Heaven," says Mencius. The Upanishads teach that all Gods are in the self but if the self is unregenerate the Gods too are desire-Gods, Ego-Gods. But in a pure heart, the Gods find a true home, a natural habitat.

So the Yogas and the Upanishads teach no apotheosis of the natural man, even though he may be a neighbour. They teach self-exceeding, self-deepening. Man has to discover the true neighbour as he has to discover the true 'I'. And the process is one and simultaneous. In the measure he discovers the true 'I', he discovers the true neighbour'. As he reaches the summit-truths about himself, he discovers that the neighbour is no other than he himself and also that he is his own neighbour. Put in more theistic and ethical terms, he realizes that a deepened 'I' is a portion of God and so is his neighbour; he should love and serve God in others.

As a man's image of his own 'I' deepens, he arrives at a progressively richer and wider definition of his neighbour too. He realizes that the neighbour is not merely his own kith and kin or the familiar figure living in the same street; he also includes the stranger, even the enemy. And a true brother is not merely a brother in faith who believes with him in the sinful nature of man, believes in the same book, in the same incarnation and prophet; the heathen, the infidel, the *kafir* too is a brother. And mind you, his brother and not his ward or pupil — why, the infidel can even be his teacher.

The spiritual neighbour begins when the personal ego begins to die. As consciousness deepens and a man's vision expands, he cannot be the same again in his conception of morality, obligation and loyalty. He rises from a limited family view to a larger tribal view, from a racial view to a cultural view, from a tribal view, whether racial or ideological, to the view of the whole human race as one family and the whole earth as one's home — Yes, one's home and not one's colony. Then from mankind, he rises to the concept of all living beings as one. With further expansion of the consciousness, he finds that he is in intimate contact with all things around, with the elements, the earth, the rivers, the trees, the whole cosmos.

We meet this view in all Gnostic religions. The Hindu psyche has been considerably shaped by this approach. To the two dimensions — individual and social — which are easily recognisable, the ancient seers of India added two other — cosmic and transcendental. The transcendental is denied by materialist schools and the cosmic is neglected even by certain religious schools. And the transcendental too is understood differently by different religions. To some the Spirit is no more than ethics and faith; to the Gnostic religions, particularly the Hindus, it is also knowledge, universality, liberation, *vijñāna* and *moksha*. Similarly, some religions think of God as an extra-cosmic being making his will known to a chosen incarnation or prophet; others regard Him as the indwelling Spirit, the secret life of the Self and open to all who approach Him sincerely.

So we see that the distinction is not merely between a secular and a spiritual approach but within this broad division, there are other sub-divisions and other important differences of inter-pretation and emphasis. Man is defined differently by different schools and they combine terms of their definition differently, and put different values on them. This in turn gives to each school a unique ethos.

In the ensuing pages, we shall discuss the Hindu approach. In their long history, the Hindus have reflected a great deal on questions of life and death, time and eternity, on man's place in the social and cosmic environment, on his terrestrial and metaphysical status. They also developed distinctive social theories. These reflections may have a contribution to make to the problems of the modern times.

The Hindu Approach

The Hindu approach has many points of contact with the approaches of other cultures, ancient and modern, religious and secular, spiritual and materialist. On individual points, it could agree with them here and disagree there but considered as a whole, it has a distinctive character and temper of its own.

The Hindu approach could be called religious but it has to be distinguished from that variety which is ascetic, pessimistic and probationary. In some religions, there is a strong bias against the world; it is regarded as no more than a transit camp; the world cannot be improved and it is not worth improving. There is a strong note of this view in Hinduism too and from time to time it gave birth to movements which are predominantly other-worldly. But in its long history, the Hindu genius has reconciled the two terms and given us a synthesis between this world and the other-world which is mutually enriching.

The outer mind is likely to deny God but it is also possible to invoke the life of the Spirit in a way that it annuls life on the earth. The Hindu spirituality tries to avoid these extremes. "May I not deny Brahma and may not Brahma deny me", is the constant prayer of a student of the Upanishads. The higher Truth is called upon and brought down to raise up earthly life and not to obliterate it.

So in Hindu thought, there is no fundamental opposition between this life and the other life. What is here is there and what is there is here. The two worlds, the here and the hereafter, the Heaven and the Earth, are closely linked. They exist simultaneously here and now in the soul, in the cave of the heart. They interpenetrate. If we live a worthy life here, we shall live a worthy life there. This world is no unregenerate place; it is a place of action and duty; it is *karma-kshetra* and *dharma-kshetra*.

Hinduism reconciles the two worlds and the two lives in another way too. It says that if a man is a meeting-point of several principles then the aim of life can be no less than the fulfilment of those principles; if he is a body, a mind and a Spirit then the objects of his pursuit should correspond to these constituents and bring fulfillment to them. So Hinduism believes that man has four objects of pursuit, *purushārthas*, — *kāma*, *artha*, *dharma* and *moksha*. The words are difficult to translate but the first two stand for emotional happiness and economic well-being and the last two stand for the larger life of the Spirit. In a whole and wholesome life, they work in unison and stand for an integral and full life of the world informed by a concept of duty and truth, both leading to spiritual liberation.

But the "wholesome" does not mean a "whole" of certain measurable quantities of these miscellaneous principles — so much of the body, so much of the mind and so much of the Spirit. It only means that we must allow due varieties and multiple expressions. Probably, in some cases one principle will be stronger than the other; then in these cases they should follow the good proper to that principle. For example, those in whom the Spirit principle is strong will find a bodily life burdensome and the deeper object of their endeavour can only be a more intense life of the Spirit; on the other hand, those in whom the body principle is predominant cannot properly and adequately follow any other life. Any such attempt in the name of spirituality will be forced and artificial. One should follow the truth of one's nature, the truth for which one is ready. In doing this, "one incurs no sin", as the Gita declares.

But while fully admitting this life of the world, Hinduism like all other religions does not accept this life as the final term. Terrestrial life has for its background in one form or another an eternal life. The tree of life has its roots above, teaches the Gita. Without this background and these roots in the eternal, this life will be a fury and fever signifying nothing. This life has its source in the eternal and the transcendental and it is fed and fertilized by it constantly. Cultures which lose sight of this source-life lose the sense of significance, purpose, assurance and worthwhileness of this life even though they may live in affluent, outer circumstances.

Not only the individual but a society too receives this infusion, this influx, this inundation from above and is renewed by it. Like the individual, a culture too is supported by the deathless life of the secret Self; and in so far as it receives its influences without distortion, it too shares in its immortality though immortality does not rule out renewal through physical death and replacement. The deathless in a culture is called 'dharma' by the Hindus. It is what holds a society together, gives it cohesion and makes it living and lasting, and which also uplifts it and make it great and fulfilling.

Time Dimension: *yugas*

The idea of renewal, of resurrection of man and the world is an ancient idea. The Stoics believed in the periodic appearance, disappearance and reappearance of the world, the present world coming to an end by a conflagration and then followed by a renovation and construction, a *palingenesia*, a new birth. The time between one catastrophe and another was called a *'periodos'* a great year. 'Period' etymologically means a 'going round'. The change could be conceived as a mere repetition, but the repetition could also be a part of a larger evolution, a change on a higher curve.

The same idea is put forth in another way also. The Spirit is 'eternal', yet it has a temporal expression too; the Imperishable puts on perishable forms, usages and ideas of an age and even evolves through them — if one can use the word 'evolve' at all for the Timeless Purusha. It puts forth one idea, one potentiality in one age and withdraws it in another; and while getting ready to dissolve it, it is also secretly planting the seeds of another.

We find this idea in a high development by the Hindus. Their scriptures sing of the Timeless as well as of Time, of *akāla* and *kāla*. And their conception of time is not niggardly; on the other hand, it is astronomical. It is on a scale at whose immensity "even soaring fancy staggers".

Here we need not discuss the time-theory of the Hindus except to refer to one of its small sub-division which is further divided into four periods or *yugas* — Kritayuga or Satayuga, Tretāyuga, Dvāparayuga, and Kaliyuga. Kritayuga is the highest; it may be called the Golden Age. It is dominated by the quality of *sattva*, of light and truth. Dharma in its full glory is the ruler in this age. Then passing through two more periods of declining dharma, through what may be called silver and copper ages, we arrive at Kaliyuga, the iron age. It is dominated by *rajas* and *tamas*, qualities of unrest and darkness. At present, the world is passing through this period.

We should remember one important thing about the Time of Hindu conception. It is not a neutral medium in which things happen and through which man merely passes; on the other hand, it is a Spirit, a psychic force, an active shaping influences; it has its characteristic ethos and potentiality. Even the Timeless Spirit, God, is subject to the influence of Time, *kāla*; in Kritayuga, God, "the refuge of yogis and the indwelling Spirit of all creatures", is white-complexioned; in Tretāyuga, He is red-complexioned; in Dvāparayuga, yellow and in Kaliyuga, He is black-complexioned.

At present, the world is passing through the Kali phase. The mind of this age is outward-going. Its intuition for the invisibles and the intangibles of life are obscured. Its mind is dominated by the physical and the material even though in its scientific thought it may have reached a point where matter dissolves and becomes some kind of energy. Its ethics is utilitarian and sensuous. It sees things in their diversity and separateness; but even if and when it does arrive at some unity it is of the nature of uniformity and it is soul-killing.

Not that the Kaliyuga has no God, no Religion, no Yoga but they too are not without its impress. Godhead is no longer a living spiritual experience; it becomes an intellectual concept, an abstract notion, a religious dogma, a *casus belli*. Sanatana Dharma gives way to tribal ideologies built round historical personages and known as historical religions. Even Yoga is used by a materialist culture for achieving greater efficiency and greater productivity, for decreasing nervous and mental tension. Yogic *āsanas* are reduced to "sexercises". They believe they would rise to *Rāma* through *kāma*.

It is not possible to transcend the influence of the Time-spirit *en masse* but there are individuals who even in the Kaliyuga belong to the Satayuga and carry an inner atmosphere proper to that *yuga*. By cultivating the *sāttvika* qualities of light and truth and justice through Yoga, worship and austerity and reflection, one changes his 'age'. While living in Kali age physically, in his mind and soul he inhabits more exalted ages. The renewal of man by God, of earthly life by Heaven, is admitted in all religious traditions.

This time horizon has given Hindu thought a roomy ethos. It has given it a range and sweep not found elsewhere. A larger perspective also brings detachment. It teaches that we should not make too much of our present problems and institutions, that Time is the lord of everything, that Time creates and Time destroys. It teaches that we should not be overwhelmed by the problems of the day, by passing intellectual and spiritual fashions, ideologies, cults, and by self-styled incarnations and prophets. It teaches that we should not believe too readily in the glib promises of the politicians, the learned jargons of the scholars, the spiritual blueprints of the savants.

Of course, this larger wisdom need not inhibit all necessary effort. For the same wisdom tells us that there is a law of karma in everything, that no effort is wasted, that whatever we do and think with good intentions and in sincerity and knowledge never goes waste; whether we know it or not, it is taken up in its own time and resumed. The efforts and thoughts of today become the destiny of tomorrow.

Other religious traditions do not give man the same elbow-room. Religions of Semitic origin recognize the transcendental principle but they grant man only a brief interlude. After this interlude, there is the Doomsday, the final judgement and the final punishment. The world according to Christianity began in the year 4004 BC* — there is a difference of opinion whether it was summer or winter of that year — and it is already due for destruction. All the signs are there. In fact, it is over-surviving. It should have come to an end 2000 years ago.

The time-perspective lends its own ethos to different religious traditions. The Hindu view is detached, the prophetic tradition is committed; the first approach lends a sense of leisure, the second of urgency and even a sense of precipitancy. The prophetic view is no teaser of mind and imagination but it demands an exercise of faith which is excessive. The Hindu view is 'wise' but this wisdom may become a resort of a lazy mind.

Cosmic Dimension

Another feature which distinguishes Hindu approach from several other religions is, as we have already mentioned above, its cosmic view of man. Man's separateness is more apparent than

---

*According to a Jewish calender still in vogue, the world was created on October 7, in the year 3761 BC, on the night between Sunday and Monday, at 11 hours, $11\frac{1}{3}$ minutes p.m.

Christian theologians did nothing to widen this perspective. Gabriel de Mortillet gives us 32 different estimates of the duration between the creation of Adam and the birth of Jesus. The highest estimate is 6984 years and the lowest 3784 years.

real. He is a member of a larger nexus. He is shaped by influences originating in the farthest reaches of the universe. These influences are not merely corporeal; they are also biological and psychic. Man's world is not merely physical with the immensity of which the modern sciences have made us familiar and which confirm ancient Hindu reflections. Behind the material, there is also a subtle world which itself emanates from a larger causal world. The subtle and the causal worlds have their own modes of existence and follow their own laws and these are not the laws of space and time with which we are familiar on the physical plane. In man the three worlds meet. In the ancient language of Hindus, man is a citizens of the three worlds: *bhūḥ, bhuvaḥ, swaḥ.*

This view teaches man a new 'togetherness' — not merely the togetherness of mankind but of all creatures and beings, including those removed in time and space and even in consciousness. He realizes that he is in a sparrow, in a cow, in a camel, in a lion, in plants and even in minerals. He realizes a sense of fellowship with all living creatures and even with what is ordinarily considered as the inanimate world. He realizes that the elements, the earth, the fire, the wind, the sun, the directions, the stars are his kins. All are astir with life; all life is one; he is in all beings; he carries the whole cosmos within him.

This expanded vision demands a radical change in our world-view and loyalty. Our world now includes not only ourselves and our blood relations, not even only our party or church or *ummah*; it includes the whole mankind, all living creatures, all elements. With this vision, we can no longer look upon them as mere 'factors of production'; they are not meant merely for human domination and exploitation. They are part of us. They sustain us and we in turn should sustain them. We have obligations towards them and they have their rights. Those who violate those rights violate the *rita*, world's inner, spiritual balance. This violation brings about violation of our own reality and harmony. It sets up forces of Nemesis; we are pursued by hybris, by forces of our own karma.

This vision of unity does not abolish diversity. In fact, it teaches a new respect for diversity. The individual is no part of a mechanical unit, no cog in a machine; he is a member of a spiritual unity; he has his role to play, his contribution to make. He has his rights, obligations, place and destiny.

This cosmic view is different from the one which modern Science teaches. It does not abolish or submerge the individual. In fact, it invests him with a new significance. The individual is a window which opens out on the universal. It is instinct with the universal life. Traditions which teach us the cosmic view also teach us the 'occult' view of individual objects and events.

In this view, nothing is unimportant: where we sit, where we stay, what direction we face, when we start a journey — everything is significant. Winds, hills, rivers, springs, ravines, plants, trees, all have their mood, their colour. They are personalities, psychic powers, even deities. In this view, nothing is a chance happening, calculable effects of causes working externally. Everything that happens is a sign, an augury, a portent; it has a destiny and an appointed time, nothing is fortuitous.

In this view, events have an inner significance which is not measurable by their outer importance. A new idea, a silent thought of an obscure person may be more important than the eloquent pronouncements of statesmen or the preaching of learned clergymen.

Take for example the fateful day of 12th October, 1492, the day when the New World was discovered. In its own time, it was a small event but it led to big consequences. The newcomers had guns, horses, love of gold and Christian self-righteousness. Among the few things they had for export were communicable diseases like syphilis, tuberculosis, smallpox and a sense of sin. All combined to depopulate a whole hemisphere which housed at the time of its discovery 90 to 120 million people according to latest estimates. The local people, their arts, their skills, their cities, their freedom, their life-style — all were swept away in an avalanche. Everything happened with such suddenness and so naturally that neither the victors nor the victims knew what was taking place.

The Five Great Sacrifices

The two dimensions, transcendental and cosmic, have lent to Hinduism an ethos which distinguishes it not only from materialist-secular culture but even from some religious cultures. Hinduism conceives life as a *yajña,* a self-offering, an inter-change and inter-flow of energies, a glad and thankful return to Gods and elements of gifts that are freely received from them. It emphasises various kinds of unities: unity with one's forefathers, unity with all living beings and with nature, unity with Gods. It prescribes five daily sacrifices, *pañcha mahāyajñas*, as a memorial and a reminder to those unities.

The first *yajña* is Self-knowledge and self-study. It is the foundation of all other *yajñas*. This is called *brahma-yajña*. This is the offering to *brahma*. Daily reading of scriptures is its external aspect.

The second *yajña* is *pitri-yajña*, offering to one's ancestors. Life is a stream and we must bear witness to this continuity. In Hindu thought, there is no generation gap. We are in our ancestors and they are in us and we shall continue to live in our progeny. It is not merely a blood-unity; at heart, it is a spiritual unity. It is a unity of the *dvija*, twice-born.

This *yajña* is common to widely different cultures, Chinese, Greek, Roman. Plato exhorts us not to "forget the yearly tribute of respect to the dead", and to omit "nothing that conduces to a perpetual remembrance of them". But we do not find this *yajña* in proselytizing religions. The reason is simple. According to their beliefs, the true life of the Spirit begins with conversion. So they have to deny their forefathers who were pagans, heathens, infidels, idolators, polytheists, fire or sun worshippers, who were benighted, who qualified for hell. So while Hinduism stresses ancestral unity, proselytizing religions stress disunity, discontinuity for their special reason.

The third is *deva-yajña*, offering to Gods. The divine is a most important dimension of the human, a truth which an outward mind does not sufficiently see. We should invoke Gods, remember them daily. The relationship between men and Gods is not a one-way traffic; Hinduism has used an image which suggests reciprocity, mutuality. We invite Gods in our midst and they partake in our feast. We nourish them and they nourish us. We strengthen and increase their power within us by praise, adoration, remember-ance, purity, discrimination and in return they bestow on us strength, joy, intelligence and immortality. *Deva-yajña* is in reality an offering to our own higher nature, the secret Godhead within us.

The fourth is *bhūta-yajña*, offering made to elements and all creatures. Daily, in traditional homes, cakes and food-morsels are offered to Agni, to cows, to birds. This should remind us of unity that binds us all together, the animate as well as the inanimate world. We are part of a greater whole and we work in unison, in wholesome co-operation. We are not strangers, much less enemies. Man is not created just for lordship. All beings and creatures have their rights, their due place. When we begin denying this place to the animal world and to what we call the inanimates, we end by denying it to fellow-men, to non-believers, to Africans, to Red Indians, to class-enemies, to our own less fortunate brothers in society. We deny soul to the elements, to birds and beasts; and this soullessness comes back to us in cruelty, exploitation and injustice. The modern economic theories and practices which exploit nature and animals for maximum profits have their continuity in the Biblical doctrine of man's lordship over Nature. In the Bible, the words are used to convey a large, poetic sense; in any case, they are capable of a nobler inter-pretation. But they have been turned into a cruel and wicked doctrine which offends against the deeper spiritual sense and is destructive of man's environment — ecologic, social and psychic. Transgression against the elements, the mother earth, the animals, the soil sets up forces of Nemesis which eventually destroy man himself.

The last *yajña* is called *nri-yajña*, which is an offering to men. It is homage paid to the unity of mankind, which has its roots in the larger fraternity of Nature. The larger human brotherhood is expressed by various images in different religions: by the image of a 'stranger' in the Jewish religion, by 'neighbour' in the New Testament, by 'guest' in Hindu religious literature. Old Hinduism preached that God himself is the visitor in the guise of a guest.

These five daily *yajñas* are the foundation of the highest morality and spirituality taught by the ancient Vedic seers. Those who first offered their food to Gods, forefathers, elements, all living creatures, fellow-men, and those who first fed their aged parents, their children, their dependents and servants before they themselves ate were called *yajñaśishṭāśinaḥ* or *vighasāśinaḥ*, eaters of the remains of sacrifices. An unnamed blessing and a transforming element entered into their food and turned it into ambrosia, *amrita*. They became deathless and they lived in deep peace and reconciliation with their Gods, their world, their fellow-men and with themselves.

Social Organisation: *varṇa-āśrama dharma*

So far we have discussed the larger Hindu world-view and life-view. It is a religious view fundamentally but it differs in some important ways from views of some other religions. These wider differences in outlook and perspective lead to differences in social practices. True, people do not live by the theories of their respective cultures but try to solve their current problems as best as they can, problems which are about the same everywhere. This explains fundamental human unity even in the midst of their widely different beliefs and usages. But ideas too have their importance, particularly when they are not merely mental but express deeper psychic types and racial peculiarities and mind's deeper urges and vision. Such ideas have a shaping influence on the psychology of a people and affect their polity and social ordering. Here we shall refer to one or two Hindu concepts which are more strictly social and psychological though they too are rooted in the metaphysical and derive from the larger definition of man.

If a man is neither wholly Spirit, nor mind, nor body and if a society is composed of men who embody these principles in different combinations and who express them differently in different stages of life, then the principles and forms of social ordering and organisation too have to be multiple. Hinduism conceives man and society as tetrads. There are four *āśramas* or stages in the life of an individual, and four *varṇas* or divisions of a society. The two concepts are closely related for they are founded on the same truth — the truth of certain fundamental psychological quality mirrored more fully at one stage in the life of an individual or in a particular order of the society. So in this scheme, the individual evolution reflects the larger social ordering and the social order reflects the unfoldment of the Spirit in the individual.

We shall take up the concept of *varṇa* first. It is inadequately translated as 'caste' but for want of a better word we may retain this so long as we keep in mind its inadequacy. Caste in its present meaning stands merely for something rigidly social but the concept of a *varṇa* is psychological and metaphysical though it has also a social facet. It is a natural self-division of a society based on a dominant psychological trait and spiritual quality.

The caste institution has created great misgivings; and the castes as they exist mock the original principles on which they were based. A lot of accretion has gathered around them and they also do not agree with the modern temper. Originally, caste was based on the principles of live and let live. It was meant to promote justice, freedom and efficiency in a society.

Castes were based on the familiar fact that men differ in their nature, potentiality, endowment and temperament. Some are more cerebral, others more manual. The intelligence of some is more abstract, of others more practical. Some can pursue more distant ends, for others that will not be a sufficient motive. Some are more active, others more contemplative.

It is not intelligence but a certain quality that pertains to it which determines a man's caste. As men rise in the power of abstraction and impersonality, they rise in the scale of caste. A Shudra is loyal to men, a Brahmin to principles. The two truths are not opposed but complementary. One mentality is more concrete and personal, the other more impersonal. One mentality has softer, more passive and receptive qualities; the other is more discriminative and reflective.

The activity of a Shudra is informed by *yama* and *niyama*; it is intent and devoted. A Vaishya shares these qualities but his activity is also more enterprising. It goes out in search of new pastures. A Shudra establishes concrete relationship with men around and is unselfish in these relationships. A Vaishya also establishes relationship with the soil, with the elements, with animals. He serves them intelligently and unselfishly. By his service, he creates wealth which he shares with other orders of the society which do not have his kind of talent and function.

A Kshatriya pursues still more abstract values. He serves order and justice. He protects the weak and tames the strong or rather the headstrong. He protects the society from external aggression and also from internal subversion. He lives for justice and in this pursuit his own life counts for nothing.

A Brahmin is a teacher. He is detached and contemplative. He turns away from everything that is small and sordid. He stands for the principle of austerity and symbolises higher life. He is looking for the imperishable in the midst of the perishable.

The divisions given above may be too idealistic but they have a validity and no society can do without them altogether. They are necessary for the self-articulation of a society and they are found in one form or another in all societies. When people follow their natural bent of mind and cultivate their inborn gifts, the results are the best for the society as well as for the individual. These are natural divisions and there is no question of high and low and of mutual prejudices. But if these natural divisions become permanent social divisions maintained by a rigid tradition, then they lose vitality and inner life and sanction.

When people belong to castes socially to which they do not belong naturally, the results are bad. Social stability and individual happiness demand that social and natural divisions should be in tune with each other; but if there is any large-scale hiatus between them, it leads to what the Gita calls the "confusion of castes", *varṇasaṁkara*. It creates bitterness and bad blood all around.

There was a time when caste was a positive thing and it strengthened the society. Caste promoted economic security, political stability and cultural self-determination. It was another name for community life. One had a profession as soon as one was born and was trained in its skills from the beginning — unlike the present times when one does not know his profession till the end of his life and the spectre of unemployment haunts him all through. The individual also found security and protection in a community. As one of its organic members, he could not be pushed around easily. The atomised individual of modern societies has no cushion. He is at the mercy of any tyranny that might come up.

Above all, a caste was the vehicle of a great cultural life. It followed its own customs and usages; it followed even its own laws; it celebrated different events of life like birth, death, courtship, matrimony in its own way; it followed its own beliefs and modes of worship; it had its own saints and Gods. The society was a commonwealth, a federation of self-determined communities. Hinduism encouraged this variety and plurality because it believed that in living in different ways, they lived the same life and in worshipping through different modes, they worshipped the same Reality. This attitude promoted harmony, co-existence and cultural freedom.

But monolithic ideas of religion, worship, God, morality, state, party do not feel comfortable with communitarian and caste concepts and practices. The excessive zeal of monolators has time and again led to genocide and undermined local community life. Imperialism and the spirit of modern commercialism too have reinforced the forces of uniformity. Today, the atomized individual feels helpless before the might of the State, Corporations, and political parties.

The modern spirit of the age is against caste though they have reappeared under a new guise and in many cases in a worse form. It is not a question of 'democratic' and 'equalitarian' temper of the new age, as some thinkers tell us. The fact is that castes have lost their old functions. True life has gone out of them and they have become mere shells. When castes were living things, they ensured to all freedom, equality, security, fearlessness, community life, continuity, cooperation, stability, cohesion, spiritual well-being — values which alone form the true criterions for judging a good polity and society. In those days, there was no question of prejudice and exclusion. Bhishma advised Yudhishthira that a king should have a Council of Ministers which should include "four Brahmins of inner and outer purity, who know the Vedas and who are also fearless; eight Khstriyas of good physique and who also are proficient in wielding weapons; twenty-one wealthy Vaishyas and four Shudras of blameless character and inner self-control". If a Kshtriya king failed to give protection to the people and to their culture, then he could be replaced by one who could even if he was a Shudra. For "what is the use of a bullock who can carry no load, or a cow which yields no milk". A king even though he is a Khshtriya but who cannot perform a king's function is "like a wooden elephant, a leather deer, a barren woman, a waste land, a rainless cloud". On the other hand, a person even if he is a Shudra but who can protect the people "from increasing hands of robbers, who can punish licentious living, who can uphold the *varṇāśrama dharma* is worthy of a king's respect" for he brings "succour to men in great difficulties, and is like a boat to a drowning person".

With regard to equality too, the caste-societies of nobler days do not suffer by comparison. The Brahmins who were the highest caste were perhaps the poorest in economic goods. Their's was an aristocracy of intellect and austerity. The fact is that these societies cared for a different kind of equality; that all should rise up, all should evolve to greater spiritual heights. In societies where *sattva* qualities prevail, where people are taught to care for truth, excellence and worship, the average quality of life of every one is higher and all tend to be Brahmins — or at least only those are Brahmins who have those qualities. But in times and societies where the emphasis is on things and commodities and where the mind is outward-going, it is the Vaishya and Shudra spirit that prevails. Even the culture, religions, sciences and education of these societies are more like trades and professions than true vocations of the Spirit. Look at modern societies. They have a lot of intellectual activity but very little Brahminhood. A lot of inhuman research is going on in the laboratories of America and Europe on monkeys and other animals. This is mere butchery masquerading as science. There is neither wisdom nor humanity in their sciences and research.

According to old Hindu thought, the two *yugas*, Satayuga and Kaliyuga, have no proper castes. In the first *yuga*, all including the Shudras tend to be Brahmins; in ages when Dharma has considerably declined, even the Brahmins become like Shudras. They have nothing but arrogance and pride; knowledge, austerity and compassion fall away from them.

More correctly speaking, modern societies are outside the pale of *varna-āśrama dharma*. There are no true Brahmins and Kshatriyas, nor true Vaishyas and Shudras. Mere wealth, industry and commerce do not make a Vaishya class. In spiritual thought, the foundation of wealth is not exploitation of fellow-men and fellow-creatures and the destruction of Nature's resources for maximum personal profits. A true Vaishya creates wealth through service, by working in consonance with the nature of things, by entering into their rhythm. He earns properly and shares widely.

Similarly, a Shudra too is a highly spiritual concept. There is a Shudra in all of us and in early stages of life, we are all Shudras. The qualities that characterize a Shudra — the qualities of discipline, work, devotion, loyalty, faith — are the foundations of all other spiritual qualities. In Yoga, they find their acme in a devotee who becomes a servant or slave of God. Some of the greatest God-men of India have come from the Shudra-class. The mere fact that a man is a wage-earner and that his wages are depressed and that he is culturally dispossessed does not make him a Shudra in the spiritual sense of the term.

The principle which gives us the four castes also give us the four *āśramas* or stages in the life of an individual. Each person passes through different stages of life which are characterized by different capabilities and excellences. There is no abstract 'best' which one should follow at all stages but every stages has its own 'best' which one could profitably and more naturally express.

Hinduism divides a man's life into four stages. The first period is that of learning. In this period, one should acquire skills and knowledge and become integrated in the cultural life of the society. In this period, a man's senses are keen and his memory sharp and he is a quick learner. In this period, he is also capable of a natural identification with his elders and teachers, an indispensable condition of learning in early years; one is naturally and spontaneously 'docile' which etymologically means 'teachable' and which also gives us the words 'disciple' and 'discipline'. Alas! as a man grows, he loses the quality of discipline and forgets the role of a pupil. These have to be re-learnt through Yoga.

When a man has acquired skills and reached mature vitality, he enters the life of a householder which is the second stage or *āśrama*. In this stage, he supports the economic fabric of the society and contributes to the continuance of the race. Not the number but the quality of wisdom, bravery and proficiency and intelligence are preferred in the progeny.

In the last two stages, a man enters into increasing detachment from the world. He disengages himself from bodily affections which his natural vitality no longer supports. There is no sight more pitiable than the old trying to live like the young, a body weak in vitality but still strong in desire and ambition. There is time for everything. In the younger days, when the bodily principle is strong, the spiritual principles is in abeyance. But with age when the bodily principle is receding the spiritual principle should become more alive and one should seek Spirit's life and freedom unencumbered by inordinate demands of the body.

At this stage one can also no longer be oblivious of the shadow of death which looks distant and unreal when one is young and which one can easily ignore at that stage. But as one grows older, one finds his kith and kin, friends and dear ones more and more on the other side. It is time for him to contemplate on death and seek the meaning of life.

He becomes a sannyasin, a recluse. He has no possessions, no abode, nothing that he will call his own; he stores nothing.

His allegiance is to Truth alone, to the Self in all, and not to any ideology. He is no missionary of any creed or doctrine. He should not be confused with modern intellectuals seeking promotions and careers, who are merchants and mercenaries in spirit. He lives a life of austerity. He has no patrons; he fears none and frightens none. He is a friend of all.

As the same principle governs the individual and the social, the wider social order is reflected in the individual stages too and vice-versa. The individual in the different stages of life repeats the spiritual and psychological qualities that we find on a larger scale in the division of the society into castes. As we have already said, a man is a Shudra in his early stage. He has activity, exertion, faith, loyalty; he serves; he learns; he has discipline; he is teachable; he performs his duty. In the second stage, he becomes a creator of wealth, a supporter and nourisher of the society and its different institutions. In the last stages, he should become more detached, more contemplative and pursue more abstract qualities like Self-knowledge. He should become a Brahmin as best as he can.

Even while pointedly mentioning the principle of diversity and differentiation, the truth of unity is not neglected. "Though divided into four, *āśrama* is known to be one by the wise" — *vyastamekam chaturdhā hi brāhamaṇāḥ aśramān vidhūḥ*, declares the *Mahābhārata*. The four *āśramas* meet in the individual. This observation has several implications. It means that it takes a combination of the qualities of all the orders to make a person complete. Even a Brahmin is not complete without the qualities of a Shudra. It is for this reason that Mahatma Gandhi tried to inculcate in all who joined his camp the qualities of a Shudra: discipline, work, service. Nations in which these qualities are neglected, nations which avoid necessary physical work, which cannot undertake selfless service, become weak in their very foundation.

It also means that the highest experience of which the Upanishads speak, the *turīya* state which is the witness of all other three states of consciousness — waking, dream and sleep states —

the state of which the foundation is *yama* and *niyama*, and is open to all *varṇas* and *āśramas*. *Moksha* is no respecter of persons. *"Teshāmapetatrishṇāṇām nirṇiktānām śubhātmanām chaturtho' panishad dharmaḥ sādhāraṇaḥ iti smritiḥ."* It also means that by being true to any one vocation and principle proper to oneself, one gets the merits of all, reaches the highest end of life. "Fulfilling the truth of one *āśrama*, one attain to the *summun bonum*, high, good; some reach it by renouncing the world, others by living in forests; some by living the ideal life of a householder; and others by living the life of a *brahmachārin*."

Brahmanism which is the main stream of Hinduism emphasized the truth of the diversity of human nature and the unfoldment of a man's nature through successive stages. But there has been another important stream called Shramanism, equally a part of Hinduism, which did not give the same importance to this principle. It preached *moksha* to all and sundry, and its mendicant order — the highest order — was open to any one who cared to join it. This led to some crying evils. Young men were drawn to the order prematurely without adequate preparation. Life became monkish. Young men willfully took to a life of celibacy even when their nature was not ready for it. It smacks of violence and involves a certain kind of mutilation. In this respect, Brahmanism shows a more lively understanding of human nature and its approach is more psychological. It does not teach one morality and one spirituality to all. People who join a religious order prematurely, without adequate preparation, while they inflict suffering upon themselves bring bad name to the order and even to religion itself.

Index

active life, contemplative life is not an adjunct of, 37; lower and higher expressions of, 73.

Africa, Islam threatens Christian influence in, 160.

ahiṁā, increasingly deeper meanings of, 34.

Akbar (Mughal emperor), was influenced by the Bhakti Movement, 123.

Al-Ghazzali, tried to reconcile Sufism with Prophetic Islam, 163-164.

Allah, mullahs, qazis and military generals questioned names given to him by infidels, 123; meaning 'the god' was plural (and not singular) in origin, 161; female counterpart of, 161; masculine form of Goddess Al-Uzza retained in one of the names of, 161.

Al-lāt, Goddess of (Pagan Arabs), was female counterpart of Allah, 161.

Al-Uzza, Goddess (of Pagan Arabs), Allah's name Al-Aziz retains her in masculine form, 161.

Alvar saints, full-blown *bhakti* found in, 114.

anātma, a deep spiritual truth conveyed by Buddha in the great concept of, 135; not absence of Self but presence of

Ego meant by, 135; has as wide a domain as that of *ātman* of the Upanishads, 136, 138-139; a key-word and a fundamental concept in Buddhistic *sādhanā*, 139-40.

anātmavāda of Buddhism, spirit of *bhakti* opposed to, 123.

ancient seers of India, added cosmic and transcendental dimensions to individual and social dimensions of mankind, 233-234.

animals, Jesus did not feel the wails and tears of, 121; eaten for no more than theological reasons, 224.

animal world, the Bible lacks compassion towards, 121; implications of denying due place to, 243.

Arabia, male chauvinism of Muhammad abolished the Goddesses of, 161.

asambhūti and *sambhūti*, paths of, 139.

Asia, Western conquest opened Europe for, 201-202.

asteya, increasingly deeper meanings of, 34.

āsurika forces, warning against use of *smriti* by, 44-45.

ātma-smriti, highest culmination of *smriti* in spiritual *sādhanā*, 43,

Bhisma, advises Yudhisthira that his Council of Ministers should include members from all castes, 248.

Bible, the word 'desirelessness' does not even occur in, 74; compassion towards God's animal creation missing from, 121; called "The Greatest Love" but full of fanaticism and bigotry, 166; physical description of God in, 170; non-Biblical saints mentioned in, 206.

Bible and Quran (Biblical literature), difference between teachers in the Upanishads and the teachers in, 170-171; messengers (known as prophets) occupy the centre of the stage in, 171.

Boccaccio, Giovanni, wrote story ridiculing the Christian institution of Confession, 156.

bondage, spiritual life is release from, 71; called by many names to bring out different nuances of, 76-77; according to Jains, 76.

brahmacharya, Indian teachers on the science of, 193-194; no forced celebacy in, 194.

brahmavāda, gives way to mayāvāda in the Upanishads, 146.

brahma-vihāras (Great Abidings), Rāja-Yoga retains utility of, 19; practice of four, 19-20; increasingly more emphasized in later developments of Buddhism, 19; countered not only by their opposites but also by their lower versions, 19-20.

Brahmanic tradition, discipline of householders in, 194.

Brahmanism, is the mainstream of Hinduism, 252; diversity of human nature and its unfoldment in stages emphasized by, 252; does not teach one morality and one spirituality to all, 252.

Brahmin(s), characteristic qualities of, 246; aristocracy of intellect and austerity, 248.

brotherhood, Christian and Muslim idea of, 162-163; expressed differently in different religions, 243-244.

Buddha, on science of liberation, 80; spoke often about state of liberation but in negative terms, 86; split between body and mind, Nature and God, samsāra and nirvāṇa occurred in the time of, 127; the Self retained in disguised form by, 128-129; spiritual or moral principle missing from world-view of some contemporaries of, 129; deep spiritual truth (taught) in the concept of anātma by, 135; Gods become cheer-boys of the teachings of, 147; Gods played great role in the life of, 148-149; Gods bow often to, 149; Shramanic tradition followed by, 194.

buddhi (intellect), Gita on three kinds of, 94; several spiritual cultures speak disparagingly about, 100; nearest to knowledge of the Purusha, 100-101; its meaning in Sāmkhya, 101; its meaning in the Upanishads, 101; a definite and separate category in Indian spirituality, 102; universality is an important quality of, 103; lower manifestations of, 103; shows cunningness of 'meek piety', 103-104.

years at most and 3784 years at
least between creation of Adam
and birth of Jesus, 239n.
desire, a whole twin-life designated
by, 55; is an insatiable fire
enveloping wisdom, 57;
supported by ego and nescience,
66; has within it the seed of its
opposite, 78; subtle, mentalized
forms of, 82; purification of, 82.
Dharmashastras, use physical and
spiritual elements of human love
to support the fabric of society,
191.
dhyāna, five stages of, 22-23;
different truths revealed by
different bhūmis of, 24.
Divinity, experienced differently at
different levels, 101-102.
doctrine of karma, Buddhist and Jain
view of Gods in keeping with,
147.

Eastern spiritual wisdom, received
respect and recognition from
humanists, universalists, and
men of science and reason in the
West, 167; a welcome
development in Western society
is respect for, 167.
Eckhart, snubbed the man who spoke
of God being one, 163.
Ego-Gods, birth of, 153; come fully
into their own in theological
disguise, 153; pieties, morals
and spiritual truths become the
worship of, 153-154; abound in
most unsuspected places, 154;
become worse when codified in
a theology, 154-155; egos fight
in human affairs in the name of ,
158; impure worship goes to,
165; abide in the unregenerate
self, 232.

Egypt (ancient), country of
multiplicity of Gods, remained
free from religious persecution,
165.
Elements (of Nature), forces of
Nemesis set up by transgression
against, 243.
Elohim, doubly plural (God) in
origin, 161.
Encyclopaedia of Religions and
Ethics, part of Christian
Apologetics but concedes
religious tolerance to Hinduism,
202.
enforced celebacy, Hinduism spared
morbidities and extravagance
and excesses of, 194.
Equality (in Yoga), several connected
meanings of, 52; is not apathy
or impassivity, 52-53; is the
psychological counterpart of a
great ontological truth, 53; true
establishment of, 53-54; not
satisfying if it is a response of
the ego based on training and
fortitude, 54-55; begins with
desirelessnes, 55-56; prajñā or
wisdom-view of things is
another pillar of, 56; fruit as
well as root of deepened
consciousness, 58; practised
differently in different systems
of sādhanā, 58-59; as prescribed
in the Upanishads, 59; Gita
gives the highest synthesis of
the living practices of, 59.
Europe (under Christianity), some
great values denied by
renunciation in, 67;
overwhelmed by the motto of
One God, One Mediator, One
Church and One Book, 160; old
Gods destroyed and stamped out
in, 160; religious excesses

Hindu tolerance, theological basis of, 202-203.

Hindu Yoga, more akin to the mystic way in other religions, 27.

Hinduism, has never been exclusively brahmanical, 122; *bhakti* is one of the greatest elements in, 122; *bhaktas* and *santas* strengthened the culture of, 123; spared morbidities and extravagances and excesses of enforced celebacy, 194; outsiders attracted by the spirit of tolerance in, 202; Christian Apologetics concedes religious tolerance to, 202; absence of intolerance not incidental in, 202-203; 'liberal' Christian theologians plan a new encounter with, 210; a Sufi's derogatory description of, 221-226; mystic experience of saints confirms the pantheism of, 224; no worshipper at the shrine of historicity of prophethood, 225; worships only the "eternal" in the "temporal", 225; caste system is not the whole and sole of, 225; never developed theocracy and its concomitants, 228; social dimension neglected in some later developments of, 229; men is the meeting point of several principles in, 234; theory of *yugas* or time dimension in, 236-239; Time not a neutral medium but an active shaping influence in, 237-238; sees the law of karma operating in everything, 239; Five Great Sacrifices (*mahāyajñas*) in, 242-244; life conceived as a *yajña* in, 242; provides reciprocity and mutuality between Gods and

men, 243; sees God himself visiting in the guise of a guest, 244; men and society conceived as tetrads in, 245; psychological and ethical basis of caste in, 245-246; plurality and variety in social life encouraged by, 247; man's life-span divided into four stages by, 250-251; Brahmanism is the main stream of, 252; Shramanism is equally a part of, 252.

historical (prophetic) religions, born in time and will die in due course, 225; in Kaliyuga, Sanatana Dharma gives way to, 227.

Huetti, Robert, inspired by the Lord to cut off his right hand, 27. See 'inspiration'.

human beauty, reminds of the beauty that never fades, 190.

human brotherhood, expressed differently in different religions, 243-244.

human love, in the language of Yoga, 192.

Huxley, Aldous, on a man who was divinely inspired to cult off his brother's head, 27. See also Huetti and 'inspiration'.

Ibn al-Arabi, on romantic love as "a secondary phenomenon", 195.

iconoclasm, an aspect of the Semitic approach to religion, 225.

Illusionism (*māyavāda*) of Shankara, *bhakti* opposed in spirit to, 123.

India, no opposition between Science and Spirit in, 91; Bhakti Movement renewed and gave new authenticity to the spiritual life of, 119-120; country of multiplicity of Gods, 165;

role of virtue and knowledge, 81; *prajñā* according to, 99.

James, William, confused by translation of *smriti* as memory, 42n.

Jesus, tears and wails of animals sacrificed in the Temple not felt by, 121; Jewish world influenced by ideas from East and West by the time of, 159; believed in 'one' God and 'salvation only for the Jews', 159 and n.

Jewish calender, creation (of the world) dated to 3761 BC in, 239n.

Jewish history, marked by prophecies, 26.

Jewish world, some ideas and monastic institutions borrowed from Buddhism by, 159; Greek influence had great fertilizing effect on the ideas of, 159; influenced by ideas from East an West by the time of Jesus, 159.

Jews, measurement of different limbs of God popularized by, 165.

Judaism, born in and nurtured on the prophetic ethos, 26.

Justification by Faith, blood-bath caused by the Christian doctrine of, 156.

Kabir and Nanak, classical spirit breathed by the *bhakti* of, 113; on the domain of *māyā*, 138-139; love of the Formless by, 196.

Kali (Goddess), Ramaprasad and Ramakrishna worshipped God as Mother in the form of, 115.

Kaliyuga, at present the world is passing through the phase of, 237; mind dominated by the

physical and the material in, 237-238; its impress on God, Religion and Yoga, 238; religion centered round historical personages in, 238.

karma, Hindu theory compared with Muslim theory of, 223.

Karma-Yogin, equality as practised by, 59.

Kashyapa, Purna, no spiritual or moral or logical principle in the world-view of, 129.

Kathopanishad, on paths of *preyas* and *sreyas*, 181.

Katyayana, Prakrudha, no spiritual or moral or logical principle in the world-view of, 129.

Keshakambali, Ajit, no spiritual or moral or logical principle in the world-view of, 129.

knowledge, no spiritual or profane subjects in but only spiritual or profane approach to, 90; Gita on different levels of, 93-94; Yogic thought on different levels and kinds of, 94; Gita on three kinds of, 94-95; different contents and modes of, 95.

Krishna, love in transcendental form embodied by, 195-196; simplicity and directness of Mira's love for, 196.

Krishna of Kurukshetra, some people call for going back from Krishna of Vrindavana to, 124.

Kshatriya, characteristic qualities of, 246.

Law of Karma, no elect, no eternally damned, no final judgement, and no permanent hell-fire in, 31-32; places our destiny in our own hands, 32.

'liberal' Christian theologians, find in

commandments, 187; grows
with growth of self-awareness,
187-188; soul-principle takes up
the guidance of, 188-189.
Moses, destruction of the Hittites,
Amorites, Canaanities and others
ordered by the God of, 87.
Muhammad (Prophet), Goddesses
were doing very well in Arabia
before the advent of, 161;
Goddesses of Arabia abolished
by the male chauvinism of, 161;
Muslim mystics did not quarrel
with the utterances of, 163.
mūrti-worship, found good enough
by saints of the highest order,
224.
Muslim invaders, Bhakti Movement
tried to tame the fanaticism and
ferocity of, 123.
Muslims, the worst idolators, 225.

neighbour, service of God seen as the
service of, 230; white man's
burden and Christian missions
emerge from an insufficient
view of, 232.
Nemesis, violation of the world's
inner balance sets up forces of,
240; transgression against the
Elements, mother Earth, animals
and the soil sets up forces of,
243.
Neo-Equality, moral and
metaphysical rehabilitation of
lower truths of life by, 61.
New Testament, higher truths of
Universality, Liberation and
Self-knowledge missing from,
24; no controversy about One
God and Many Gods in the
Gospel part of, 159; spiritual
deterioration starts in the Acts
part of, 160.

new (Christian) theology, not so new
as it believes, 219.
New World, doings of Christian
newcomers in, 241.

old Gods, destroyed and stamped out
in Europe under Christianity,
160; demolished by St.
Augustine, 172.
Old Testament, 'One God' gets
repeated emphasis in, 158;
speaks with soulful contempt of
the Gods of foreigners, 158-159;
accounts of many saints of non-
Jewish origin contained in, 159.
One Book, Europe under Christianity
overwhelmed by the motto of,
160.
One Church, Europe under
Christianity overwhelmed by the
motto of, 160.
One God, theology of, 88; experience
of relationship with, 101-102;
has been the bee-in-the-bonnet
of Semitic religions, 158; of
Moabites, Ammorites, Hittites,
Hivites and others, 159; Europe
under Christianity overwhelmed
by the motto of, 160; ideology
of domination represented by
the doctrine of, 162; prophets
and men of action rather than
mystics created the idea of, 163;
easier to understand than One
Reality called by many names,
164.
'One God' and 'Many Gods',
discussion of controversy about,
158-159; 'our True God' and
'their False Gods' is another
facet of, 158.
One Mediator, birth of the concept
of, 160; Europe under
Christianity overwhelmed by the
motto of, 160.

'white man's burden', a diluted
version of the Church's God-
given mission, 219, 232.

Whitman, Walt, on God of animals,
169n.

Wilberforce, use of force for
conversion of heathens in India
advocated by, 201, 216-217.

words, have outer and inner or lower
and higher or narrower and
broader meanings, 105.

worship, outward and under-
developed form of, 222.

Yahweh, Cardinal Danielou on stages
in the abode of, 207-208;
reaches complete and final
Temple in Christianity, 208.

Yoga, says vast life is locked in the
soul, 11; purpose of, 14;
retracing of steps in, 23-24, 36;
uses thought to conquer thought,
23-24, 36; seeks permanent
change in consciousness, 26-27;
on pitfalls of 'inspiration' and
prophethood, 28; seeks
purification at various levels, 32-
33; several methods of chitta-
śuddhi proposed in, 36; requires
purity not only of morals but
also of contemplation, 38; leads
to knowledge of things as they
are, 40-41; renunciation at the
centre of many systems of, 64;
renunciation as taught by, 64-65;
Liberation belongs to the last
stages of, 73; teachings of, 74;
conquest of kleśas is the central
problem of, 79-80; highest
concept of God provided by, 86-
87; aims at liberating larger
consciousness from its bondage,
89; is joy-cultivation (sukha-
sādhanā), 109; no dichotomy

between reason (buddhi) and
faith (śraddhā) recognised by
the Indian system of, 111; unity
of spiritual life salvaged in, 144;
methods to enter depths of the
heart where (Vedic) Gods had
retired, 145; human love in the
language of, 192; narrowing of,
229; not words but their level of
consciousness more
fundamental in, 231, 'love thy
God and love thy neighbour' is
the mantra containing all truths
of, 231; teaches not apotheosis
of natural man but self-
exceeding and self-deepening,
232; is used by materialist
culture in Kaliyuga, 238.

Yoga of Equality (samatva-yoga),
known as upekshā in Buddhist
Yoga, 60-61.

'yoga of sex' (illumination through
copulation), claims hoary
ancestry in Indian Tantras and
the temples of Khajuraho and
Konarka, 193.

Yoga of withdrawal, functions of
dream-like world in, 98.

Yogic Equality, to be distinguished
form Neo-Equality taught by
modern teachers of Yoga, 61.

Yogic literature, much emphasis on
purity in, 38; smriti means
'mindfulness' in, 42.

Yogic sādhanā, moral life is the fruit
and meaning of, 35; a recurring
experience of, 130.

Yogic samādhi, seeks knowledge of
mind's most divine part, 12;
discussed under two heads, 14-
15, Pātañjala Yoga on levels of
true, 17; no eschatological or
apocalyptical spirit in, 26;
defined as concentration of

S